101 Random Stuff You Never need to Know

A whimsical journey through the facts and curiosities you never knew you needed

B N William

TABLE OF CONTENTS

Coffee vs. Tea in the World	01
The Mystery of Left-Handedness	05
The World's Shortest War	09
Animals in Space	11
The Invention of the Potato Chip	13
The Great Emu War	15
The Color of Carrots	19
Bizarre Ice Cream Flavors	21
The World's Longest Place Name	22
The High-Heeled Shoe Origins	24
Crazy Laws of South Africa	27
Fruit or Vegetable Debates	33
The Beatles and the 'Let It Be' Legacy	35
Platypus: Nature's Oddball	38
The Mystery of Spontaneous Human Combustion	40
Competitive Pillow Fighting	41
Berghain: The Temple of Techno	43
The London Beer Flood	45
The Art of Fingerprinting	47
The Loudest Sound in Recorded History	49
The Historical Practice of Dueling	52
The Mystery of the Bermuda Triangle	55
Vacation to North Korea	57
The Wife Carrying Championship	61
The Dancing Plague of 1518	63
London's Great Stink of 1858	67
Crazy Laws of the Africa	69
The Great Molasses Flood of 1919	71
The History of Toilet Paper	72
The World's Deepest Postbox	30
Why We Say "Bless You" After Sneezing	75

Crazy Laws of the Asia	76
The Mystery of Crop Circles	78
The Science of Brain Freeze(this one is missing)	81
The Origins of the Piñata	83
Unusual Olympic Sports of the Past	85
The Legend of the Fountain of Youth	87
Why Bananas Are Berries, But Strawberries Aren't	90
The Invention of Bubble Wrap	91
Phantom Islands of Ancient Maps	92
The Great Escape Artist: Houdini	94
The World's Largest Omelet	95
The Mystery of Sailing Stones	97
The Mystery of the Voynich Manuscript	98
The Enigma of the Zodiac Killer	101
The Curious Case of the Cottingley Fairies	106
The Phenomenon of Aurora Borealis	107
The Secrets of Stonehenge	110
The Disappearance of Amelia Earhart	112
The Legend of Bigfoot	114
Hiroo Onoda: No Surrender	117
The Mystery of the Mary Celeste Ship	121
The Lost Treasure of the San Miguel	124
The Curious Concept of Schrödinger's Cat	126
Munch, The Scream	128
The Simpsons Predicts the Future	131
Crazy Laws of the Middle East	135
The Riddle of the Sphinx	139
Reel vs Real: The Truth Behind Gangster Movies	141
Tom and Jerry: The Psychological Perspective	144
The Legend of El Dorado	146
The Mystery of the Loch Ness Monster	148
The Curse of Tutankhamun's Tomb	150
The Mysterious Disappearance of the Roanoke Colony	152

The Legend of the Jersey Devil	**156**
Pepsi vs. Coca-Cola: The Cola Wars	**159**
The Original Formula of Coca-Cola	**162**
The Origin of Football	**163**
Castro's Exploding Cigar	**166**
Left- and right-hand traffic	**168**
Starbucks in Italy	**170**
Crazy Laws of the United States	**172**
The Mysterious Shroud of Turin	**179**
The Riddle of the Hanging Gardens of Babylon	**181**
The Legend of the Kraken	**183**
Oswald's, Soviet Adventure	**186**
The Ha Giang Loop	**190**
The Puzzle of the Antikythera Mechanism	**193**
Tupac in Puerto Rico	**195**
From Trenches to Middle-earth: J.R.R. Tolkien's Journey	**198**
We Didn't Start the Fire: The Time Capsule in a Song	**201**
Belgians in the Congo	**204**
The Enigma of the Toynbee Tiles	**210**
The Legend of the Mothman	**215**
The Mysterious Hum of Taos, New Mexico	**218**
The Curious Case of Kaspar Hauser	**221**
Churchill's Greatest Quotes	**223**
The Secret Society of the Freemasons	**228**
Why is Bob Dylan So Weird	**232**
The Legend of the Chupacabra	**234**
The Unexplained Sounds of the Bloop	**236**
The Mystery of the Devil's Kettle Falls	**239**
The Phantom Time Hypothesis	**243**
The Mysterious Stone Spheres of Costa Rica	**245**
The Legend of the Lost City of Z	**247**

The Unexplained Disappearance of the Eilean Mor	250
The Oslo Hotel Murder Mystery	252
Crazy Laws of the europe	255
Georgia Guidestones	262
Why Do Cats Purr?	265
Steve Jobs Commencement Speech	266

Join us on your favourite platform,
Scan the QR code on
your phone or tablet

Welcome, curious reader, to the whimsical world of "Trivia Book: 101 Random Stuff You Never Need to Know"! Here, we embark on a quirky journey through the lesser-known alleys of history, culture, and the downright bizarre. This book is your ticket to a carnival of curiosities, a maze of wonder, where the ordinary becomes extraordinary, and the mundane turns magical.

Dive into the playful depths of the unknown, from the mysteries of the animal kingdom to the oddities of human behavior. Marvel at the eccentricities of history, the peculiarities of nature, and the amusing quirks of our daily lives. Each page is a new adventure, a new puzzle to ponder, a fresh giggle waiting to escape.

So, grab your favorite beverage, find a cozy nook, and prepare to be delighted, bemused, and thoroughly entertained. This is not just a trivia book; it's a celebration of the weird and wonderful tapestry of life. Enjoy the ride!

1 - Coffee vs. Tea in the World

In the grand battle of wake-up brews, two champions reign supreme: coffee and tea. Globally, mornings (and sometimes afternoons) hinge on this critical choice – a steaming espresso or a soothing Earl Grey? It's a tale of two beverages, each with a fan base as fervent as sports enthusiasts. Coffee lovers tout their drink as the elixir of high energy, painting the world in shades of robust Arabica and adventurous Robusta. On the other side, tea aficionados find solace in their delicate infusions, celebrating everything from the humble green leaf to exotic chai spices. The world map could well be redrawn as lands of beans and leaves, with each nation tipping its mug to one side or the other.

But it's not just about a caffeine kick; these drinks steep in cultural significance. Coffee is the lifeblood of bustling cities, the fuel for breakneck deadlines and artistic endeavors. It's the protagonist in the story of late-night studies and early morning rushes. Tea, meanwhile, is the essence of tranquility and tradition – a cup is an invitation to pause, reflect, or bond. Whether it's the Japanese tea ceremony, steeped in Zen and artistry, or the British afternoon tea, a legacy of leisure and gossip, tea transcends the leaf to become a ritual. Together, coffee and tea don't just perk up our day; they brew a rich tapestry of global culture, one sip at a time.

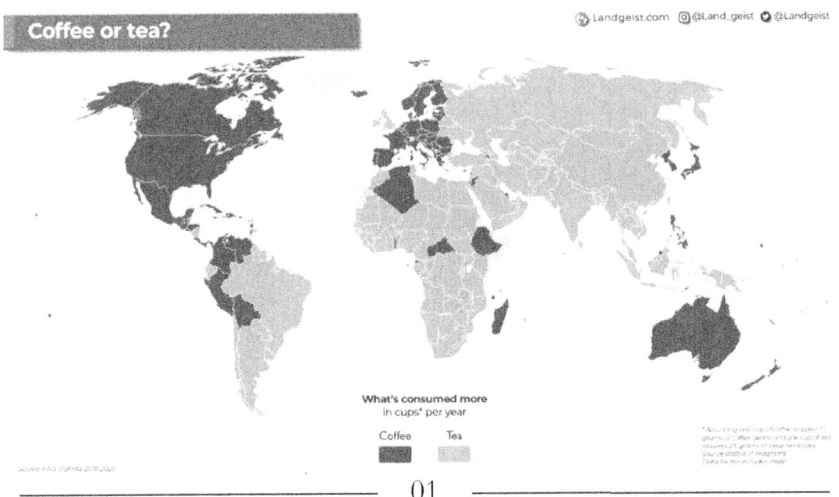

The tale of consumption unfolds, as seen on the graph. The East, steeped in tradition, bows to the leaf: China, with its ancient tea rituals, sips more tea than any other, followed closely by the aromatic brews of India and the strong, black infusions of Turkey. Meanwhile, the Nordics, with their long, dark winters, are a stronghold of coffee culture. Finland leads the charge, their cups perennially brimming with the dark, rich liquid, followed by their Scandinavian neighbors, Norway and Iceland, where coffee is less a beverage and more a way of life. It's a world divided not by borders but by beverage preference, where the number of cups per capita tells a story more intricate than any census.

- Tea Time Travel: Legend has it that tea was discovered by Chinese Emperor Shen Nong in 2737 BC when leaves accidentally blew into his pot of boiling water.
- Tea for Immortality: Ancient Chinese believed tea to be a key ingredient for the elixir of immortality.
- A Steeped History: The earliest recorded tea party dates back to the 3rd century AD in China, where it was a social event for the upper class.
- Boston's Brew Rebellion: The Boston Tea Party of 1773 wasn't about flavor but protest—colonists dumped tea into the harbor to rebel against British taxation.
- High Tea or Low Tea?: The British 'afternoon tea' tradition was started in the 1840s by the Duchess of Bedford, not because of hunger, but boredom.
- Matcha Do About Nothing: Japanese Samurai warriors prepared and drank matcha as a pre-battle ritual for its calming and focus-enhancing qualities.
- Bean There, Done That: Coffee was supposedly discovered by an Ethiopian goat herder named Kaldi, who noticed his goats became energetic after eating certain berries.
- Java Jives: The term "cup of joe" is said to have originated from American soldiers (G.I. Joes) in WWII who were known to consume large amounts of coffee.

- Espresso Yourself: The word 'espresso' comes from Italian and means "expressed" or "forced out," referring to the way espresso is made by forcing boiling water through pressed coffee grounds.
- Turkish Delight: In Turkey, coffee was so important that a woman could divorce her husband if he failed to provide her daily quota of coffee.
- Coffee House Coups: The first European coffee houses, which opened in the 17th century, were often referred to as "penny universities" because for a penny one could buy a cup and listen to stimulating conversations.
- Arabian Beginnings: The world's first coffee house, Kiva Han, opened in Constantinople (now Istanbul) in 1475.
- Dutch Courage: The Dutch were pivotal in spreading coffee's popularity in Europe after they began cultivation in their colony in Java, Indonesia.
- Pope's Approval: Coffee gained popularity in Europe after Pope Clement VIII declared it delicious, quashing any religious controversy.
- Leaves of Change: The trade of tea leaves was so significant in the 19th century that it shaped historical events, including the Opium Wars between Britain and China.
- Revolutionary Brew: Coffee became America's preferred drink after the Boston Tea Party, as drinking tea became unpatriotic.
- The Bean Belt: All coffee is grown in the Bean Belt, the area between the Tropics of Cancer and Capricorn.
- The Civilized Stimulant: In the 18th century, tea replaced ale as the English drink of choice because it was considered a more 'civilized' stimulant.
- Coffee in Space: Coffee is so beloved that it has even made it into space; astronauts enjoy specially made 'space cups' to sip coffee in zero-gravity.
- Caffeinated Conquests: During the 17th and 18th centuries, coffee plants were so valuable that European powers would go to great lengths to acquire and cultivate them in their colonies.

Tea and coffee consumption

The table below offers a snapshot of coffee and tea cultures around the world, measured per capita—"by head"—to give an average consumption indicator for each country.

Tea

Country	Amount (kg per capita)	Trivia
Finland	12.0	Workers are granted two coffee breaks per day by law.
Luxembourg	11.1	Located in the heart of Europe's coffee-loving region.
Netherlands	8.2	Dutch coffee addiction influenced Indonesian coffee cultivation.
Sweden	7.7	Fika, an extended coffee break, is a part of the culture.
Denmark	7.4	Black coffee, locally roasted, is gaining preference.
Norway	6.8	Alcohol prohibition era boosted the coffee culture.

Coffee

Country	Amount (kg per capita)	Trivia
Turkey	3.2	Workers are granted two coffee breaks per day by law.
United Kingdom	2.2	Located in the heart of Europe's coffee-loving region.
Ireland	2.1	Dutch coffee addiction influenced Indonesian coffee cultivation.
Pakistan	1.5	Fika, an extended coffee break, is a part of the culture.
Iran	1.5	Black coffee, locally roasted, is gaining preference.
Russia	1..4	Alcohol prohibition era boosted the coffee culture.

In the cosmic tussle for the title of Healthiest Brew, coffee flexes with its antioxidants, linked to reducing the risk of several diseases, while tea counters with its reputation for less caffeine and a calming effect, thanks to theanine. The health-conscious crowd often goes green (tea, that is) for a detox, while the productivity hackers guzzle coffee to fuel their hustle. But let's spill the beans: isn't the choice often just a matter of which warmth hugs your insides better on a chilly morning or which cup whispers the sweetest promise of alertness?

As the world shrinks, our mugs expand with choices, brimming with single-origin coffee and hand-rolled oolong teas. The modern connoisseur might debate over notes of chocolate in their Nicaraguan roast or the grassy undertones of a Gyokuro shade-grown tea. Globalization has not only made these options accessible but has turned them into statements of sophistication. So, whether you wrap your hands around a steamy latte or a porcelain cup of sencha, remember: you may never need to know the intricate origins of your morning pick-me-up, but isn't it a delightful way to stir up a mundane day?

2 - The Mystery of Left-Handedness

"When nothing goes right, go left"—and that's precisely what about 10% of the population does every day when they pick up a pen or swing a bat. Lefties, in their stylish defiance of the right-handed majority, have long been the enigmatic figures of classrooms and cafeterias. With a world that seems to be engineered for the right-handed, from scissors to can openers, left-handers navigate daily life with a kind of suave adaptability that could only be described as a superpower.

"Lefties in great demand but limited supply!"—the rarity of left-handedness makes it a hot commodity in certain professions. Think of those left-handed pitchers in baseball throwing curveballs that seem to defy physics. Or the artists whose right-brain dominance showers them with creative genius—Leonardo da Vinci and Michelangelo, anyone?

And to all left-handers who've ever heard, "God made everyone right-handed, only the truly gifted overcome it"—take it as a compliment. Lefties have muscled their way through a right-centric world, and history is all the richer for it. They've ruled kingdoms, shaped art and culture, and have even been statistically more likely to become U.S. presidents. So while you may never need to know which of your friends are quietly calculating the best angle to use a right-handed desk, isn't it amusing to ponder the mysterious allure of the left-handed legend?

The ten most famous left-handed people

- Leonardo da Vinci: Not only was he a left-handed master artist, but he also had a voracious curiosity that led him to write extensive scientific studies about everything from the flow of water to the way birds fly.
- Marie Curie: The famed left-handed scientist was the first woman to win a Nobel Prize and remains the only person to win a Nobel in two different sciences (Physics and Chemistry).
- Barack Obama: The former U.S. President, besides being left-handed, is known for his love of basketball and has a tradition of filling out NCAA brackets for March Madness.
- Oprah Winfrey: This media mogul and philanthropist, while being a lefty, was also the first female African-American to become a billionaire.
- Bill Gates: The co-founder of Microsoft and philanthropist, who writes with his left hand, was a college dropout from Harvard University.

- Aristotle: The ancient philosopher might have been left-handed, and he also wrote on a diverse range of subjects, from physics to poetry, and even dream interpretation.
- Napoleon Bonaparte: The French military leader and emperor, known to be left-handed, also imposed the metric system and left a set of civil laws known as the Napoleonic Code, which has influenced legal systems around the world.
- Albert Einstein: The theoretical physicist who developed the theory of relativity was left-handed, and interestingly, he was also a talented violinist.
- Jimi Hendrix: Arguably the greatest electric guitarist in the history of rock music and a lefty, famously re-strung his guitars upside down to play left-handed, which contributed to his unique sound.
- Julius Caesar: The Roman general and statesman was left-handed and is also credited with the Julian calendar, the predecessor to the Gregorian calendar most of the world uses today.

The path of left-handers through history has been as twisted as a corkscrew – and sometimes just as sharp. Lefties have been celebrated, stigmatized, and mystified, making their mark in a world that's often felt like it's spinning the wrong way.

In the days of yore, left-handedness was often seen with a mix of suspicion and intrigue. The Latin word for left, "sinister," is a tell-tale sign of the superstition that once surrounded left-handers. In medieval times, lefties were often associated with witchcraft and nefarious dealings. A left-handed compliment? Not exactly the praise you'd want!

Delving deeper into the medieval mindset, left-handers often found themselves unfairly entangled in witch hunts. The prevalent belief was that left-handed people were consorting with the devil. During witch trials, if a suspect was discovered to be left-handed, it was considered further evidence of their pact with dark forces. In some cultures, left-handed children were forced to switch hands, as using the left was seen as a sign of moral and character weakness. Even the Bible contains passages that associate the right hand with favor and power and the left with weakness or evil. This cultural bias ingrained a sense of mistrust towards left-handers that persisted for centuries.

Fast forward to the Renaissance, and things start to look a bit brighter for our left-handed luminaries. Artists like Leonardo da Vinci, a lefty himself, were celebrated for their unique perspective – both literally and figuratively. Da Vinci's backward writing, where he penned notes from right to left, is a classic example of left-handed adaptation and mystery.

But the plot thickens in more recent times. Up until the 20th century, many schools would force left-handed children to write with their right hand, a practice rooted in a mixture of tradition and misguided discipline. The tides of change, however, have turned significantly in modern times, with left-handers now being celebrated for their unique approach to problem-solving and creativity.

Left-handers have navigated a history as complex as a labyrinth, from superstitions to being celebrated for their uniqueness. Each lefty is a living chapter of this intriguing story, full of resilience and distinctiveness. Remember: you may never need to know the entire saga of left-handedness, but it's a fascinating snippet to add to your collection of curiosities.

3 - The World's Shortest War

Talk about a brief battle! The World's Shortest War, clocking in at a mere 38 minutes, sounds more like a sitcom episode than a chapter in the annals of history. This blink-and-you-miss-it conflict, known as the Anglo-Zanzibar War, occurred on August 27, 1896, and holds the Guinness World Record for the shortest war in history.

- A London Tube Journey: Traveling from Heathrow Airport to King's Cross Station on the Piccadilly Line? That's about a 50-minute ride, comfortably surpassing the duration of the war.

- Baking a Lasagna: Preparing and cooking a decent lasagna can take upwards of an hour. In the time it takes for the cheese to bubble and brown, a whole war was fought and concluded!

- An average episode of the U.S. version of "The Office" lasts about 22 minutes. You could barely fit in two episodes before the war, which lasted just 38 minutes, would have been over. It's a humorous thought that a conflict between nations was shorter than watching Michael Scott's antics in a couple of episodes!

The war was sparked by a classic case of political drama. When the pro-British Sultan of Zanzibar passed away, his nephew, Khalid bin Barghash, seized the opportunity to claim the throne, much to the chagrin of the British  who favored another candidate. The British, not ones to dilly-dally, issued an ultimatum: step down or face the consequences. Khalid, feeling rather bold, decided to hunker down in the palace.

The clock started ticking on August 27, 1896, at 9:02 AM, when the British naval forces, positioned in the harbor, opened fire on the palace. The bombardment was swift and brutally effective. By 9:40 AM, the flag of Khalid was down, and the shortest war in history was over. The aftermath? A demolished palace, one sunken yacht, two British soldiers injured, and approximately 500 Zanzibari casualties. Khalid managed to escape and took refuge in the German consulate before being captured later.

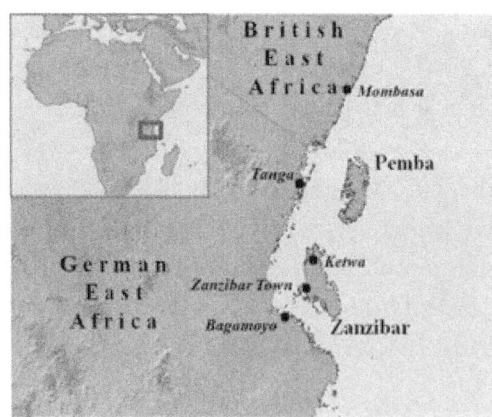

The Anglo-Zanzibar War, though fleeting, left a lasting impression. It highlighted the might of the British Empire at the time and marked the end of one of the shortest reigns in history. So, while you may never need to know the ins and outs of this historic 38-minute skirmish, it's a remarkable tidbit to drop during a lull in conversation — who wouldn't be intrigued by a war that lasted less than the average commute?

4 - Animals in Space

Buckle up for a cosmic safari! The history of animals in space is not just a tale of human ingenuity, but a testament to the bravery of some unlikely astronauts. Long before humans set foot on the Moon, our furry and feathered friends were the pioneering space travelers, helping us understand if life beyond our planet was possible.

The Canine Cosmonauts: The Soviet space program sent the first canine cosmonauts, including the famous Laika, the first animal to orbit Earth in 1957. Though Laika's mission was one-way, she paved the way for human spaceflight.

Buzzing into Orbit: Believe it or not, fruit flies were the first Earthlings to reach space. In 1947, they were launched aboard a U.S. V-2 rocket to study radiation exposure at high altitudes.

Monkeys and Apes: The United States sent several monkeys and apes into space in the 1950s and 60s to study the biological effects of space travel. Ham, a chimpanzee, became famous in 1961 for his suborbital flight, demonstrating tasks during the flight before safely returning to Earth.

Félicette, the Astrocat: In 1963, France sent Félicette, a stray Parisian cat, into space. Félicette returned safely after a brief suborbital flight, making her the first and only feline astronaut to date.

Spacefaring Frogs and Newts: The amphibious set has also seen its day in orbit.

NASA's Orbiting Frog Otolith experiment in 1970 involved sending frogs to space to study weightlessness's effects on the inner ear.

Spiders Spinning in Zero Gravity: In 1973, two garden spiders named

Arabella and Anita lived aboard Skylab, spinning webs in space so scientists could study how zero-gravity affected their abilities.

Mice, Fish, and Even Jellyfish: Modern space missions have seen a diverse range of animals, including mice, fish, and jellyfish, helping researchers understand long-term effects of space on living organisms.

A Celestial Menagerie: The International Space Station has become a floating laboratory for studying various organisms, including worms and tardigrades, known for their resilience in extreme conditions.

The legacy of these animal astronauts lives on, not only in the advancements they contributed to space exploration but also in the ethical discussions they inspire about our responsibilities to our fellow Earthlings.

While you may never need to know the details of each animal's journey into the cosmos, their stories add an intriguing and sometimes heartwarming chapter to the annals of space exploration. These intrepid creatures have provided invaluable insights, making them unsung heroes of the space age.

5 - The Invention of the Potato Chip

Crisp, crunchy, and irresistibly addictive, potato chips are a snacker's delight. But did you know their origin story is as flavorful as the chips themselves? Let's slice into the history of this beloved snack.

A Chef's Revenge Turned Culinary Icon: The potato chip was born not out of a recipe, but from a diner's complaint and a chef's stroke of cheeky genius. In 1853, at Moon's Lake House in Saratoga Springs, New York, a customer complained that his potatoes were too thick and soggy. Chef George Crum, irked by the criticism, decided to slice the potatoes paper-thin, fry them to a crisp, and salt them heavily, hoping to make them inedible. To Crum's surprise, the customer adored the creation, and the "Saratoga Chips" became an instant hit.

From Kitchen Accidents to Snack Sensations: What started as a kitchen mishap turned into a snack revolution. The original recipe for Saratoga Chips was simple – thinly sliced potatoes fried until crisp in hot oil, then seasoned with salt.

The data vividly illustrates how countries in the Western hemisphere lead the way in per capita consumption of potato chips. This trend underscores the cultural affinity for this savory treat in these regions, where potato chips have become not just a snack, but a staple of leisure and social gatherings. Let's take a closer look at which countries are reaching the most into the chip bag!

Country	Consumption (Kg per capita)
United States	6.7
United Kingdom	5.4
Canada	4.2
Australia	3.8
Spain	3.4

- First Flavored Chips: The first flavored potato chips were barbecue, introduced by Joe 'Spud' Murphy, the owner of an Irish chip company, in the 1950s.
- A Global Phenomenon: Different regions have unique flavors; for example, the UK has prawn cocktail and Worcester sauce flavors, while Japan offers flavors like seaweed and wasabi.
- The Largest Bag of Chips: In 2013, Corkers Crisps created the world's largest bag of potato chips, weighing in at 2,515 pounds.
- A Space Age Snack: In 1995, Pringles sent a can of chips into space aboard the space shuttle Columbia, making them the first potato chips in space.
- Record-Breaking Crunch: The world's longest potato chip, created by a Japanese company, measures over 25 inches long.
- Potato Chip Day: National Potato Chip Day is celebrated in the United States on March 14th every year.
- Economic Impact: The potato chip industry is a multi-billion-dollar industry, with Americans spending over $7 billion a year on potato chips.
- The Sound of Freshness: The distinctive crackle sound when a potato chip bag is opened is designed by manufacturers to enhance the sense of freshness and quality.
- The Power of Packaging: The modern potato chip bag is a result of years of innovation; it's designed to prevent light and air from degrading the chips and to keep them fresh longer.

A Snack for Science

Beyond being a beloved snack, potato chips have intriguingly found themselves at the center of scientific intrigue. In one notable study, researchers delved into the sensory experience of eating potato chips. The study, conducted by scientists at the University of Oxford, focused on how the sound of the crunch affects our perception of the chip's freshness and quality. They discovered that the louder and crisper the crunch, the more we perceive the chip as being fresh and high quality. This research has implications not just for food science, but also for how manufacturers design packaging and market their snacks.

But the science of potato chips doesn't end there. Another study explored the psychological aspect of chip consumption, examining the "hedonic treadmill"

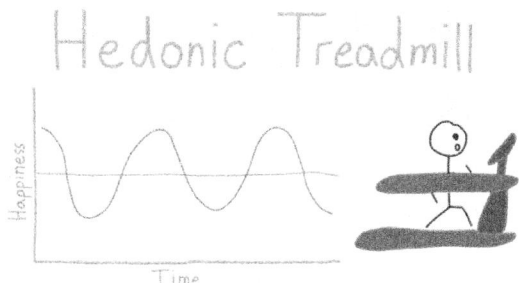

a concept where we rapidly get used to positive life changes, requiring more to maintain a level of happiness. It turns out, eating potato chips (or any favorite food) frequently can reduce the pleasure we derive from them over time, a classic case of too much of a good thing.

So, the next time you're enjoying a bag of your favorite potato chips, **remember: you may never need to know** the intricate science behind that satisfying crunch or why they seem less appealing the more you eat. But isn't it fascinating to think that such a simple snack can be a window into complex scientific principles? Potato chips, it seems, are not just a treat for the taste buds but also food for thought!

6 - The Great Emu War

Strap in for a tale that sounds more like a quirky comedy script than a chapter from a history book. The Great Emu War of 1932 is an episode in Australian history that is as bizarre as it is true, featuring a feathered foe unlike any other.

Post World War I, Australia faced an unexpected adversary

– emus. These large, flightless birds were wreaking havoc on the wheat crops in Western Australia, leading distressed farmers to seek government intervention.

In a move that seems straight out of a slapstick movie, the Australian government deployed the military, armed with Lewis machine guns, to manage the emu population. The operation was led by Major G.P.W. Meredith of the Seventh Heavy Battery of the Royal Australian Artillery

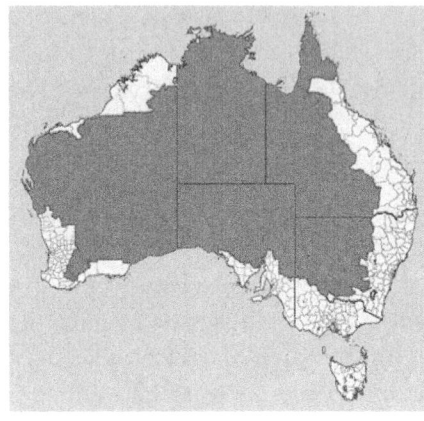

The "war" officially began in November 1932. However, the emus, with their surprising agility and speed, proved to be elusive targets. The birds' guerrilla tactics, scattering into small groups, made them a challenging enemy for the trained soldiers.

The map provided illustrates the vast expanse of Australia, a continent where the emu, the country's iconic flightless bird, roams. With the rich outback and extensive farmlands, emus had (and still have) a vast territory to traverse, which in the 1930s included the Western Australian wheatbelt, the stage of the Great Emu War. This expansive area, marked by the yellow regions on your map, signifies the agricultural lands that the emus invaded, leading to the infamous conflict. The emus' extensive range across the Australian landscape, coupled with their impressive adaptability, made the military operation to curb their population all the more challenging. Today, the emu continues to be a symbol of the wild, untamed spirit of Australia, occupying a significant swath of land that stretches across the continent.

After several days of the campaign, the military found they had expended a large amount of ammunition but had little success in reducing the emu population. The operation was deemed ineffective and costly.

- Machine Guns vs. Birds: The military used two Lewis machine guns and 10,000 rounds of ammunition, which proved largely ineffective against the emu onslaught.
- Media Mockery: Newspapers dubbed the operation "The Emu War," and headlines lampooned the futile attempts of the soldiers with puns and jokes.
- Emus' Winning Streak: The emus' surprising agility meant that they could run at speeds of up to 50 km/h, making them difficult targets for the military.
- A Tactical Withdrawal: After a month of the military's involvement, the operation was called off, citing only a few hundred emus were killed, far short of the thousands anticipated.
- Bounty on Birds: Following the military withdrawal, a bounty system was put in place, which proved to be more successful, with thousands of bounties claimed over a six-month period.
- Political Backlash: The operation's failure led to criticism in the Australian parliament, with one senator comparing the emus to Zulus and the military engagements to a war.
- Emu War Veterans: Soldiers who participated joked about forming "Emu War Veterans" associations to remember their unique military service.
- Environmental Concerns: The war raised questions about human impact on wildlife and the environment, as the emu invasions were partly due to the clearing of large areas for agriculture.
- Tourist Attraction: Today, the Great Emu War is a point of quirky historical interest and tourism in the small towns of Western Australia.
- Continued Nuisance: Despite the war's end, emus continue to be a nuisance in some farming regions, causing debates on wildlife management.
- Memorialized in Games: The Great Emu War has inspired board games and video games, memorializing the event in pop culture. need some specific example
- The Great Emu War has indeed been immortalized in the realm of gaming, capturing the whimsical side of this historical event. One such example is the card game "Emu War!"

- by This and That Games. In this game, players take on the role of Australian farmers who work together to fend off the emus, reflecting the collective effort that characterized the actual event.
- Another nod to the Great Emu War can be found in the video game "Call of Duty: Modern Warfare II," where there is a passing mention in one of the game's levels, adding a touch of historical humor to the gameplay.

As the sun set on the battlefields of the Western Australian wheatbelt, the Great Emu War drew to a close – not with a triumphant victory, but with a humbling acknowledgment of defeat. The military, despite their firepower and strategy, conceded to the emus, whose guerrilla tactics and astonishing speed had left the soldiers outmaneuvered. The birds, it seemed, had outlasted human ingenuity, and the government was forced to wave the white flag.

In the aftermath, the government switched tactics from military might to economic incentives, establishing a bounty system that proved to be more effective. Farmers, now turned bounty hunters, claimed their rewards for each emu captured, bringing some relief to the beleaguered agricultural sector. Though the emus were never fully vanquished, their disruptive forays into farmland were curtailed, restoring a semblance of peace and order.

The Great Emu War remains a peculiar chapter in Australia's history, often revisited with a mix of amusement and disbelief. It's a story that serves as a whimsical reminder of nature's unpredictable power and humanity's limitations. And while you may never need to know the intricate details of this feathered fiasco, it's an amusing morsel of history, a testament to the fact that sometimes, truth really is stranger than fiction.

7 - The Color of Carrots

Prepare to have your mind peeled back layer by layer as we dig into the colorful history of the carrot. This common vegetable, now synonymous with a vibrant orange, actually began its culinary journey sporting a very different hue.

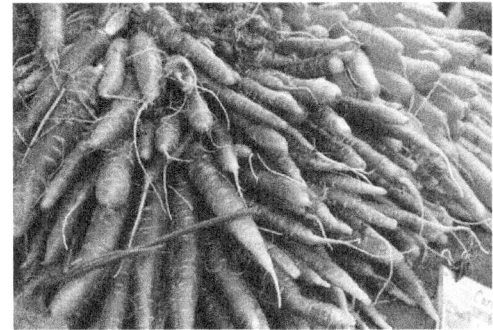

Believe it or not, carrots weren't always orange. The wild ancestors of the carrots we know today were likely purple or white. These early varieties were grown in Central Asia and the Middle East.

A Dutch Transformation: It was the Dutch in the 17th century who developed the orange carrot we are familiar with today. As the story goes, it was cultivated as a tribute to the House of Orange, the Dutch royal family, which led the struggle for Dutch independence.

Initially, however carrots were grown for their aromatic leaves and seeds rather than their roots. They were used medicinally before being recognized as a food source. Ancient Greeks and Romans appreciated them for their medicinal properties, and they weren't necessarily eaten as part of a meal.

- **Ancient Ancestry:** The earliest carrots were cultivated around 900 AD in Persia which is considered the true birthplace of the carrot.
- **A Spectrum of Shades:** Besides purple and white, there were also black, red, and green carrots, each with its own unique taste and texture.
- **Nutritional Powerhouses:** Carrots are high in beta-carotene, fiber, vitamins K1, potassium, and antioxidants.
- **A Visual Boost:** Beta-carotene in carrots is converted into vitamin A by the body, essential for good vision.

- **A Flavor Enhancer:** Carrots were used in sweet puddings before sugar became widely available in Europe.
- **War-time Heroes:** During World War II, carrots were used in Britain to sweeten food when sugar was rationed.
- **Culinary Flexibility:** Carrots are used worldwide in various dishes, from raw in salads to cooked in stews and soups.
- The Giant of the Veggie World: The largest carrot ever recorded was over 19 feet long and grown by John Evans in 1998 in Alaska.
- **Carrots Go to Space:** Seeds of the carrot were among the few food plants taken to the Moon by Apollo astronauts to provide fresh food.
- **A Tinge of Myth:** Contrary to popular belief, eating massive amounts of carrots doesn't significantly improve night vision.
- **Symbolism and Superstition:** In medieval times, carrots were thought to ward off spirits, particularly in the British Isles.
- **A Literary Snack:** The author of "Peter Rabbit," Beatrix Potter, was the first to popularize the idea of rabbits loving carrots.
- **A Colorful Comeback:** Heirloom and rainbow carrots have seen a resurgence in popularity for their vibrant colors and taste.
- **Carrot Tops:** The green tops of carrots are edible and can be used in salads or as a garnish.
- **Festivals of Orange:** 'Carrot festivals' are celebrated in many parts of the world, including Holtville, the "Carrot Capital of the World," and in Ohakune, New Zealand, which has a giant carrot sculpture.

As you peel, chop, or bite into the crunchy texture of a carrot, remember: you may never need to know its colorful lineage or the fact that it's been to space and back. Yet, every slice of this vibrant vegetable carries with it millennia of history and an evolution as rich and layered as its flavors. It's a humble reminder that sometimes, the most ordinary things hold extraordinary tales.

8 - Bizarre Ice Cream Flavors

Step right up to the wondrous world of ice cream, a place where vanilla and chocolate have made room for a cavalcade of the bizarre and the deliciously strange. This frozen treat, once a luxury for the elite, has undergone a metamorphosis as wild and varied as the flavors now on offer.

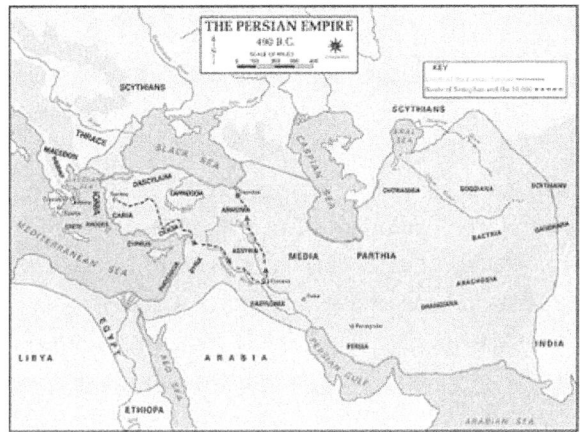

Ice cream's journey begins over a thousand years ago, with origins claimed from China to ancient Persia. Originally, it was snow mixed with fruit and honey, evolving through the Renaissance with the the addition of milk and cream, until the first ice cream parlor opened in 18th century America. Since then, the quest for new flavors has taken a route as inventive as the human palate allows.

Traditional Tastes with a Twist: From Italy's zestful limoncello to Japan's matcha green tea ice cream, traditional flavors have long been the backbone of this chilled delicacy. In Turkey, the stretchy, taffy-like dondurma is made with mastic and salep, while the Philippines boasts of a vibrant purple yam ice cream called ube.

Fast forward to today, and the ice cream world has exploded with innovation. From the subtle to the scream-inducing, there's a flavor to challenge even the most adventurous of taste buds.

- **Garlic Ice Cream:** Hailing from the Gilroy Garlic Festival in California, this pungent treat melds the heat of garlic with the coolness of ice cream.

- **Charcoal Black Coconut:** A gothic twist on tropical flavors, this ice cream gets its color from activated charcoal.
- **Lobster Ice Cream:** Straight from the shores of New England, this savory-sweet concoction is a true seafood lover's delight, featuring buttery lobster folded into the mix.
- **Horse Flesh:** Japan offers this controversial flavor, a daring choice for those looking to push the boundaries of culinary comfort.
- **Pear with Blue Cheese:** An artisanal blend found in select gourmet shops, combining the sweetness of pear with the tangy kick of blue cheese.
- **Wasabi Ice Cream:** Another Japanese innovation that offers a frozen fiery kick that's both cooling and nose-tingling.
- **Bacon Ice Cream:** For the breakfast enthusiast, salty-sweet bacon bits meet the creamy base in an unexpected harmony.
- **Beer-Flavored Ice Cream:** Breweries have dived into the trend, churning out ice cream with the malty, hoppy notes of a good ale.

As culinary artists continue to experiment with ice cream, the future promises even more extraordinary flavors. Will it be savory squid ink or the refreshing zing of kombucha ice cream? Only time will tell.

So, the next time you find yourself in the frozen aisle, pondering a pint of pickle-flavored ice cream, remember: you may never need to know the full spectrum of ice cream's wild flavor adventures, but isn't it exhilarating to taste the creativity and cultural stories that each scoop offers? In the realm of ice cream, it seems, the only limit is the imagination.

9 - The World's Longest Place Name

Prepare for a linguistic journey as we venture into the land of lengthy labels. Nestled in the beautiful landscapes of New Zealand is a hill with a name so long, it holds a Guinness World Record. It's a place name that's not just a tongue twister, but a tale in itself.

A Maori Marvel: The hill is known to the locals as **Taumatawhakatangihangakoauauotamateaturipukakapiki maungahoronukupokaiwhenuakitnatahu**

which in the Maori language translates roughly to "The summit where Tamatea, the man with the big knees, the climber of mountains, the land-swallower who traveled about, played his nose flute to his loved one." With 85 characters, it is one of the longest place names in the world and a testament to the Maori's cultural love for descriptive and poetic nomenclature. What a mouthful!

A Signpost Sensation: The hill's signpost has become something of a tourist attraction in itself, with visitors flocking to take a photo with the sign bearing the hill's lengthy name.

Where Legends Echo: This name commemorates the deeds of a legendary hero, Tamatea, a figure famed in Maori mythology for his explorations and adventures across the land.

It's a name that challenges even the most skilled linguist, and hearing it pronounced correctly is music to the ears – a rhythmic and harmonious blend of vowels and consonants.

<u>Here are some runner-up candidates:</u>

Llanfairpwllgwyngyllgogerychwyrndrobwllllantysiliogogogoch, Wales - This town's name was extended in the 1860s to attract tourists. It translates to "St Mary's Church in the hollow of the white hazel near a rapid whirlpool and the Church of St Tysilio of the red cave."

Chargoggagoggmanchauggagoggchaubunagungamaugg, United States - A lake in Webster, Massachusetts, with a name derived from the Nipmuc language, and is often said to mean "Fishing Place at the Boundaries – Neutral Meeting Grounds." It has been dated to at least 1921.

Tweebuffelsmeteenskootmorsdoodgeskietfontein, South Africa - A farm in the North West Province of South Africa, with a name that means "The spring where two buffaloes were cleanly killed with a single shot." The name dates back to the early 20th century.

Azpilicuetagaraycosaroyarenberecolarrea, Spain - A place in the Basque Country, the name is in the Basque language and relates to the geography and historical ownership of the land. The exact origin date of the name is not well-documented but reflects the Basque tradition of descriptive place naming.

Pekwachnamaykoskwaskwaypinwanik, Canada - A lake in Manitoba whose name means "where the wild trout are caught by fishing with hooks" in the local Cree language. Its name is likely as old as the Cree naming tradition itself.

These places, with their lengthy and often challenging names, carry with them stories and traditions that are integral to their local heritage. While you may never need to know these names by heart, they offer a delightful glimpse into the linguistic and cultural richness that defines places across our globe.

10 - The High-Heeled Shoe Origins

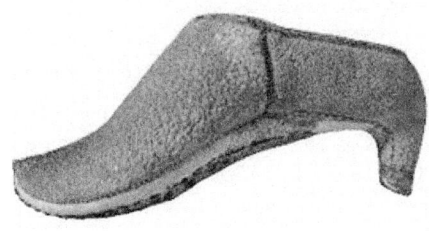

Step into the history of high-heeled shoes, and you'll find a path that's as elevated and intriguing as the heels themselves. These fashion staples, now often associated with femininity and glamour, have a story that strides through various cultures and centuries.

The origin of high heels can be traced back to the 10th century in Persia. Soldiers wore heels to help secure their feet in stirrups. The heel provided stability while riding and shooting arrows.

Heels were introduced to Europe during the 1600s, possibly through Persian diplomats. European aristocrats quickly adopted them, not for utility but as a status symbol. The height of the heel was indicative of one's social ranking – the higher the heel, the higher the status.

Initially, high heels were not gender-specific. Both men and women of the European aristocracy wore them. King Louis XIV of France was known for his love of heels, often adorned with elaborate decorations and sometimes encrusted with miniature battle scenes.

In the 18th century, men's fashion shifted towards more practical clothing, and heels were seen as impractical. This is when high heels started to be associated more with women's fashion.

Over the centuries, the style and height of the heel have evolved. The 19th century saw the introduction of the stiletto, with its slim and high heel, a stark contrast to the chunky and lower heels of the previous centuries.

The invention of the sewing machine and new materials like plastic helped in the mass production and design variation of high-heeled shoes in the 20th century.

In modern times, high heels have transcended their functional origin to become a powerful symbol in fashion and popular culture, often associated with femininity, power, and elegance.

Despite their popularity, high heels have also been at the center of debates around gender norms, fashion vs. comfort, and health implications.

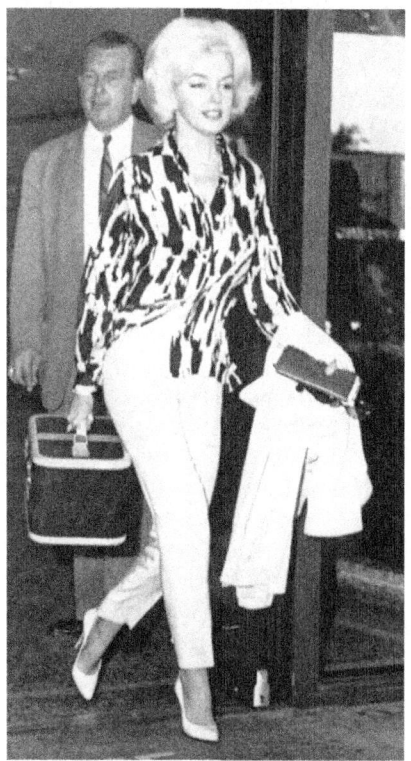

Iconic figures like Marilyn Monroe and Audrey Hepburn have immortalized high heels in popular culture, influencing generations of fashion.

"I don't know who invented high heels, but all owe him a lot"

As you ponder the towering presence of high heels in fashion history, remember: you may never need to know how these elevated shoes climbed their way into the wardrobes of the elite and the common folk alike, but it's a fascinating example of how fashion evolves with culture and time.

11. Crazy Laws of South America

Buckle up for a wild ride through the legal landscape of South America, where a tango beat might be mandatory, but showing your belly button isn't. Prepare to be surprised, amused, and maybe even a little bewildered as we uncover the wackiest, quirkiest, and downright strange laws this vibrant continent has to offer. From llama love triangles to pig-naming restrictions, get ready to toss out your travel guide and embrace the unexpected! So, put on your dancing shoes, pack your sense of humor, and hold onto your hats, because the legal safari through South America is about to begin!

- **Ecuador:** Ladies, feel free to dance away in public, just keep that belly button under wraps! Who knew the key to decency was all about the navel?

- **Colombia:** Shopping for knives? No problem! Carrying them around? Big no-no. It seems in Colombia, the journey from shop to home must be a mysterious one.

- **Peru:** Young bachelors, think twice before bringing home a female llama or alpaca. It's not just about space, it's the law! This law reflects a unique aspect of Peruvian culture and animal rights, focusing on the relationship between young men and these domestic animals.

- **Panama:** Back in the '80s, your workout gear could land you in trouble. White t-shirts and beige trunks were a no-go. Fashion police, or actual police?

- **Bolivia:** A rule that makes Thanksgiving dinners less awkward – no romantic entanglements with a woman and her daughter at the same time.

- **Argentine:** Don't forget your tango tracks! It's not just about the beat, it's a legal requirement. Tango or bust!

Argentine DJs are legally required to play a certain amount of tango music. This law highlights the cultural significance of tango in Argentina and ensures its presence in modern entertainment venues.

- **Venezuela**: It's illegal to take photos of military buildings or other strategic locations. This law is about national security but can catch unsuspecting tourists off guard.

- **Brazil**: The law prohibits selling watermelons in certain regions to prevent littering and pest issues.

- **Chile**: Classical music must be played in public buses, a law intended to promote cultural enrichment and a pleasant commuting environment.

- **Uruguay**: Dueling is legal as long as both parties are registered blood donors. This quirky law juxtaposes a traditional practice with modern health considerations.

- **Paraguay**: Dueling is legal here too, provided both duelists are legal adults and have registered as organ donors.

- **Guyana**: It's illegal to dress as the opposite gender in public, a law that reflects traditional views on gender roles and attire.

- **Suriname**: It's forbidden to name a pig 'Napoleon'. This law hints at historical sensitivities and the symbolic power of names.

- **Falkland Islands:** It's illegal to ride a llama in public. While llamas are common in South America, this law ensures their well-being and public safety.

- **Guyana**: There's a curfew for kites - they can't be flown at night. This unique regulation is likely for safety and public order.

- **Peru**: Forget those cheesy pick-up lines, fellas! Wooing a condor in Peru is illegal, protecting these majestic birds from unwanted advances and ensuring their peaceful skyward soar.

- **Bolivia**: Feeling festive? Unleash your inner pyromaniac, responsibly! Bolivia's "Law of the Devil" allows controlled bonfires to symbolically chase away evil spirits during Carnival. Just mind the marshmallows and safety regulations.

- **Suriname**: Don't underestimate the power of a name! Naming your pet turtle "Leonardo" might be cute, but in Suriname, reptiles can't share titles with historical figures. Choose wisely, little shell-dweller!

- **Colombia**: Coffee break with a kick? In some Colombian towns, adding milk to your brew is considered an abomination. Embrace the black gold in its purest form, or prepare for some raised eyebrows and friendly banter.

- **Chile**: Feeling stressed? Take a deep breath and listen to the trees! Chile boasts a unique "Law of the Forest," protecting native woodlands and promoting their therapeutic effect on stressed-out city dwellers. Nature walk, anyone?

- **Ecuador**: Sleepwalking into an adventure? Fear not! Ecuador recognizes "somnambulic sleepwalking" as a legal defense, protecting those who commit crimes while deep in their dreamworld. Talk about a legal lullaby.

- **Argentina**: Feeling competitive? Grab your mate and your chessboard! Argentine schools legally include chess in their curriculum, fostering strategic thinking and mental agility from a young age. Checkmate, boredom

- **Brazil**: Singing in the shower? Belt it out loud! Public singing is not only tolerated but encouraged in some Brazilian towns, transforming everyday spaces into impromptu karaoke rooms. Let your shower serenade take flight.

- **Venezuela**: Feeling the rhythm? Bust a move, comrade! Dancing is mandatory in some Venezuelan schools, celebrating the joy of movement and cultural heritage. Put on your salsa shoes and join the fiesta!

- **Paraguay**: Need a break from the digital world? Unplug and unwind! Paraguay boasts a "Digital Detox Day," encouraging citizens to ditch their devices and reconnect with nature and human interaction. Take a breath, the notifications can wait.

- **Ecuador**: Forget the confetti guns, fiesta-goers! Throwing flour during Carnival celebrations is strictly prohibited in some Ecuadorian towns. Opt for colorful costumes and lively music – there's plenty of joy to be shared without the powdery pandemonium.

- **Brazil**: Feeling generous? Think twice before tipping in restaurants! Gratuity is often included in the bill in Brazil, so showing your appreciation with an extra "obrigado" is enough. Save your reais for souvenirs or that extra caipirinha.

- **Argentina**: Need a midnight snack? Don't expect a 24-hour bakery bonanza! Bakeries in Argentina have mandatory closing times, ensuring bakers get their well-deserved rest. Plan your pastry purchases accordingly, or embrace the sweet dreams for a change.

- **Chile**: Got a sweet tooth with a social conscience? Opt for fair-trade chocolate in Chile! A law incentivizes the sale and consumption of ethically sourced cocoa, supporting sustainable practices and happy cacao farmers. Choose treats that taste good and do good.

- **Peru:** Calling all bookworms! Embrace the literary life in Peru. Public reading is actively encouraged in some plazas and parks, transforming these spaces into open-air libraries. Pack your favorite novel and join the bookish buzz.

- **Colombia:** Forget the selfie stick, focus on the sunset! Taking photos of certain architectural marvels is prohibited in Colombia, protecting cultural heritage and ensuring everyone enjoys the view without intrusive camera clicks. Capture the beauty in your mind, not just your lens.

- **Venezuela:** Need a laugh? Embrace the power of humor! In some Venezuelan towns, telling jokes and sharing funny stories is considered a civic duty, spreading joy and fostering community spirit. Let your inner comedian shine!

- **Ecuador:** Feeling the urge to climb? Think twice before scaling those ancient ruins! In Ecuador, protecting historical sites is paramount, and unauthorized climbing can land you in legal trouble. Stick to designated paths and appreciate the wonders from afar.

- **Argentina:** Got a green thumb? Don't plant just any tree! Argentina has laws restricting the planting of certain invasive species, protecting the delicate ecosystem. Choose native flora and help your garden flourish responsibly.

- **Brazil:** Feeling the wanderlust? Explore, but respect boundaries! Crossing into indigenous territories in Brazil without proper authorization is illegal, protecting the cultural integrity and way of life of these communities. Travel responsibly and learn about their traditions before venturing further.

Each peculiar law, whether it's about dance, romance, or even llama management, paints a unique picture of the societies from which they spring. So, while you may never need to know that serenading a condor in Peru is off-limits, or that in Argentina, a chess match might be part of the school day, these laws offer a whimsical window into the diverse tapestry of South American life. They remind us that the world is full of surprises, if only we look closely enough.

12 . The Beatles and the 'Let It Be' Legacy

In the quirky world of culinary classification, the "Fruit or Vegetable" debate takes the salad bowl! This gastronomic conundrum has perplexed chefs, gardeners, and trivia buffs alike, turning the produce aisle into a courtroom of botanical bewilderment. Let's peel back the layers of this delicious debate!

Let's start with the tomato, the reigning champion of this juicy controversy. Botanically speaking, tomatoes are fruits—berries, to be exact, since they grow from the flower of the tomato plant and house seeds. However, in the culinary courtroom, they often stand trial as a vegetable, thanks to their savory flair and compatibility with salads and sauces.

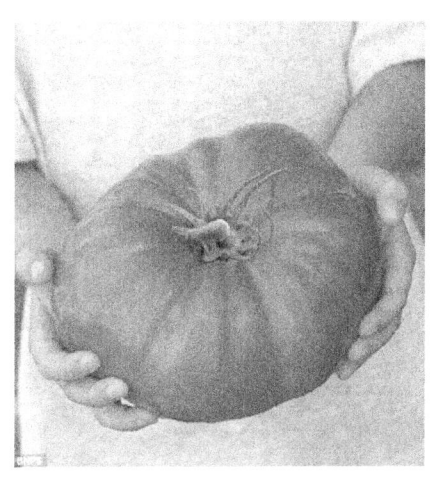

Next up, cucumbers. These crisp, cool characters are botanically fruits too. Surprising, isn't it? They sprout from flowers and hold seeds within their elongated bodies. But when it comes to their role in the kitchen, they lean more towards the veggie side, starring in salads and becoming the mainstay of pickles.

Let's not forget about the avocados, those rich, creamy darlings of the toast world. They're technically berries by botanical standards. However, their buttery texture and versatile nature have blurred the lines in the culinary world, making them a favorite in both savory and sweet dishes.

Then there are the peppers—bell, jalapeño, chili, you name it. These vibrant characters are indeed fruits, born from the blossoms of the pepper plant and wrapping seeds within their colorful walls. But slice them up, and they're more likely to join the ranks of vegetables, adding a punch to everything from stir-fries to pizzas.

Pumpkins, the beloved symbols of autumn and Halloween, also join the fruit parade. They develop from flowers and cradle seeds, making them botanical fruits. But in our kitchens, they often masquerade as vegetables, lending their sweet, earthy flavors to soups, pies, and roasted dishes.

Lastly, there are peas, those tiny green pearls tucked away in pods. Another surprise twist—they're fruits! Developing from the ovary of a pea flower, they're encased in a pod that's the hallmark of leguminous fruits. Yet, in our meals, they're often grouped with vegetables, bringing a pop of sweetness and color to our plates.

This fruit-or-vegetable debate is more than a trivial pursuit—it's a playful dance between botanical definitions and culinary traditions. It's a reminder that in the flavorful world of fruits and vegetables, things aren't always as straightforward as they seem. So next time you ponder over a tomato or dissect a cucumber, remember, **you may never need to know** whether to label it a fruit or a vegetable, but isn't it amusing to explore the twist and turns of nature's bounty?

13 . The Beatles and the 'Let It Be' Legacy

The Beatles, a name synonymous with revolutionizing music and culture, embarked on a project in 1970 that would unknowingly become a poignant swansong to their era-defining journey. This project, centered around the album "Let It Be," originally titled "Get Back," is a bittersweet chronicle of unity, creativity, and the eventual disbanding of the Fab Four.

The Making of 'Let It Be': A Studio Odyssey

The Beatles entered the studio to record "Let It Be" with an idea to return to their roots – live, no-frills recording, a deviation from the elaborate studio techniques used in their previous albums. The recording sessions, held in Twickenham Film Studios and Apple Studios, were initially intended to culminate in a live performance.

However, these sessions, laden with creative differences and interpersonal tensions, painted a vivid picture of a band at a crossroads. Paul McCartney's vision often clashed with others, particularly George Harrison, leading to temporary walkouts and palpable strain. Despite these challenges, the album birthed iconic tracks like "Let It Be," "The Long and Winding Road," and "Get Back."

The Rooftop Concert: A Historic Goodbye
In an impromptu decision, the Beatles performed their final live show on the rooftop of the Apple Corps building in London. This unexpected concert, amidst the London skyline, was a fitting,

albeit unscripted, farewell performance for a band that had become a cultural cornerstone.

- **Unconventional Studio:** The album was initially recorded in a film studio, a departure from the traditional recording studio setting.
- **George's Walkout:** George Harrison briefly quit the band during these sessions, citing discontent with the atmosphere.
- **Billy Preston's Contribution:** American musician Billy Preston was brought in to play keyboards, bringing a new dynamic to the group.
- **Paul's Leadership:** Paul McCartney often took the lead during the sessions, which caused friction with other band members.
- **Ringo's Solo Album:** Ringo Starr used the same sessions to work on his solo album.
- **John and Yoko:** John Lennon's relationship with Yoko Ono was a point of contention, with her constant presence in the studio.
- **Lennon's Disinterest:** Lennon showed a lack of interest in McCartney's "back-to-basics" approach.
- **McCartney's Frustration:** McCartney's frustration with the sessions was evident in his more assertive demeanor.
- **Film Crew Tensions:** The presence of a film crew documenting the sessions added to the band's stress.
- **Improvised Lyrics:** Some songs had lyrics improvised on the spot, showcasing the band's creative process.
- **Abbey Road Interruption:** Work on 'Let It Be' was paused to record and release 'Abbey Road'.
- **Phil Spector's Involvement:** Controversial producer Phil Spector was brought in to complete the album, much to McCartney's dismay.
- **'The Long and Winding Road' Controversy:** McCartney was unhappy with Spector's orchestral overdubs on this track.
- **Apple Rooftop:** The rooftop concert was the Beatles' first live performance in over two years.
- **Unplanned Performance:** The rooftop concert wasn't planned until days before it occurred.

- **Police Intervention:** The concert ended with the police arriving due to noise complaints.
- **Hidden Microphones:** Microphones were hidden around the rooftop to capture audience reactions.
- **Final Group Performance:** This concert marked the last time the Beatles performed live together.
- **Lennon's Closing Remark:** John Lennon famously quipped, "I'd like to say thank you on behalf of the group and ourselves, and I hope we passed the audition," at the end of the rooftop concert.
- **Release After Breakup:** 'Let It Be' was released a month after the Beatles publicly announced their breakup.

In the annals of music history, the Beatles' "Let It Be" is more than an album; it's a narrative of unity, creativity, and the inevitable evolution of artistic paths. Remember: while you may never need to know every chord and conflict of the Beatles' "Let It Be," it's a fascinating snippet of music history, echoing the enduring legacy of the Fab Four.

14. Platypus: Nature's Oddball

In the tapestry of nature's creations, few animals raise as many eyebrows or questions as the platypus. This semi-aquatic mammal from Australia is like nature's own piece of surrealist art - a hodgepodge of parts that somehow form a functioning, fascinating creature.

The platypus, with its duck-like bill, beaver-like tail, and otter-like body, baffled European naturalists when first discovered, some even thought it was a hoax. It's one of the few mammals that lay eggs instead of giving birth to live young, a characteristic it shares with the echidna.

Male platypuses have a rare feature for a mammal: they are venomous. They have spurs on their hind feet that can deliver a venom capable of causing severe pain to humans. Platypuses hunt underwater where they can't see or hear.

They close their eyes, ears, and nose, relying instead on electrolocation. They detect their prey by sensing electric fields generated by muscular contractions.

The platypus is a monotreme, an ancient branch of mammals that lays eggs. After hatching, the young are fed with milk, but there's a twist - platypuses don't have nipples. The milk oozes out of the mother's skin, and the babies lap it up.

Platypuses are often considered a living link between reptiles and mammals. They possess both mammalian and reptilian traits, providing invaluable insights into evolutionary biology.

- Currency Star: The platypus proudly features on Australia's 20-cent coin, cementing its status as a national treasure.

- Stamp of Approval: In 1974, Australia issued a postage stamp featuring the platypus, further acknowledging its significance.
- Museum Marvel: Platypus specimens are a popular exhibit in Australian museums, drawing interest from both locals and tourists.

Literary Limelight: The platypus has been the subject of various children's books, often portrayed as a quirky and lovable character.

Cartoon Celebrity: This unique mammal has appeared in several cartoons and animated series, captivating audiences worldwide.

- **Symbol of Biodiversity:** The platypus is often used in conservation messages as a symbol of Australia's unique biodiversity.
- **Educational Icon**: Many Australian schools use the platypus in educational materials to teach about evolution and animal classification.
- **Zoo Favorite:** Live platypuses in zoos, especially in Australia, are crowd favorites, providing a rare glimpse of this elusive creature.
- **Sports Mascot:** The platypus has been a mascot for various Australian sports teams, celebrated for its distinctiveness and resilience.
- **International Recognition:** Beyond Australia, the platypus has been featured in international nature documentaries, highlighting its unusual characteristics and drawing global attention.
-

While you may **never need to know** the intricacies of the platypus's peculiar lifestyle, this creature is a wonderful reminder of nature's ability to surprise, delight, and perplex, showcasing the diversity and wonder of the animal kingdom.

15. The Mystery of Spontaneous Human Combustion

Spontaneous Human Combustion (SHC) is a phenomenon as baffling as it is unsettling. Imagine, people suddenly bursting into flames without any apparent external source of ignition! This enigma has perplexed experts and sparked the imagination of many, leading to a blend of scientific investigation, skepticism, and a touch of the supernatural in popular culture.

An Inexplicable Blaze

- Spontaneous Human Combustion refers to cases where a person reportedly catches fire and burns without an apparent external source of ignition. Descriptions often involve the victim being consumed by flames while their surroundings remain relatively undamaged.
- SHC isn't a new phenomenon. Historical records dating back to the 17th century document instances of people seemingly erupting into flames. One of the earliest recorded cases is that of the Countess Cornelia Di Bandi, who, according to reports in 1731, was found almost completely incinerated in her room, with the furniture around her unscathed.
- Even in modern times, there are sporadic reports of SHC. Cases like that of Mary Reeser in 1951, where she was found reduced to ashes in her apartment with only a leg remaining, continue to baffle investigators and ignite public curiosity.
- The scientific community remains skeptical about SHC, often attributing these cases to external sources of fire, such as cigarettes. The 'wick effect' theory suggests that the human body can act like an inside-out candle, with the clothing of the victim absorbing melted fat and acting as a wick.
- The mystery of SHC has found its way into various forms of media, including literature, television shows, and movies, often portrayed as an inexplicable and horrifying act of nature or linked to supernatural elements.

Trivia Tidbits:

- Charles Dickens Controversy: Dickens used SHC in his novel "Bleak House," which led to public debate about its plausibility.
- Forensic Puzzles: In SHC cases, often the extremities like feet and hands remain unburned, adding to the mystery.
- Medical Hypotheses: Some medical theories suggest that SHC might be linked to alcoholism, obesity, or the production of flammable gases in the body.
- Theories Abound: Explanations range from paranormal activity to buildup of static electricity within the body.
- Cinematic Thrills: SHC has been a plot device in horror and thriller genres, adding an element of unpredictable terror.

Remember: while you may never need to know the ins and outs of Spontaneous Human Combustion, this eerie enigma serves as a chilling reminder of the many mysteries that science has yet to fully unravel.

16. Competitive Pillow Fighting

In the playful and somewhat surreal realm of unusual sports, Competitive Pillow Fighting stands out as a testament to human creativity in turning everyday activities into a sport. This seemingly lighthearted activity packs a surprising punch of competitiveness and skill, making it a delightful addition to the world of unconventional sports.

Competitive Pillow Fighting involves participants engaging in pillow combat, trying to outmaneuver and out-hit each other. It's not just a sleepover staple anymore but a legitimate competitive event, complete with rules, tournaments, and enthusiastic spectators.

A Sport with a Soft Touch:

- Origins and Evolution: Originating as a fun, informal game, competitive pillow fighting has evolved into organized events.

The Pillow Fight League, founded in Toronto in 2004, is one notable example that popularized the sport.

Rules of the Game: Standard rules involve competitors standing on a mattress or designated area, trying to knock each other off balance using standard bed pillows. Matches typically last a few minutes and are judged on aggression, defense, and technique.

Global Reach: The sport has gained international attention, with events held in countries like Canada, the United States, and Japan. The annual International Pillow Fight Day, celebrated in cities worldwide, is a testament to its growing popularity.

Equipment and Safety: Safety is a priority. Pillows used in competitions are usually soft and of a standard size to prevent injury. Participants often wear protective gear like helmets and knee pads.

Diverse Participation: Competitors come from various backgrounds and ages, making it a sport that celebrates diversity and inclusivity.

Pillow fighting championships have popped up in various countries, attracting participants of all ages. These events often feature a festive atmosphere, with the playful nature of the sport inviting laughter and camaraderie among competitors and audiences alike.

Contrary to its seemingly whimsical nature, competitive pillow fighting requires strategy and technique. Participants must balance offense and defense, mastering the art of the pillow swing and anticipating their opponent's moves.

While you may **never need to know** the intricacies of competitive pillow fighting strategy, this whimsical sport is a delightful reminder of the creativity and fun that can be found in transforming ordinary activities into extraordinary experiences.

17. Berghain: The Temple of Techno

Berghain, a nightclub in Berlin, has become a cultural phenomenon and an emblem of the city's vibrant nightlife. Known for its techno music and exclusive door policy, it's a place shrouded in mystique, drawing party-goers from around the globe.

A Nightlife Legend:

Origins and Location: Berghain is situated in a former power plant in Friedrichshain, Berlin. It opened its doors in 2004 and quickly became renowned for its intense techno parties and progressive electronic music.

Architectural Marvel: The club's industrial architecture, with its cavernous spaces and 60-foot ceilings, creates an atmosphere that's both imposing and inviting for an immersive music experience.

World-Class Sound System: Berghain is celebrated for its impeccable sound quality, boasting a sound system that makes it a mecca for audiophiles and techno enthusiasts.
Iconic Door Policy of Berghain

Berghain's door policy, a blend of mystery and exclusivity, has become almost as famous as the club itself.

At the helm of this selective entry process is Sven Marquardt, a figure who has risen to almost mythical status in the world of nightlife. Sven Marquardt, a former East Berlin punk and photographer, became the face of Berghain's door policy. His intimidating presence and distinctive look, complete with facial piercings and tattoos, make him an iconic figure.

Marquardt is not just a bouncer; he's also an accomplished photographer with a keen eye for aesthetics. This artistic background is said to influence his approach to selecting club-goers.
There's no known formula for gaining entry to Berghain. Marquardt and his team make split-second decisions based on a variety of factors, from the individual's vibe and style to the composition of the crowd inside.

The Rules of Engagement

- No Guarantees: Regulars and celebrities alike have been turned away. Entry is never guaranteed, regardless of status or prior visits.
- Dress Code: While there's no official dress code, Berghain regulars often sport a specific style – typically understated, black, and leaning towards fetish or alternative.
- Behavior at the Door: Quiet confidence is key. Over-eagerness, loud groups, or being overly intoxicated can decrease your chances of getting in.
- Marquardt aims to curate a crowd that contributes to the club's unique atmosphere – a melting pot of individuals who share an appreciation for techno music and the club's liberal ethos.

- The selective policy helps maintain Berghain's reputation as a sanctuary for true lovers of techno and club culture, free from judgment and inhibitions.
- Berghain's reputation has made it a bucket-list destination for clubbers worldwide, contributing to Berlin's status as a global party capital. Despite its popularity, Berghain has faced challenges, including issues with licensing, gentrification debates, and controversies related to its door policy.

Remember: While you may **never need to know** the experience of the heart-pounding moment of facing Berghain's doorkeepers, understanding the club's iconic entry ritual offers a glimpse into the enigmatic world of Berlin's techno temple. The door policy isn't just about exclusion; it's a testament to Berghain's commitment to preserving a unique cultural and musical experience.

18. The London Beer Flood

Raise a glass (with caution) to the London Beer Flood of 1814! Imagine, if you can, a day in London where the streets don't flow with the Thames, but with something far frothier and much more delicious (though sadly not for everyone). Picture this: it's October 17th, and the Meux and Company Brewery is bubbling with excitement – not just from the hops, but from a vat the size of a whale filled with over 135,000 gallons of prime London brew. But alas, this wasn't your average happy hour – this vat, with the structural integrity of a soggy crumpet, decided to call it quits, sending a tsunami of suds cascading through the streets.

Homes? Flooded. Pub walls? Crumbled like stale biscuits. And worst of all, eight poor souls found themselves victims of this boozy deluge. It was a day that redefined "drowning your sorrows," and let's just say the only fish swimming in those streets weren't the kind you'd want on your plate.

Now, while the tragedy of the London Beer Flood can't be forgotten, it's also a chance to raise a (metaphorical) glass to the resilience of Londoners. They mopped up the suds, rebuilt their walls, and maybe even salvaged a few pints from the wreckage (because, let's face it, Londoners wouldn't waste good beer, even if it came with a side of disaster).

5 Quick Facts About the London Beer Flood of 1814:

1. The "Big One" of Brewing Blunders: The vat that burst wasn't just some average beer barrel - it was the largest vat in the entire brewery, holding the equivalent of 5 Olympic-sized swimming pools worth of porter! Talk about a foamy fiasco.
2. A River Runs Through It (Literally): The flood wasn't just a puddle - it surged down the streets at an estimated 35 miles per hour, demolishing houses and flooding basements up to 6 feet deep. Imagine a tsunami of brown ale instead of seawater!
3. From Brew Pub to Brew Flood: Ironically, the Tavistock Arms pub, whose wall crumbled under the beer weight, was actually owned by Meux & Co. brewery. Talk about bad business for the suds slingers!
4. Heavenly Hiccups?: Some Londoners believed the flood was a divine punishment for excessive drinking, while others blamed gremlins or even witches. Guess even in a beer-soaked disaster, people gotta find someone to blame!
5. Tax Break Bonanza: The brewery, facing bankruptcy after the incident, actually got a massive tax rebate from the government for the lost beer. Turns out, even disastrous floods can have a silver lining (as long as it's lined with silver coins)!

So, the next time you raise a pint in a cozy London pub, remember the day the beer flowed like a river. It's a story that reminds us that life, like a good brew, can be full of unexpected twists and turns. Just make sure your glass is always half full, even if it's with the memory of a sudsy, tragic, yet oddly unforgettable day in London history.

Cheers to the past, and always drink responsibly! And remember: **You may never need to know this!**

(P.S. No need to try recreating the London Beer Flood at home, please. A good beer deserves to be enjoyed responsibly, not unleashed in a tidal wave of chaos.)

19. The Art of Fingerprinting

Picture ancient Babylon, where merchants pressed their unique fingerprints into clay tablets as a sign of authenticity. Little did they know, these imprints would one day unlock secrets in crime scenes centuries later.

Fast-forward to the Renaissance, where Marcello Malpighi, an Italian doctor, peered at the patterns on human skin under a microscope. He was onto something, but the crime-solving piece of the puzzle was still missing.

It wasn't until the late 1800s in colonial India that fingerprints found their true calling. Sir William Herschel, realizing their unique and unchanging nature, began using them for contracts and legal documents.

- Historic Conviction in Argentina: In 1892, Francisca Rojas of Argentina became the first person to be convicted of a crime based on fingerprint evidence. Her bloody thumbprint was found at the scene of her children's murder, leading to her confession.
- FBI's Fingerprint Database: The FBI's Integrated Automated Fingerprint Identification System (IAFIS) is one of the largest biometric databases in the world, containing over 70 million subjects in its criminal master file.
- Unlocking Personal Devices: Fingerprint technology is widely used in personal devices like smartphones and laptops, exemplifying its reliability and security. Apple's introduction of Touch ID in 2013 popularized this technology.

- Border Security Applications: Fingerprinting is crucial in border security, used in systems like the US-VISIT program to enhance national security and ensure accurate identification of travelers.
- Solving the 'Boston Strangler' Case: In 2013, advancements in fingerprint technology helped to confirm Albert DeSalvo's identity as the infamous Boston Strangler, solving a mystery that spanned decades.
- Identification in Natural Disasters: Post-disaster victim identification often relies on fingerprints, a key method used in the aftermath of events like the 2004 Indian Ocean tsunami.
- Banking Security: Fingerprinting technology is increasingly used in banking, both to access vaults and for customer identification, enhancing security and reducing fraud.
- Theft Prevention in Art Galleries: High-value items in museums and galleries are sometimes protected with fingerprint recognition systems, deterring theft and aiding in recovery if stolen.
- Unique Fingerprinting for Twins: Even identical twins, who share the same DNA, have distinct fingerprints, an important factor in criminal investigations and paternity cases.
- Notable Cold Case Solved: Fingerprint analysis helped solve the 1999 murder of Sherri Holland, with the killer being identified and convicted over 20 years later, demonstrating the long-term value of preserved fingerprint evidence.

The Future of Fingerprinting: As technology evolves, so does the art of fingerprinting. Researchers are exploring ways to detect fingerprints on metal, even after they've been wiped off, pushing the boundaries of this age-old science.

Fingerprinting, with its intricate patterns and unique identifiers, is more than just a tool for law enforcement; it's a fascinating intersection of biology, technology, and history. As you look at your own fingertips, remember: **you may never need to know** the whorls and ridges that make you distinct, but they hold stories and secrets that have unlocked some of history's most perplexing mysteries. Fingerprinting, in its silent, unassuming way, continues to leave an indelible mark on our understanding of identity and security.

20 - The Loudest Sound in Recorded History

Buckle up for a sonic boom through history as we explore the loudest sounds ever recorded. From volcanic eruptions to man-made kabooms, these events didn't just break the sound barrier; they shattered windows, rattled minds, and left an echo through time. So, put on your imaginary earplugs, and let's turn the volume up to 11 on history's loudest moments.

Krakatoa's Cataclysmic Bang, 1883: Picture this: it's 1883, and Krakatoa, a seemingly peaceful island in Indonesia, decides to go out with a bang – literally. The volcanic eruption was so explosively loud, it ruptured eardrums over 40 miles away and was heard as far as 3,000 miles. That's like a sound blast traveling all the way from London to Moscow! The shock waves circled the globe multiple times, and the eruption was deemed the loudest sound recorded in human history. Talk about nature's own rock concert!

The Tunguska Event, 1908: Fast forward to 1908, Siberia, where a massive explosion flattened 770 square miles of forest. No, it wasn't an alien visitation, but likely a comet or meteoroid that decided to

The Tsar Bomba, 1961: Enter the Cold War era, where the Soviet Union thought, "Why not create the biggest bomb ever?" And so, the Tsar Bomba was born – a 50-megaton nuclear behemoth. Detonated over a remote Arctic archipelago, the explosion was not only seen and felt over 620 miles away but also shattered windows in Norway and Finland. The shock wave was so powerful it circled the Earth three times. Mother Nature's Krakatoa record had a man-made contender!

- Krakatoa's Vocal Performance: When Krakatoa erupted, it was like Mother Nature decided to try out for the loudest rock band ever. The eruption's sound wave traveled the globe not once, but seven times!
- Krakatoa's Ash Art: The eruption was so powerful it turned the skies into a canvas, painting sunsets red around the world for years. Talk about a lingering encore!
- Eardrum Enemy: Krakatoa's eruption was so loud, it ruptured eardrums of sailors 40 miles away. Who needs earplugs when you've got Krakatoa?
- Barometric Bombast: The eruption caused a spike in barometric readings globally. Weather stations were probably like, "Did someone just drop the bass?"
- The Tunguska Mystery: The Tunguska event is like the Sherlock Holmes of explosions – a mystery that keeps on puzzling. No crater was found because the object likely disintegrated in mid-air. Cosmic airburst? More like a space sneeze!

- Nocturnal Daylight: The blast was so bright, it lit up night skies in Asia and Europe. Who needs a night light when you've got a comet?
- The Tsar Bomba's Overachievement: When the Tsar Bomba went off, it was like someone said, "Let's break every record." It was the largest man-made explosion ever, equivalent to about 3,800 Hiroshima bombs.
- Window Wrecker: The bomb's shockwave broke windows hundreds of miles away. Talk about a long-distance relationship!
- Mushroom Cloud Tourism: The Tsar Bomba's mushroom cloud was so high (about seven times the height of Mount Everest), it could be seen from Norway. It's not every day you get a mushroom cloud on the horizon!
- Blast from the Past: The shockwave circled the Earth three times. It's like the Earth said, "I liked that beat, play it again!"
- Weighty Matters: The Tsar Bomba was so heavy (27 tons) that the plane carrying it had to be modified. Even the parachute that slowed its descent was a heavyweight champ.
- Seismic Scares: The bomb registered on seismographs worldwide. Earthquake detectors were probably like, "Is it just me, or did the Earth just drop a beat?"
- Krakatoa's Underwater Encore: In 2018, a volcano believed to be a child of Krakatoa erupted, causing a deadly tsunami. Krakatoa's family keeping the tradition alive!
- Tunguska's Eco Impact: The Tunguska explosion knocked over an estimated 80 million trees. It was like nature's version of bowling, with a strike too powerful for the alley.

remember: **you may never need to know** the specifics of decibels or the physics of sound waves, but these events remind us of the awe-inspiring, and sometimes terrifying, power of both nature and human invention. They are thunderous reminders of moments when the Earth, and mankind, cranked the volume dial to the max. Just be thankful that history doesn't come with a volume button – some of these events are best left on mute!

21 - The Historical Practice of Dueling

Step back in time to the age of honor, where settling a dispute meant not a court battle, but a duel. Picture this: gentlemen (and sometimes ladies) donning their finest, choosing their weapons, and facing off at dawn to defend their honor. Dueling, a practice as steeped in ritual as it is in risk, has a history that's as sharp and pointed as the swords and pistols used. So, let's journey through the annals of this bygone tradition, where the clink of swords was the sound of justice, and a well-aimed shot could settle the gravest insults.

A Point of Honor: Dueling began in medieval Europe as a way for knights to resolve disputes. It was less about who was right and more about who was left standing.

Choose Your Weapon: By the 18th century, pistols became the dueling weapon du jour, although swords were still in vogue for the traditionalists. It was like choosing between an Xbox and a PlayStation, but deadlier.

Dawn's Early Light: Duels were often held at dawn. Why? Less chance of being interrupted by the law and the early morning light was just right for aiming.

A Deadly Affair: Famous participants in duels include Alexander Hamilton and Aaron Burr. Spoiler alert: it didn't end well for Hamilton. Guess he didn't throw away his shot, but he sure missed it.

Rules of Engagement: The Code Duello, a set of rules for dueling, dictated everything from the appropriate distance between duelists to the correct way to issue a challenge. It was like the rulebook for Fight Club, but with more ruffled shirts.

Ladies on the Field: Dueling wasn't just a gentleman's game. Women, known as "petticoat duelists," also participated, defending their honor with as much fervor as the men.

A Decline in Popularity: As the 19th century rolled in, dueling began to lose its luster. It was seen as uncivilized, and legal systems started frowning upon this lethal form of conflict resolution.
The Last Duel

In 1967, France witnessed what is commonly believed to be the last formal duel in its history, a curious anachronism in the modern age. The duel was between two prominent political figures: Gaston Defferre, the mayor of Marseille, and René Ribière, a member of the French parliament. The cause of this unusual event was a personal insult hurled during a heated debate in the National Assembly.

The dispute arose when Defferre, known for his sharp tongue, reportedly told Ribière to "shut up, stupid!" during a parliamentary session. In an era when such insults could no longer be settled by a duel, Ribière took exception to the remark and challenged Defferre to uphold his honor through the traditional means.

Dueling, though archaic and largely symbolic by the mid-20th century, was Ribière's chosen method to restore his sullied honor.

The duel was fought with épées, a choice befitting the tradition of French dueling. It took place in a private estate near Neuilly-sur-Seine, away from the public eye. The combatants, adhering to the age-old code of dueling, faced each other not in anger but as a matter of principle. The duel, supervised by a former army colonel, lasted four minutes, a relatively long duration by fencing standards. Ribière was wounded twice, but both men survived the encounter.

This incident, occurring in the post-war era, marked the end of the historical practice of dueling in France. While it may seem out of place in the context of the 20th century, the duel between Defferre and Ribière serves as a fascinating reminder of the enduring influence of tradition and honor in French culture. It stands as a testament to the changing norms of conflict resolution and the decline of dueling as an acceptable means to settle personal disputes. This event in French history not only serves as a curious anecdote but also marks the symbolic closure of a long-standing martial tradition.

As we holster our pistols and sheathe our swords, remember: **you may never need to know** the intricate dance of a duel or the etiquette of challenging someone to a fight to the death. But the practice of dueling, with its mix of bravado, honor, and danger, adds a swashbuckling chapter to our history. It's a reminder of a time when personal honor was worth risking it all, even if today it seems like an echo from a more tempestuous past. Dueling, in its own way, was history's dramatic way of saying, "Let's sort this out, once and for all."

22. The Mystery of the Bermuda Triangle

Bermuda Triangle, a region steeped in mystery, maritime myths, and a fair share of unexplained disappearances. Located in the western part of the North Atlantic Ocean, bounded by Miami, Bermuda, and Puerto Rico, this loosely area has been the subject of intrigue and speculation for decades.

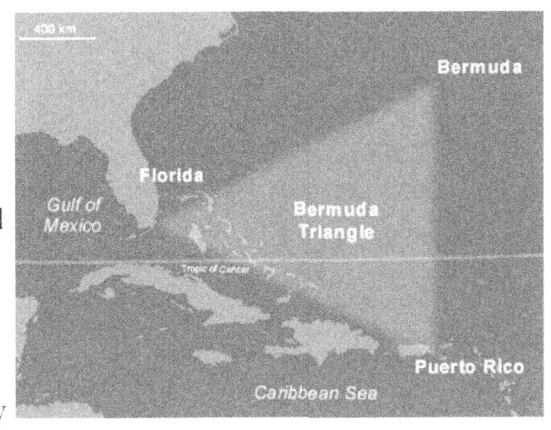

The Bermuda Triangle's notoriety began in earnest in the 20th century. Perhaps the most famous incident was the disappearance of Flight 19 in 1945, a training flight of five TBM Avenger torpedo bombers from the US Navy. The flight, along with its 14 crew members, vanished without a trace, fueling speculation about supernatural forces at play. The rescue plane sent to find them also disappeared, adding another layer to the mystery.

Over the years, numerous ships and aircraft have seemingly vanished when traversing the Triangle. The USS Cyclops in 1918, a massive Navy cargo ship with over 300 men aboard, disappeared without sending a distress signal. The civilian tanker SS Marine Sulphur Queen vanished in 1963, with theories ranging from paranormal activity to more scientific explanations like methane hydrates releasing gas and reducing water density.

While the idea of mysterious forces is compelling, scientists have offered more mundane explanations for the Triangle's mysteries. These include human error, bad weather, and the Gulf Stream's strong ocean currents. The region is also one of the few places on

Earth where a compass points towards true north rather than magnetic north, potentially confusing navigators.

But let's not let science get in the way of a good story! Here are five of the more outlandish theories that have added to the Bermuda Triangle's lore:

- Alien Abductions: Some theories suggest that extraterrestrials are fond of this particular corner of the Atlantic for their Earthly rendezvous. Perhaps aliens have a thing for tropical climates and are just misguidedly trying to invite humans to an intergalactic beach party.
- The Lost City of Atlantis: Ah, Atlantis, the go-to explanation for anything underwater and mysterious. According to this theory, the fabled city is lurking beneath the Triangle, and its advanced technology is disrupting navigation systems. Because, of course, ancient Atlanteans had the foresight to inconvenience 20th-century technology.

- Time Warps and Portals: Some believe the Triangle houses a portal to another time or dimension. It's like nature's own version of a sci-fi wormhole, except it probably doesn't lead to a parallel universe where everyone has their doppelgänger.
- Underwater Crystal Pyramids: Apparently, there are gigantic crystal pyramids under the Triangle, remnants of Atlantis (again with Atlantis!), and they are supposedly larger than the ones in Egypt. It's unclear if they come with an ancient curse or a gift shop.

- Methane Gas Explosions: A slightly more scientific but still wild theory involves massive underwater methane explosions. The idea is that these gas blowouts can sink ships and down planes. It's like blaming a giant, invisible sea monster with really bad indigestion.

Despite modern navigation technology and improved understanding of the natural world, the Bermuda Triangle continues to captivate the imagination. It remains a symbol of the unexplained, a place where the boundaries between fact and fiction blur. Remember: while you may never need to know the exact coordinates of the Bermuda Triangle or the details of every disappearance, the mystery itself is a reminder of the vast, unexplored mysteries that still exist in our world.

23 - Vacation to North Korea

So, you've chosen a North Korean vacation? You brave, foolhardy explorer, you! Buckle up, buttercup, because this trip is less "beachside piña colada" and more "balancing on a tightrope while juggling live ammunition." But hey, where else can you witness synchronized goose-stepping grannies or watch a statue competition judged by Kim Jong-un's pet unicorn (rumored, not confirmed)?

Dress Code: Ditch the blue jeans, comrade. They're about as welcome as a South Korean flag at a birthday party for Dear Leader. Think beige, think shapeless, think "I'm blending in with the furniture (literally, those sofas haven't moved since 1984)."

Photography: Hold your horses, shutterbugs! Snapping pics willy-nilly is like asking if the Supreme Leader enjoys karaoke renditions of Gangnam Style. Stick to landscapes and approved monuments – imagine Big Ben, but with way more scowling portraits and suspiciously shiny surveillance cameras.

Tour Guide Trivia: Ever wished you had a human GPS with zero personality and a side of paranoia? Meet your North Korean guide! Ask too many questions about, say, the "accidental" disappearance of Uncle Jong-un, and you might find yourself starring in the next Pyongyang Prison Revue.

Passport Play: Sayonara, sweet passport! Upon arrival, your precious travel document goes on a solo vacation, returning only when you do. Think of it as an extended spa weekend in the Ministry of State Secrets. Just make sure it's in tip-top shape – a dog-eared passport is basically an invitation to a "friendly chat" with the Thought Police.

The Unfortunate Tourist and the Forbidden Photo

Otto Warmbier, a 21-year-old University of Virginia student, embarked on a tour of North Korea in December 2015. It was a trip fueled by youthful curiosity and a yearning to experience this enigmatic, Respect the Leaders: Bowing before Kim Il Sung and Kim Jong-Il is less of a suggestion and more of a mandatory Olympic sport. Not feeling the solemn genuflection? Try practicing your best robot impression – anything less enthusiastic might land you a starring role in a re-education camp drama.

Telecommunication Tales: Your phone? Dead as disco in Pyongyang. It'll take a vow of silence during your stay, only returning to the land of the living upon your departure. Think of it as a digital detox, sponsored by the Department of Information Control.

Guided Adventures Only: Solo exploration? About as likely as finding a double latte in a state-run bakery. Every step, every visit, is choreographed tighter than a synchronized swimming routine for competitive walruses. Embrace the group hug, comrade, it's the only way to fly (or, rather, shuffle in an orderly line).

Honoring the Leader: Flower-laying ceremonies and statue-bowing marathons will be your new Olympic event. Get ready to polish your respectful demeanor – think Miss Congeniality meets a military parade. Just remember, a single tear of boredom could be misconstrued as a revolutionary plot.

Silent Nights: Forget nightclubbing your way into the next Great Proletariat Dance-Off. Music and dancing are about as welcome as a capitalist shopping spree in the Supreme Leader's personal supermarket. Think library-level decibel requirements, enforced by humorless guards with megaphones and questionable fashion choices.

Car Care: A dirty car is basically a walking (or, rather, driving) middle finger to Dear Leader. Keep that paintwork gleaming, comrades, or prepare for a "friendly" traffic stop that involves more paperwork than a rocket launch application.

Bonus tip: Pack your sense of humor (preferably dark and gallows-worthy), your dancing shoes (for the mandatory synchronized line-dancing sessions), and an extra-large dose of curiosity (but keep it well-concealed, like a state secret under your bed).

isolated nation. Little did he know, a seemingly harmless prank would turn his adventure into a tragic nightmare.

Warmbier, along with his tour group, stayed at the Yanggakdo International Hotel, a towering monument to Pyongyang's grandiose architecture. In the final hours of his trip, Warmbier committed an act that, in his Western sensibilities, felt like a mischievous souvenir mission. He attempted to remove a propaganda banner from the hotel staff-only restricted floor.

Whether driven by youthful impulsiveness or a naive misunderstanding of North Korean laws and sensibilities, his actions triggered a chain of events with devastating consequences.

His attempt was quickly detected by hotel security. In a country where loyalty to the regime and respect for state-sanctioned symbols are paramount, Warmbier's act wasn't just petty theft; it was seen as a direct challenge to the authority of the state. He was detained, interrogated, and swiftly convicted of subversion, a charge often leveled against those deemed politically threatening to the North Korean regime.

The court sentenced Warmbier to 15 years of hard labor, a sentence that sent shockwaves through the international community. The world watched in disbelief as the young American, who had simply made a foolish choice, was condemned to a harsh fate in a notorious labor camp. The Warmbier case brought renewed focus on the opaque legal system and harsh punishments within North Korea, sparking condemnation and raising concerns about the treatment of foreign visitors.

Months later, after what appeared to be prolonged negotiations, Warmbier was released in a coma and returned to the United States. The sight of the once-vibrant young man, now unresponsive and suffering from extensive brain damage, only intensified the outrage directed at the North Korean government.

While the exact cause of Warmbier's condition remains unclear, medical reports linked his injuries to torture and neglect during his imprisonment. His tragic death in June 2017 served as a stark reminder of the potential dangers lurking beneath the carefully curated facade of North Korean tourism.

The Warmbier case wasn't just a personal tragedy; it cast a harsh light on the human rights abuses and restrictive laws within North Korea. It serves as a cautionary tale, urging both tourists and international communities to approach the country with utmost caution and awareness of the severe consequences that can arise from even seemingly minor transgressions.

Warmbier's story, etched in international memory, stands as a powerful reminder of the importance of cultural sensitivity, respectful travel practices, and the crucial role of diplomatic engagement in bridging the gap between vastly different political systems. His unfortunate fate compels us to tread carefully, prioritizing safety and understanding whenever venturing into the complex and often unpredictable world of North Korea.

You may **never need to know** how to survive in North Korea but if you do, you might just return with enough stories to fill a propaganda handbook (but write it in invisible ink, just in case). Good luck, comrade! You'll need it.

24. The Wife Carrying Championship: A Hilarious Finnish Tradition in the Heart of the Countryside

Nestled amidst the idyllic Finnish countryside, in the small town of Sonkajärvi, lies a peculiar yet utterly entertaining spectacle: the annual Wife Carrying Championship. This event, far from being just a test of muscle power and endurance, is a hilarious celebration of love, humor, and Finnish eccentricity.

The origins of this quirky championship are steeped in local legend, with some tales hinting at a playful tradition of young men "stealing" wives from neighboring villages. Today, however, the event is purely consensual and joyous, with couples voluntarily participating in the race, embracing the competitive fun and lighthearted absurdity of it all.

The Wife Carrying Championship has transcended national borders, attracting participants from across the globe. Couples from various countries flock to Finland not only to compete but also to be part of this unique cultural phenomenon, making it a truly international spectacle.

From the classic piggyback ride to the more daring Estonian style where the wife hangs upside down with her legs around the husband's shoulders, competitors employ a diverse range of techniques to navigate the challenging course. This variety in styles adds an extra layer of strategy and, of course, hilarious possibilities to the race.

The race is far from a simple sprint. The 253.5-meter course is designed to test not just individual strength but also teamwork and balance, with obstacles like water traps, hay bales, and hurdles ensuring that victory comes with a good dose of laughter and shared effort.

In a delightful twist, the winning couple is awarded the wife's weight in beer! This unconventional prize adds to the lighthearted fun of the event and serves as a sweet (or should we say, hoppy?) reward for the victors' impressive athleticism and teamwork.

The championship is just one part of a larger festival that pulsates with music, dancing, and vibrant merriment. This festive atmosphere brings together the local community and international visitors, creating a unique and joyous celebration that transcends the limits of the race itself.

While the concept may raise eyebrows at first glance, the event is fundamentally rooted in good humor and mutual respect. It's an opportunity for couples to work together, literally uplifting and supporting each other in a display of unity and strength, all within the bounds of playful fun.

The popularity of the Finnish event has inspired similar competitions worldwide, with countries like the United States, Australia, and even Estonia hosting their own versions of the Wife Carrying Championship. This global spread speaks volumes about the infectious joy and uniqueness of this Finnish tradition.

The Wife Carrying Championship is more than just a competition; it's a joyous celebration of partnership, camaraderie, and the lighter side of life. It's a testament to Finland's love for the unconventional, a place where laughter reigns supreme, and the spirit of fun transcends cultural boundaries. Whilst you may never need to know this. It might just be your next must-see event for anyone visiting Finland or simply seeking a good dose of hilarious entertainment.

25 - The Dancing Plague of 1518, Strasbourg. Pardonnez-moi!

Hold your baguettes, history buffs, because we're revisiting the most bizarre episode of mass toe-tapping ever recorded: the Dancing Plague of 1518, Strasbourg edition. Picture this: not Munich, but the grand old French city of Strasbourg, usually known for its cathedral spire and Alsatian charm, suddenly becomes a medieval mosh pit. Think the can-can in the cobbled streets, the waltz in the bakery window, and the jig outside the Notre Dame. Talk about spontaneous combustion of the footloose kind!

Frau Troffea, the OG Queen of Footloose Fancy: It all started with her, this polka-loving pioneer. One minute she's haggling over choucroute garnie, the next she's doing the Macarena like a possessed sauerkraut seller. Soon, the rhythm bug bit the whole town, turning Strasbourg into a human disco ball with questionable fashion choices. Bakers pirouetted between baguettes, cobblers tapped out jigs instead of hammering shoes, and even the bourgeois got caught in the toe-tapping tornado. Imagine husbands waltzing with their poodles, monks doing interpretive Breton dance (with questionable hip movements), and children skipping school for impromptu breakdancing battles in the Grand Place. It was like a fever dream choreographed by a tipsy gnome after a night of too much vin d'Alsace!

Doctors Baffled, Theories Abounded: Naturally, the good burghers were scratching their heads and consulting dusty scrolls of medical wisdom. They poked, prodded, and prescribed dubious concoctions of leeches and lentil soup, but the dancing continued. Some blamed demons, others bad Camembert (always blame the cheese!), and a few even thought it was a divinely ordained Zumba class gone wrong.

(Turns out, God really digs the gavotte.)

A Month of Madness & Mystery: For a whole month, Strasbourg shimmied and shook. People collapsed from exhaustion, some even danced themselves to death (talk about dying on the dance floor, literally). Finally, in a desperate attempt to appease the rhythm gods, they carted the last twirlers off to a mountain shrine to pray for divine intervention (and maybe some decent foot massages).

The Tune Fades, the Mystery Remains: The Dancing Plague faded into history, leaving behind a shroud of rumors and theories. Was it mass hysteria? Ergot poisoning from moldy rye bread? A cosmic flash mob gone rogue? We may never know for sure, but one thing's certain: it's a reminder that sometimes, the best cure for life's anxieties is to just let loose and shake your baguette, even if it's in the middle of a medieval marketplace. Just don't blame it on bad cheese, okay?

Bonus Trivia Tidbits:

- Some historians believe the dancing was a form of religious ecstasy, inspired by a charismatic preacher. Others think it was a social protest against the harsh living conditions of the time.
- The Dancing Plague wasn't an isolated incident. Similar outbreaks of mass dancing were reported throughout Europe in the Middle Ages.
- Modern research suggests the dancing could have been caused by a combination of psychological factors, such as stress and religious fervor, and physical factors, such as ergot poisoning or even epilepsy.
- Fashion faux pas: While waltzing in a wheat field or jigging in a jewelry shop might sound romantic, the attire of the afflicted wasn't exactly haute couture. Imagine leather breeches ripped from hours of twirling, or dirndls stained with sweat and tears (of exhaustion, not joy). Talk about dancing like nobody's watching, because trust me, nobody wanted to be watching.
- Musical mayhem: Forget Spotify playlists – the soundtrack to the Dancing Plague was far less curated. Think ear-splitting bagpipes, screeching fiddles, and the off-key chanting of delirious dancers. It was a cacophony so powerful, it could shatter windowpanes and make pigeons fly away in terror.
- Dancing duo drama: Love stories couldn't escape the rhythm either. Imagine a couple waltzing into their wedding ceremony, only for the bride to collapse from exhaustion right at the altar. Talk about cold feet, literally! And forget waltzing into the sunset – these honeymooners were more likely to be carted off to a hospital (if one even existed back then).
- Animal antics: Even pets weren't safe from the dance fever. Cows mooed and stomped in impromptu jigs, sheep hopped like possessed woolly balls, and cats chased their tails in dizzying circles. It was like a barnyard ballet gone terribly wrong.

- The reluctant dancer: Not everyone embraced the spontaneous boogie. Some poor souls resisted the urge to twirl, only to be dragged into the fray by overzealous neighbors. Imagine being yanked out of your bakery to do the polka with a sweaty blacksmith – not exactly the recipe for a stress-free day.
- The dancing doctor: One physician, desperate to understand the plague, decided to fight fire with fire. He joined the dancers, hoping to observe their movements and find a cure. Needless to say, he ended up dancing for days, eventually collapsing from exhaustion himself. Talk about diagnosing yourself to death (well, not quite, but close).
- The aftermath: When the dancing finally stopped, Strasbourg resembled a hungover disco ball. The streets were littered with exhausted bodies, empty wine casks, and the remnants of broken instruments. It was a scene of post-apocalyptic revelry, leaving the city wondering: "What the polka just happened?"
- Dancing in the afterlife: Some legends claim the dancers didn't truly stop. On quiet nights, their ghostly figures can still be seen gliding through the cobbled streets, forever trapped in their macabre waltz. So, next time you visit Strasbourg, listen closely – you might just hear the faint echo of polka steps in the moonlight.
- Artistic inspiration: The Dancing Plague wasn't all doom and gloom. It inspired artists for centuries, from paintings depicting writhing bodies to poems about the madness of the masses. Think of it as a bizarre Renaissance reality show, with the whole of Strasbourg as the unwilling contestants.
- A cautionary tale: The Dancing Plague reminds us that even the most mundane things can turn into mass hysteria. It's a testament to the power of the mind and the contagious nature of emotions. So, the next time you feel the urge to bust a move, remember Frau Troffea and her merry band of jigsters – and maybe save the spontaneous disco for the dance floor, not the marketplace.

What did the blacksmith say to the baker during the Dancing Plague?

"Looks like we're finally kneading some dough in this town!"

So, the next time you feel the urge to bust a move, remember Frau Troffea or not you may never need to know this. But if you do, let loose, embrace the rhythm, and dance like nobody's watching (except maybe a few bemused ghosts and a very confused poodle). Just don't overdo it, okay?

26. London's Great Stink of 1858: When the Thames Turned Foul

Did you know London once smelled so bad it shut down Parliament? No joke, folks! In the sizzling summer of 1858, the River Thames, London's supposed lifeblood, turned into a stinking sewer, unleashing the aptly named "Great Stink." Imagine the Thames not reflecting Big Ben, but reeking like a thousand unflushed toilets on a heatwave. Gross, right?

So what caused this olfactory apocalypse? Centuries of dumping raw sewage and industrial waste into the Thames finally reached a boiling point (literally) thanks to a scorching heatwave. The result? A miasma of methane, ammonia, and other fragrant delights that blanketed the city like a pungent fog. Flies feasted, diseases spread, and even Parliament couldn't escape the stench – lawmakers gagged and fled, unable to stomach the legislative agenda for the day.

But wait, there's a hero in this smelly story! Enter Joseph Bazalgette, a Victorian engineering rockstar who refused to let London drown in its own filth. He dreamt of a mighty underground network of brick-lined sewers to whisk the stinky stuff away from the Thames and into oblivion. Despite budget woes and sneering doubters, Bazalgette pushed on, channeling his inner sewer sorcerer and creating a labyrinthine system of tunnels and pumping stations. And guess what? Bazalgette's stinky solution solved the stinky problem! By 1865, his sewer system was up and running, banishing the Great Stink to the history books and dramatically reducing disease outbreaks. Talk about a nose-worthy feat!

trivia tidbits to impress your friends:

1. The Parliament Packing Stench: The Great Stink wasn't just unpleasant - it shut down Parliament! Lawmakers literally fled the Houses of Parliament, unable to stomach the unbearable odor wafting from the Thames. Talk about a smelly filibuster!
2. Nose Plugs and Perfumed Politicians: To combat the stench, Londoners resorted to desperate measures. Nose plugs made from handkerchiefs and sponges became fashionable accessories, while politicians doused themselves in perfume just to survive parliamentary debates.
3. The Stench Heard 'Round the World: News of the Great Stink traveled far and wide, making London a laughingstock in the international press. Imagine being the city known for its Big Ben... and even bigger stink!
4. Poop Power to the People!: The Great Stink sparked a wave of public activism, with citizens demanding better sanitation solutions. This pressure played a key role in Bazalgette's sewer project finally getting the green light.
5. From Stench to Symphony: The Thames Tunnel, a pioneering underwater tunnel built during the Great Stink era, wasn't just for sewage. It also housed the world's first underwater concert in 1843, proving even smelly history can have musical moments.
6. Sewer Sleuths: Bazalgette's sewer system became a haven for Victorian "ratcatchers," who descended into the tunnels to hunt the vermin attracted by the waste. Talk about a job with unique perks (and pungent paychecks)!
7. Sewage Chic?: Believe it or not, the Great Stink briefly spawned a trend for "Thames mud" cosmetics, with creams and soaps supposedly made from the river's muck. Desperate times, desperate beauty measures, we guess!
8. A River Reborn: Thanks to Bazalgette's genius, the Thames gradually transformed from a stinking sewer to a vibrant riverine artery. Today, it hosts boat tours, kayaks, and even the occasional salmon, proving that even the smelliest situations can have a fresh start.

So there you have it, folks! The Great Stink of London: a story of human waste, engineering genius, and the importance of not treating rivers like trash cans.

Remember, you may never need to know this. next time you flush the toilet, spare a grateful thought for Bazalgette and his stinky legacy – it's the least we can do after he saved London from its own... well, you know.

27 - Crazy Laws of Africa

Chad: Thinking about taking a snapshot in Chad? You'll need to pause and get a permit first. It's a must-do for anyone looking to capture the country's vistas and moments.

Sudan: Navigating social interactions in Sudan comes with its own set of rules. For instance, men and women can't sit together without a chaperone, adding a layer of formality to their meetings. Moreover, aiding an injured person carries a weighty responsibility—if they don't survive, you could be held partly accountable.

Kenya: Animal lovers, Kenya's got your back! Here, it's illegal to slaughter an animal in view of another, a law that speaks volumes about their approach to animal welfare. And for those thinking about organizing an animal fight, think again—it's a legal no-go.

Ghana: Aspiring actors in Ghana face a unique dilemma—too many roles might land you behind bars! On a different note, car enthusiasts can't tint their car windows, a rule that keeps things transparent, quite literally.

Morocco: Morocco takes its marital and religious laws seriously. Engaging in sexual relations outside of marriage is off-limits, and religious discussions, especially about Jesus Christ or possessing an Arabic Bible, are strictly regulated.

Egypt: Not in the mood to vote? In Egypt, that's not an option—abstaining can lead to imprisonment. The country also has strict rules against public displays of affection and religious conversion efforts.

Eswatini (Swaziland): Fashion police alert in Eswatini! Wearing mini skirts or tops that show off your stomach is a fashion faux pas that's also illegal.

Sierra Leone: For those who love jogging in groups, Sierra Leone might not be your ideal workout destination. Group jogging is banned, considered as something that could lead to unruly behavior.

Zimbabwe: In Zimbabwe, be mindful of your gestures, especially around state motorcades. Any offensive signs could land you in legal trouble.

Tanzania: Tanzania's legislators face a unique dress code: no fake eyelashes or nails. Also, collecting and disseminating data without proper authorization is a strict no-no.

Uganda: Female civil servants in Uganda adhere to a specific dress code. Sleeveless tops, tight-fitting dresses, and certain hairstyles and nail styles are off the table.

Equatorial Guinea: For bibliophiles, Equatorial Guinea presents a challenge. Reading foreign books, magazines, or literature is against the law, reflecting the country's stance on external cultural influences.

Eritrea: In Eritrea, you need to register your religious choices with the government. Practicing a religion without official acknowledgment is illegal.

Mauritania: A change of faith, particularly renouncing Islam, is a serious matter in Mauritania. Those who don't repent within three days face severe consequences.

Nigeria: In Nigeria, importing fruits, drinks, and wine is a surprising legal no-go. In a world leaning towards trade liberalization, this law stands out.

South Africa: Planning to buy a TV in South Africa? Don't forget your license. This unusual requirement is necessary for any television purchase.

Madagascar: In a quirky twist of law, pregnant women in Madagascar are not allowed to wear hats. It's a unique regulation that certainly raises eyebrows.

As we journey through the diverse and dynamic continent of Africa, we uncover laws that are as varied and vibrant as the cultures they represent. From restrictions on fortune-telling to mandates on witchcraft, these laws offer a glimpse into the rich tapestry of African societies. Remember, while you may **never need to know** that in some parts of Africa, it's illegal to carry a frog in a bank, these unique laws are a testament to the continent's rich cultural heritage and diverse societal norms. Africa, with its myriad of customs and traditions, continues to enchant and educate us in the most unexpected ways.

28. The Great Molasses Flood of 1919

In the annals of bizarre disasters, few events can top the Great Molasses Flood that occurred in Boston on January 15, 1919. This unusual catastrophe unfolded in the North End neighborhood of the city, and to this day, it remains one of the most extraordinary and tragic incidents in Boston's history.

The calamity began at the Purity Distilling Company, where a massive tank containing over 2.3 million gallons of molasses burst. The rupture unleashed a tidal wave of molasses, estimated to be about 25 feet high at its peak, traveling at 35 miles per hour. The wave of thick, sticky syrup quickly engulfed the streets, wreaking havoc with its immense force and surprising speed.

The flood demolished buildings, overturned vehicles, and uprooted the elevated railway tracks. The impact was so severe that it crushed and drowned 21 people and injured over 150 others.

The aftermath of the flood was overwhelming, with several city blocks coated in a thick layer of molasses. The cleanup operation took weeks, with hundreds of people working to restore the area. It was said that for years after the disaster, the scent of molasses lingered in the North End.

Investigations into the disaster revealed that the tank had been poorly constructed and inadequately maintained. The tragedy led to changes in safety standards and regulations for industrial storage tanks, marking a significant development in the history of American industrial safety.

While the likelihood of encountering a molasses flood in your daily life is slim, this peculiar event in Boston's past serves as a sticky reminder of the unexpected twists that history can take. Remember: you may

Investigations into the disaster revealed that the tank had been poorly constructed and inadequately maintained. The tragedy led to changes in safety standards and regulations for industrial storage tanks, marking a significant development in the history of American industrial safety.

29. The History of Toilet Paper

In the grand timeline of human ingenuity, the chapter on toilet paper is a must-read, offering a glimpse into how civilizations have tackled a universal need. This tale of cleanliness starts not in a modern bathroom, but in ancient times and travels across cultures and centuries.

Ancient Origins and Far Eastern Innovation: Our story begins in China, where the first documented use of toilet paper dates back to the 6th century. By the 14th century, during the Ming Dynasty, the production of toilet paper for the imperial court was in full swing, with records showing an annual supply of over 720,000 sheets of the delicate product.

A World of Alternatives: Before the widespread use of paper, various materials served the purpose. In Ancient Rome, a communal sponge on a stick was quite the hit. Meanwhile, in other parts of the world, natural elements like leaves, grass, and even corn cobs were the order of the day.

Enter the Modern Roll: The journey of toilet paper as we know it began in the 19th century. Joseph Gayetty introduced one of the first packaged toilet papers in the U.S. in 1857, infused with aloe and marketed as a medicinal item. However, it was the Scott Paper Company that truly revolutionized the industry, bringing the concept of the perforated toilet paper roll to households in the late 1800s.

A Staple of Modern Hygiene: Today, toilet paper is a ubiquitous presence in bathrooms worldwide, available in various textures and even colors. The evolution of this humble product reflects changing attitudes towards hygiene and convenience. From luxury item to household staple, the history of toilet paper is a testament to human resourcefulness in addressing one of life's basic needs.

While the topic might not come up in polite conversation, remember: you may never need to know the full history of toilet paper, but it's a curious and amusing tale that underscores the ingenuity behind even the most mundane aspects of daily life.

30. The World's Deepest Postbox

Imagine sending a postcard from the ocean's depths – a reality made possible by the world's deepest postbox, located off the coast of

Susami, a small town in Wakayama Prefecture, Japan. This underwater mailbox is not just a novelty but a testament to human creativity and the love for the extraordinary.

Submerged in the Name of Communication: Plunged 10 meters (about 33 feet) beneath the surface, the postbox was established in 1999. It was initially proposed by the town's postmaster as part of an event to promote the local diving industry. Little did he know, it would become a world attraction.

A Watery Way to Send Greetings: Divers from around the globe flock to Susami to post waterproof cards to their loved ones. As of 2015, over 38,000 pieces of mail had been sent from this unique box, a number that continues to grow.

Official Recognition: The postbox has been recognized by the Guinness World Records as the deepest of its kind in the world. It's not your typical postal experience, combining the thrill of diving with the charm of traditional mail.

A Quirky Tourist Attraction: This submerged postbox is emptied once a day by a local dive shop. It's a blend of whimsy and practicality, serving both as a tourist attraction and a functional mail drop-off point. Special waterproof postcards and pens are available for those eager to send their underwater messages.

The World's Deepest Postbox is more than just a place to mail a letter; it's a symbol of the lengths (or depths) to which humans will go to add a bit of magic to everyday activities. Remember: you may never need to know how to scuba dive to send a postcard, but in the small town of Susami, they've turned mailing a letter into an underwater adventure.

31. Why We Say "Bless You" After Sneezing

"Bless you!" It's a common refrain heard after someone sneezes, but have you ever wondered why we say it? This seemingly automatic response is steeped in history, superstition, and a dash of medical myth.

Ancient Beliefs and Plague Fears: The practice dates back to ancient times and has various cultural origins. One belief was that a sneeze could accidentally expel the spirit from the body, and saying "bless you" would prevent this. Another theory suggests that the heart momentarily stops during a sneeze, and saying "bless you" is a sign of relief that the sneezer is still alive.

Pope Gregory I's Influence: The tradition took a significant hold in Europe during the 6th century with the outbreak of the bubonic plague. Sneezing was one of the plague's symptoms, and Pope Gregory I suggested saying "God bless you" after a sneeze as a prayer for good health.

Warding Off Evil Spirits: In some cultures, it was believed that sneezing opened the body to evil spirits. Saying "bless you" was a protective measure to guard the sneezer from demonic possession. A Sign of Politeness: Over time, saying "bless you" became a social courtesy, a way of acknowledging someone's sneeze and wishing them well, much like we say "excuse me" or "sorry."

Today, saying "bless you" after someone sneezes is more of a cultural habit than a superstition or religious practice. Remember: you may never need to know the origins of why we say "bless you," but it's a fascinating example of how ancient beliefs and customs can evolve into everyday modern manners.

32 - Crazy Laws of Asia

- **Singapore:** Feeling free at home? In Singapore, walking around naked even in your own house can land you in hot water. Better keep those curtains drawn!

- **China:** Family first in China! There's a law that requires adult children to visit their elderly parents regularly. Talk about legal family bonding!

- **Japan:** Watch your waistline in Japan! The "Metabo Law" mandates yearly waist measurements for adults to encourage healthy living. Over the limit? Time for diet classes.

- **Bangladesh:** Cheating on exams in Bangladesh is a serious offense. Students can find themselves behind bars for trying to outsmart their tests.

- **Thailand:** Going commando in Thailand? Think again. It's illegal to leave your underwear at home. And watch where you step – disrespecting currency with the King's image by stepping on it could land you in trouble.

- **China:** Reincarnation in China comes with a twist – it's illegal for Tibetan Buddhist monks to reincarnate without government permission. Talk about controlling the cycle of life and death!

- **India:** Failed a suicide attempt in India? You could end up in jail. The law aims to deter such attempts but ends up penalizing the survivors.

- **South Korea:** Night owls under 16 in South Korea have to log off online games by midnight. The "Cinderella Law" aims to curb video game addiction.

- Malaysia: In Malaysia, cross-dressing is legally prohibited. The law focuses particularly on Muslim trans women, and it's used to justify their harassment, including physical and sexual assault.

- Indonesia: Be careful if you plan on engaging in any romantic liaisons in Indonesia. Adultery is illegal here, and if you're caught, you could face some serious legal consequences.

- Philippines: Fancy yourself as a bounty hunter? The Philippines is one of the few places where you can legally chase down fugitives for a reward. This echoes an old Wild West tradition, but with a modern twist.

- Vietnam: In Vietnam, it's illegal to change a light bulb unless you're a licensed electrician. Seems like a bit of an overkill for such a mundane task, but it's the law!

- Singapore: Singing in public with obscene lyrics is a big no in Singapore. If you're caught, you could face a fine or even imprisonment. Best to keep your karaoke songs clean!

- Thailand: If you're a movie buff in Thailand, think twice before bringing a VCR home. The possession of more than 120 unlicensed video tapes or DVDs is illegal, a law likely aimed at curbing piracy.

- Bhutan: Bhutan takes its environmental conservation seriously. It's mandated by law that at least 60% of the country must remain forested for all future generations. A beautiful commitment to nature, indeed.

In Asia, a continent where ancient traditions meet rapid modernization, the laws can be as diverse as the geography. Traversing from the deserts of the Middle East to the islands of Southeast Asia, we encounter a mosaic of legalities that mirror the cultural complexities of this vast region. From rules about chewing

33. The Mystery of Crop Circles

Embark on a journey into the enigmatic world of crop circles, those perplexing patterns that appear overnight in fields around the globe. These intricate designs range from simple circles to complex geometrical figures, creating a tapestry of mystery in the very grain of the countryside.

- **First Recorded Crop Circle:** The earliest recorded crop circle dates back to the 1600s. A woodcut from 1678, known as the "Mowing-Devil," shows a field of oat stalks laid out in a circle, with the devil cutting the oats.
- **Increase in Complexity:** Initially, crop circles were simple circles. Over time, they evolved into intricate patterns, some spanning over 200 meters in diameter, with detailed designs that have amazed both scientists and enthusiasts.
- **Alien Theories:** The appearance of crop circles near Stonehenge and other ancient sites fueled theories of extraterrestrial origins. Some UFO enthusiasts believe these formations are messages from alien beings or landing marks of UFOs.
- **Mathematical Marvels:** Many crop circles exhibit sophisticated mathematical properties, such as fractals and elements of sacred geometry, leading to speculation about their creation involving advanced knowledge.
- **Nighttime Creations:** Most crop circles appear overnight, adding to their mysterious nature. This has led to theories about them being created by otherworldly forces, as such complex designs would seemingly require more time and daylight to construct.

The phenomenon has influenced music as well. For example, the electronic music duo Boards of Canada has an album titled "Geogaddi" with artwork and sounds inspired by crop circles, reflecting the mysterious and ambient nature of the phenomenon.

- **Cereologist:** The study and interpretation of crop circles is known as cereology. Enthusiasts and researchers who investigate crop circles are called cereologists.
- **Media Influence:** The phenomenon of crop circles inspired various pop culture references, including movies like "Signs," which explore the alien theory behind these mysterious patterns.
- **Nocturnal Artists:** Despite the confession of Doug and Dave, crop circle creators often work at night to maintain the mystery and avoid detection, using simple tools like ropes and boards to flatten crops.
- **Global Phenomenon:** While crop circles are predominantly found in the UK, they have been reported in over 25 countries, with some of the other hotspots including the United States, Canada, Australia, and Japan.

The Doug and Dave Theory: In 1991, two men, Doug Bower and Dave Chorley, claimed they had been creating crop circles in England since the 1970s using planks, rope, and a baseball cap fitted with a loop of wire to help them walk in a straight line. Their confession demystified some of the formations but also added to the intrigue, as not all could be easily explained away.

Geometry and Precision: Many crop circles exhibit a level of precision and complexity that baffles onlookers. Some designs are based on mathematical equations and sacred geometry, leading to speculations about their creation being beyond human capabilities. The crop circle phenomenon has indeed permeated various aspects of culture, art, literature, and spirituality, often serving as a canvas for human creativity and curiosity.

Here are specific examples of how crop circles have influenced different areas:

- **Art:** Crop circles have inspired numerous artists. For instance, the intricate patterns have been replicated in large-scale sand sculptures by renowned sand artist Simon Beck. Additionally, artists like Stan Herd have created 'earthworks' or large-scale land art that resembles crop circle designs.
- **Literature:** The mystery of crop circles has been explored in fiction. A notable example is "Signs" by M. Night Shyamalan, a novel adapted into a popular film that intertwines crop circles with a story of extraterrestrial contact. Another example is "The Circle Maker" by Mark Batterson, which, while not directly about crop circles, uses the concept metaphorically to explore themes of prayer and miracles.
- **Spiritual Beliefs:** Crop circles have given rise to new spiritual movements and beliefs. For some, these formations are seen as messages from higher powers or extraterrestrial beings. Books like "The Gift" by Freddy Silva explore crop circles as spiritual phenomena, suggesting they are created by non-human intelligence as messages to humanity.
- **Pop Culture:** Crop circles have been featured in television shows like "The X-Files," which often delved into paranormal phenomena, presenting crop circles as mysterious alien signatures. They have also appeared in advertising campaigns, using their intrigue to capture public attention.
- **Folklore and Mythology:** Crop circles have become modern folklore, with communities often attributing mystical properties to them. In some areas, they are woven into local

Whether the work of mischievous humans or an unexplained natural phenomenon, crop circles continue to captivate the imagination. Remember: you may never need to know the intricacies of how these geometric wonders are formed, but they serve as a mesmerizing mystery, a blend of art and enigma etched across the fields of the world.

34. The Science of Brain Freeze

Ever found yourself in the throes of a brain freeze, clutching your head in agony, all because you dared to guzzle a slushie or inhale an ice cream like there was no tomorrow? Welcome to the icy grip of sphenopalatine ganglioneuralgia, more affectionately known as brain freeze. It's nature's way of saying, "Slow down there, frosty!"

Here's the scoop on what happens when you chill your brain out, literally

The Cold Touch: The saga begins when something freezing cold waltzes onto the warm dance floor of your mouth, giving the roof a frosty peck. This is not just any cold encounter; it's the kind that makes your brain go, "Whoa, buddy!"

The Temperature Tango: This icy caress leads to a quickstep of temperature changes—first, a rapid cooling, followed by a swift rewarming of the blood vessels in your palate. It's like turning the thermostat down and then blasting the heat, all within seconds.

Vascular Waltz: In response, your blood vessels perform a frantic dance, constricting and dilating faster than disco lights at a '70s dance-off. This results in a blood flow boogie that's off the charts.

Frosty Fun Facts!

- Migraine Connection: The same dance routine gone awry in brain freeze is thought to be a backup dancer in the concert of migraines and cluster headaches. Who knew they were related?
- Avoidance Tactics: To dodge a brain freeze, savor your cold treats with the elegance and pace of a fine dining experience. Rushing through a brain freeze is like sprinting on ice—slippery and not recommended.
- The Warmth Rescue: Got caught in the freeze? Deploy the tongue! Press it against the roof of your mouth like a warm blanket on a cold night, or sip something warm to thaw the icy tension.
- Geographical Mysteries: Ever wonder if Eskimos get brain freezes? While we might not have all the answers, adapting to colder climates might mean their brain freeze game is on a whole different level. Imagine telling an Eskimo, "Just eat it slower!"
- Ice Cream, the Silent Culprit: Not all heroes wear capes, and not all villains look villainous. Ice cream, the sweet siren of the dessert world, is often the mastermind behind the brain freeze heist. It's a cold-hearted trickster with a delicious disguise.
- The Speedy Gonzales of Pain: Brain freeze is like the Usain Bolt of headaches, sprinting from zero to "ouch" in seconds flat, but don't worry—it's also the first to cross the finish line, making its painful exit as quickly as it arrived.
- The DIY Headache Kit: Fancy a brain freeze but out of ice cream? Fret not! Slurping down a cold drink or even a snow cone in a rush can equip you with your very own DIY brain freeze. It's like a science experiment, but with more regret.
- A Toast to Warmth: In the world of brain freeze, your tongue is the superhero, and warm beverages are its sidekick. Together, they battle the icy clutches of pain, melting away the freeze with all the drama of a climactic movie scene.

Remember, while brain freeze might be a chilly nuisance, it's also a fascinating glimpse into the body's response to sudden temperature changes. Plus, it gives us all a valid excuse to enjoy our frozen treats just a tad slower, savoring every delectable moment without the brain-biting consequences. Stay frosty, but not too frosty!

35. The Origins of the Piñata

The piñata, a staple of festive celebrations, has a history as colorful and varied as its appearance. This fun party icon, typically filled with sweets and treats, has a journey that spans continents and cultures, revealing a rich tapestry of traditions and meanings.

A Multicultural Beginning: Contrary to popular belief, the origins of the piñata are not solely Mexican. The concept is believed to have originated in China, where figures of animals were filled with seeds and hit with sticks as part of New Year celebrations. The remnants were then burned and the ashes kept for good luck.

Marco Polo's Influence: The idea of the piñata was likely brought from China to Italy by the explorer Marco Polo in the 13th century. In Italy, it transformed into a tradition called "pignatta," which means "fragile pot." The Italian version was typically a clay pot, which was the precursor to the modern piñata.

- **Spanish Religious Symbolism:** In Spain, the piñata was traditionally used during Lent. The classic Spanish piñata, resembling a pineapple with seven cones, represented the seven deadly sins. The blindfolded attempt to break the piñata symbolized faith overcoming sin and temptation.

Did you know? Spanish Lent traditions date back to the early Middle Ages, originating as a period of fasting and reflection in the 40 days leading up to Easter Sunday. This practice was established to mimic Jesus Christ's sacrifice and withdrawal into the desert for 40 days. Lent in Spain, known for its profound religious ceremonies and processions.

- **Mexican Cultural Fusion:** Spanish missionaries in Mexico used the piñata to attract indigenous people to Christian teachings. They found a pre-existing tradition where a clay pot was broken on a pole to honor Huitzilopochtli, the Aztec god of war. This ritual was adapted and merged with Christian symbolism.
- **Las Posadas and Piñatas:** In Mexico, the piñata became a central part of Las Posadas, a nine-day Christmas celebration. The breaking of the piñata, filled with fruits and sweets, symbolizes the triumph of good over evil.
- **The Seven Cones:** Each of the seven cones on the traditional Spanish piñata stood for a deadly sin: pride, envy, wrath, sloth, greed, gluttony, and lust. Smashing the piñata represented the destruction of these sins and the triumph of virtue.
- **A Symbol of Hope:** The piñata, often decorated and filled with tempting items, was also a metaphor for hope and reward. The act of breaking it open while blindfolded was seen as a leap of faith, with the rewards inside symbolizing the blessings of adhering to religious faith.
- **Evolution in Design:** While traditional piñatas were shaped like pineapples or stars with cones, modern piñatas come in a vast array of designs, often reflecting popular culture and festive themes, moving away from their religious connotations.
- **Adaptation Across Borders:** The piñata tradition spread from Mexico to other parts of Latin America and eventually to North America, where it became a popular element in birthday parties and other celebrations, often devoid of its original religious significance.
- **A Festive Staple Worldwide:** Today, the piñata has shed most of its religious connotations and is widely associated with festive parties. In Mexico, piñatas are often

star-shaped, reflecting their historical religious symbolism, and are a key feature in birthday celebrations and during the Posadas at Christmas time.

The piñata, with its vibrant colors and joyous purpose, is a fascinating example of how a simple object can weave through history, adapting and evolving with each culture it touches. Remember: you may never need to know the full global journey of the piñata, but this festive artifact is a delightful symbol of cultural fusion and shared joy.

36. Unusual Olympic Sports of the Past

The Olympic Games, a grand stage for athletic prowess, have not always been limited to the standard track, field, and pool events we know today. Over the years, the Olympics have featured some rather unusual sports that have since been retired. These quirky events offer a glimpse into the Games' eclectic past.

- **Tug of War (1900-1920):** Once a serious Olympic competition, teams of eight would literally pull their weight to drag the opposing team over a line. It was a test of sheer strength and teamwork.
- **Live Pigeon Shooting (1900):** In the Paris 1900 Olympics, live pigeon shooting was an official event. Competitors shot at live

pigeons, and the winner was the one who downed the most birds. It was the only time animals were killed on purpose in Olympic history.
- **Solo Synchronized Swimming (1984-1992):** This paradoxically named event involved swimmers performing synchronized routines alone, without a team, judged on their ability to stay in sync with the music.
- **Rope Climbing (1896, 1904, 1906, 1924, 1932):** This event required athletes to climb a suspended rope using only their hands. Speed and technique were key in this demanding physical challenge.
- **Swimming Obstacle Race (1900):** Held in the River Seine, this unique swimming event had athletes climb over a pole and a row of boats, and then swim under another row of boats.
- **Plunge for Distance (1904):** A one-time Olympic event where competitors dove into the pool and remained motionless for one minute or until their head resurfaced. The winner was the one who recorded the longest distance.

- **Underwater Swimming (1900):** Athletes were awarded two points for each meter swum underwater and one point for each second they stayed below the surface.
- **Race Walking (1904-Present):** While still an Olympic sport, it's unusual in its rule that competitors must always have one foot on the ground.

- **Pistol Dueling (1906):** Athletes used wax bullets and wore protective gear. The aim was to simulate a real duel, a popular practice among gentlemen in the early 20th century.
- **Jeux Sans Frontières (1900):** Also known as 'Intercalated Games,' this was a bizarre mix of sports and disciplines, including firefighting contests and kite flying, meant to encourage international friendship.

These odd and now-obsolete Olympic sports provide a fascinating window into the changing nature of athletic competition and what constituted Olympic-level challenges in different eras. Remember: you may never need to know the rules of underwater swimming or how to win at tug of war, but these historical sports trivia offer a quirky insight into the ever-evolving nature of the Olympic Games.

37. The Legend of the Fountain of Youth

A fabled spring that supposedly restores the youth of anyone who drinks or bathes in its waters. This enduring myth has captivated human imagination for centuries, symbolizing the universal human desire for renewal and longevity.

The concept of restorative waters can be traced back to ancient times, appearing in the writings of Herodotus, the Alexander Romance, and the stories of Prester John. These tales speak of magical waters capable of reversing aging and curing sickness.

- **Juan Ponce de León's Quest:** The legend became particularly prominent in the 16th century with Spanish explorer Juan Ponce de León, who, according to popular lore, searched for the Fountain of Youth in what is now Florida. However, modern historians note that this story is likely a myth; there's no historical evidence that Ponce de León actually sought the Fountain.

- **The Fountain's Symbolism:** Over the centuries, the Fountain of Youth has come to symbolize the human quest for the elusive, magical solution to the problem of aging. It represents an eternal dream of vitality and the hope to defy the natural aging process.

- **Literature:** Edmund Spenser's epic poem "The Faerie Queene," written in the late 16th century, is one of the earliest and most notable literary works to feature the Fountain of Youth. In the poem, the fountain is depicted as a sacred place with rejuvenating waters, symbolizing purity and renewal. Similarly, in Gabriel García Márquez's novel "One Hundred Years of Solitude," the pursuit of the mythical fountain by one of the characters represents the unattainable quest for eternal life.

- **Film and Television:** The Fountain of Youth has been a recurring theme in films and TV shows, often portrayed as an elusive, mystical source of eternal youth and beauty. For instance, in "Pirates of the Caribbean: On Stranger Tides," the quest for the Fountain is central to the plot, representing the characters' desires to escape death and achieve immortality. In "Indiana Jones and the Last Crusade," the pursuit of the Holy Grail, a relic with life-giving properties, mirrors the legends of the Fountain of Youth.

- **Art:** The Fountain of Youth has been a subject of fascination for many artists throughout history. For instance, Lucas Cranach the Elder, a German Renaissance painter, created a famous work titled "The Fountain of Youth" in 1546. The painting depicts elderly people entering a pool and emerging young and revitalized, visually capturing the transformative power attributed to the mythical fountain.

-
- **Music:** The theme of eternal youth and the Fountain of Youth has also been explored in music. For example, in the realm of classical music, the German composer Engelbert Humperdinck's opera "The Miracle" features a fountain whose waters can restore youth.

- **Philosophy and Psychology:** The myth of the Fountain of Youth extends beyond mere storytelling into the realms of philosophy and psychology, where it is often analyzed as a metaphor for humanity's vain pursuit of eternal life and the unrealistic desire to escape the natural aging process.

Today, the Fountain of Youth is often used as a metaphor for anything that potentially increases longevity or rejuvenates, from medical breakthroughs to lifestyle changes.

The legend of the Fountain of Youth, while a mythical tale, encapsulates a deep-seated human aspiration to overcome the ravages of time. Remember: you may never need to know the whereabouts of this mythical spring, but its story flows through the annals of history, reminding us of our enduring quest for youth and vitality.

38. Why Bananas Are Berries, But Strawberries Aren't

Dive into the surprising world of botanical classifications where common names and scientific categories often don't match up. One of the most intriguing examples is the case of bananas and strawberries, and how, in the realm of botany, a banana is considered a berry, while a strawberry is not.

- In botanical terms, a berry is a simple fruit with seeds and pulp produced from the ovary of a single flower. It must also contain three distinct layers: the exocarp (outer skin), mesocarp (fleshy middle), and endocarp (innermost part, which holds the seeds). By this definition, bananas qualify as berries. They develop from a single ovary of a single flower and contain the three layers.

- The Case of the Strawberry: Strawberries, on the other hand, are classified as aggregate fruits. Unlike berries, which develop from one ovary, aggregate fruits form from multiple ovaries of a single flower. What we think of as the "seeds" on the outside of a strawberry are actually the fruits, each with its own seed inside, making the strawberry not a true berry in the botanical sense.

- Misleading Common Names: The discrepancy between common usage and scientific classification often leads to such confusions. In everyday language, fruits are classified based on culinary attributes, leading to a different categorization compared to the botanical one.

- Other Surprising "Berries": In addition to bananas, other fruits such as tomatoes, kiwis, and grapes also fit the botanical criteria for berries. Their structure aligns with the scientific definition, even though they are not commonly referred to as berries in everyday conversation.

- The culinary classification of fruits is based more on taste and kitchen usage rather than scientific criteria. This is why strawberries are considered berries in the culinary world, while scientifically, they do not meet the criteria.

The curious case of why bananas are berries but strawberries aren't is a perfect example of the fascinating, sometimes counterintuitive world of botanical classification. Remember: you may never need to know the specific criteria that classify fruits in botany, but this quirky piece of trivia adds an interesting twist to our understanding of the fruits we consume daily.

39. The Invention of Bubble Wrap

Bubble Wrap, the ubiquitous packing material loved for its poppable bubbles, has a backstory that's as surprising as the satisfying snap of its bubbles. This accidental invention is a prime example of ingenuity and serendipity at play.

- Wallpaper Origins: Bubble Wrap was originally conceived in 1957 by engineers Alfred Fielding and Marc Chavannes. Interestingly, it was not intended as packing material but as a type of textured wallpaper. They sealed two shower curtains together, trapping air bubbles between them, hoping it would become a trendy new home decorating item.
- From Wallpaper to Insulation: When the wallpaper idea didn't take off, Fielding and Chavannes pivoted. They marketed their invention as greenhouse insulation. The trapped air bubbles were

were perfect for trapping heat, but this application also didn't achieve commercial success.

- A Packaging Revolution: The big break for Bubble Wrap came in 1960 when IBM was preparing to launch its first mass-produced computer, the IBM 1401. Fielding and Chavannes suggested using Bubble Wrap for protecting the computer during shipping. IBM agreed, and the product found its niche, revolutionizing packaging.

- Popularity and Playfulness: Beyond its practical application, Bubble Wrap has become a cultural phenomenon. Its satisfying popping sound and feel have made it a stress-reliever and object of play. January 29th is even celebrated as National Bubble Wrap Appreciation Day.

- Evolution and Sustainability: Today, Bubble Wrap is not just a single product but a brand. It has evolved with variations like anti-static Bubble Wrap for electronics and even a version designed to be more environmentally friendly.

The invention of Bubble Wrap is a classic tale of a simple idea morphing into an essential product in unexpected ways. Remember: you may never need to know the origins of Bubble Wrap, but every time you pop those air-filled bubbles, you're partaking in a bit of serendipitous invention history.

40. Phantom Islands of Ancient Maps

Phantom islands, a term that evokes images of mysterious, uncharted territories, refer to islands that were once believed to exist but were later proven to be nonexistent or misidentified landforms. These elusive islands, often included in ancient and medieval maps, tell a fascinating story of exploration, cartographic errors, and the allure of the unknown.

- **Cartographic Creations:** Phantom islands often appeared on maps due to navigational errors, mistaken observations, or even deliberate fabrications. Before the age of accurate scientific cartography, mapmakers frequently relied on sailors' tales and unverified reports, leading to the inclusion of these non-existent lands.
- **Famous Phantom Islands:** One of the most famous phantom islands was Hy-Brasil, said to be located off the west coast of Ireland. It appeared on maps from 1325 to the 1800s and was rumored to be a cloaked island, visible only once every seven years. Another well-known example is Frisland, a phantom island that appeared on maps for over a century, believed to be located in the North Atlantic Ocean.
- **The Case of Sandy Island:** As recently as 2012, a phantom island named Sandy Island was reported in the Pacific Ocean. It appeared on maps and even on Google Earth but was later found not to exist when a scientific expedition went to its supposed location.
- **Symbol of Mystery and Adventure:** Phantom islands captivated the imagination of explorers, adventurers, and the public alike. They represented the mysteries of the unexplored world, often thought to hold riches or be home to exotic peoples or creatures.

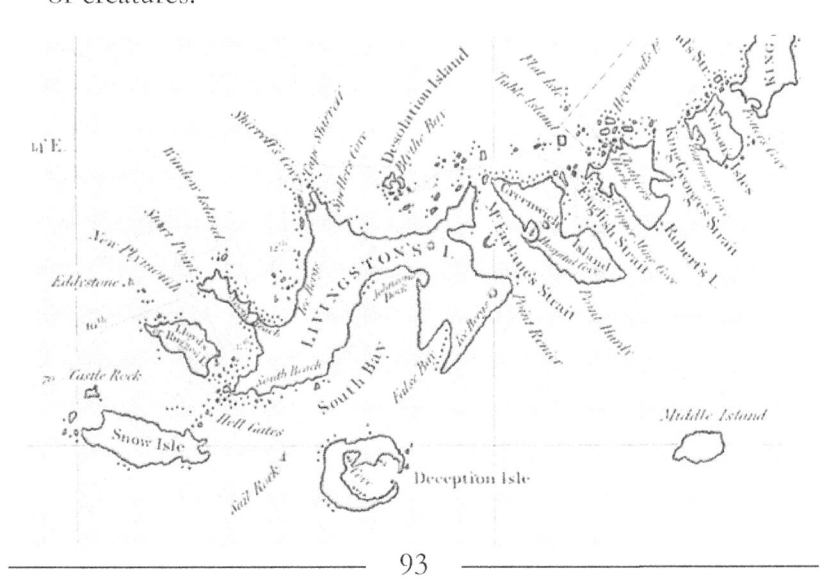

- **Influence on Literature and Culture:** These mythical islands have influenced literature and folklore, inspiring stories and legends. The idea of hidden or lost islands has been a recurring theme in tales of adventure and fantasy, capturing the human fascination with discovery and the unknown.

Phantom islands, while not real in a geographical sense, hold a significant place in the history of exploration and cartography. Remember: you may never need to know the exact coordinates of these non-existent isles, but they offer a glimpse into the adventurous spirit of early explorers and the intriguing evolution of mapmaking.

41. The Great Escape Artist: Houdini

Dive into the captivating world of Harry Houdini, the legendary illusionist and escape artist whose death-defying stunts and masterful illusions left audiences spellbound. Houdini's legacy extends far beyond his performances, making him an iconic figure in the world of magic and escapology.

From Humble Beginnings: Born Erik Weisz in Hungary in 1874, Houdini started his career as a magician under the name "Harry Houdini," inspired by the French magician Jean Eugène Robert-Houdin. He initially performed traditional card tricks before discovering his true calling: escape artistry.

Master of Escapes: Houdini's fame skyrocketed due to his sensational escape acts.

He would free himself from handcuffs, straitjackets, water-filled tanks, and even prison cells. His ability to escape from seemingly impossible situations earned him the nickname "The Handcuff King."

The Chinese Water Torture Cell: One of Houdini's most famous stunts was the Chinese Water Torture Cell, where he was suspended upside-down in a locked glass-and-steel cabinet filled with water, managing to escape without any visible means of exit.

A Crusade Against Spiritualists: Houdini also became known for his campaign against spiritualists and mediums. Using his knowledge of magic, he exposed frauds who claimed to have supernatural powers to communicate with the dead.

Death and Legacy: Houdini's death on October 31, 1926, added to his legend. He died of peritonitis, secondary to a ruptured appendix, after sustaining punches to his abdomen – an incident shrouded in mystery and speculation.

Influence on Pop Culture: Houdini's influence extends into contemporary culture, with numerous books, films, and theatrical productions based on his life. He symbolizes the power of human ingenuity and the allure of mystery.

Remember: **you may never need to know** how to wriggle out of a straitjacket or escape a water-filled tank, but Harry Houdini's story is a testament to the extraordinary limits of human skill and perseverance, inspiring awe and wonder even today.

42. The World's Largest Omelet

In the realm of culinary feats, the creation of the world's largest omelet stands as a testament to gastronomic ambition and community spirit. This massive undertaking isn't just about breaking eggs; it's about setting world records and bringing people together for a unique and memorable event.

- **A Record-Breaking Dish:** The record for the world's largest omelet was set in Santarém, Portugal, in 2012. A team of chefs and volunteers came together to cook this gigantic omelet, showcasing both culinary skills and community effort.
- **The Ingredients:** To create this colossal omelet, the team used a staggering 145,000 eggs. The process also required massive quantities of oil and a variety of seasonings to add flavor to this enormous dish.
- **The Cooking Process:** The omelet was cooked in a gigantic pan, measuring 10.3 meters in diameter. Preparing such a large omelet required not only a large number of ingredients but also specialized equipment and a coordinated effort from all those involved in the cooking process.
- **A Community Event:** The making of the world's largest omelet was more than just a culinary endeavor; it was a community event that attracted a large crowd of locals and tourists alike. It showcased the spirit of collaboration and celebration.
- **Culinary Tradition and Innovation:** This event highlighted a blend of traditional cooking methods and innovative approaches to deal with the scale of the dish. It was a unique way to celebrate the culinary heritage and creativity.
- **Guinness World Record:** The achievement was recognized by the Guinness World Records, marking it as an official world record in the culinary world.

Remember: you may never need to know the recipe for the world's largest omelet, but this extraordinary culinary feat serves as a delicious example of what can be achieved when a community comes together to crack a few (thousand) eggs and create something truly egg-ceptional.

43. The Mystery of Sailing Stones

Embark on a journey to Death Valley National Park in California, where a geological phenomenon has puzzled observers for decades. The sailing stones, also known as sliding rocks or moving rocks, are large stones that mysteriously "sail" across the flat, dry surface of the Racetrack Playa, leaving visible trails behind them without any human or animal intervention.

- **Mysterious Movement:** These rocks, some weighing hundreds of pounds, move across the playa's flat surface, leaving long, winding tracks that can stretch for hundreds of feet. For many years, no one ever saw the stones in motion, leading to a host of speculative explanations.
- Early Theories: Before their movement was understood, various theories were proposed, including strong winds, ice formation, slick algal films, magnetic fields, and even pranksters or extraterrestrial activities.
- Scientific Breakthrough: The mystery began to unravel in 2014 when researchers used GPS and time-lapse photography to discover the real cause. It turns out the stones move due to a perfect combination of ice, water, and wind.
- The Role of Ice and Wind: During winter, the playa fills with a thin layer of water, which freezes overnight and forms sheets of ice. As the temperature rises, the ice breaks into large floating panels. Light winds then drive these ice sheets, which push the rocks at a slow pace, causing them to leave trails on the

muddy bottom of the playa.
- **Variety of Trails:** The stones' trails vary in length and direction, some straight and others in curves and zigzags. The differences in movement patterns are due to variations in wind direction, ice thickness, and the stones' shape and size.

- **An Ongoing Study:** While the general mechanism of the sailing stones is now understood, researchers continue to study the phenomenon to understand the finer details of the conditions and forces at work.

Remember: you may never need to know the precise scientific explanation behind the sailing stones of Death Valley, but this natural phenomenon is a fascinating example of how seemingly magical events can often have a grounding in the intricate interplay of natural forces.

44. Voynich Manuscript

Voynich Manuscript, a mysterious book that has baffled cryptographers, historians, and linguists for over a century. This medieval codex, named after Wilfrid Voynich, a Polish book dealer who acquired it in 1912, is filled with unknown symbols, illustrations of imaginary plants, and other inexplicable content.

Unknown Language and Authorship: The manuscript is written in an unknown script that has resisted all attempts at deciphering. Its author, origin, and purpose remain a mystery, fueling various theories about its creation and meaning.

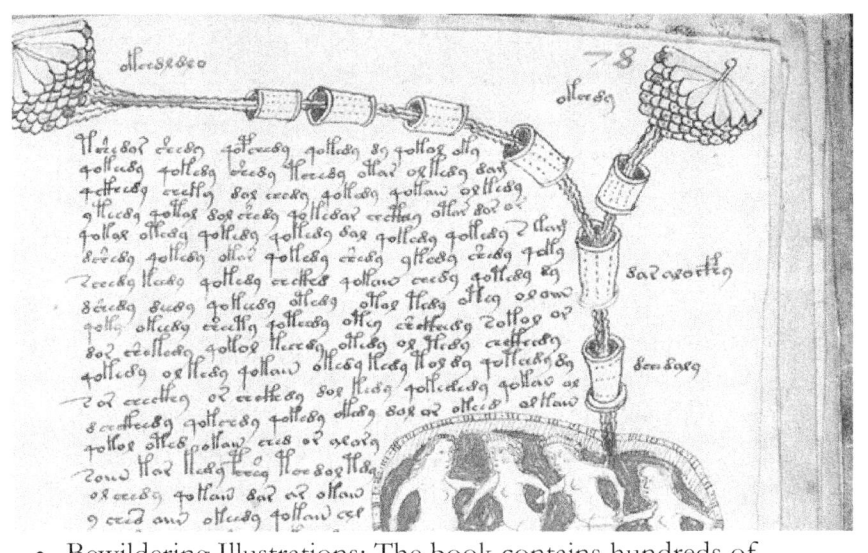

- Bewildering Illustrations: The book contains hundreds of illustrations of non-existent plants, astrological diagrams, and humanoid figures, further deepening the intrigue. These drawings seem to be of a botanical, astronomical, and medical nature but do not correspond to any known categories.

- Carbon Dating: Tests have dated the manuscript to the early 15th century (1404–1438), making it over 600 years old. This dating has dispelled some theories about its origins but has not brought researchers any closer to understanding its true purpose.

- Attempts at Deciphering: Many professional and amateur cryptographers, including those from both World Wars, have attempted to crack the code of the Voynich Manuscript. Despite these efforts, the text remains undeciphered, leading some to speculate that it may be an elaborate hoax.

The Hoax Theory:

The theory that the manuscript is a hoax has been considered, given its uncrackable code and unusual imagery. However, the sophistication and consistency of the script and the elaborate nature of the illustrations have led many to believe it is a genuine creation.

- **The Master Prankster Theory:** Some believe that the Voynich Manuscript could be the work of a medieval trickster, possibly created as a form of intellectual entertainment for the elite. Imagine a 15th-century jester with a penchant for cryptography and botanical doodles!
- **Financial Motives?:** Another angle to the hoax theory posits that the manuscript might have been created to swindle a wealthy buyer. The idea is akin to selling a map to a non-existent treasure island. In this case, it's a book of secrets that no one can read.
- **Too Complex to be True?:** Skeptics of the manuscript's authenticity often point to the book's intricate and consistent script as suspiciously perfect. It's like finding a diary written in an unknown language with no errors or corrections – either it's a work of genius or a well-crafted fake.
- **Inconsistencies in Botany:** The manuscript is filled with illustrations of plants that don't resemble any known species. It's as if someone decided to play "fantasy garden" and sketched an alien flora collection.
- **The Unbreakable Code:** The text's resistance to decipherment fuels the hoax theory. Critics argue that if it were genuine, some progress in translation would have been made by now, considering the number of brilliant minds that have tackled it.
- **Modern Cryptographic Attempts:** Even with advanced technology and cryptographic techniques, the manuscript remains undeciphered. This unyielding mystery prompts the question: is it really a code or just gibberish designed to confuse?
- **The Artistic Touch:** The elaborate illustrations, particularly the astronomical and astrological diagrams, are detailed and precise. Hoax theorists question why a forger would invest so much time in such complex artwork if the aim was simply to deceive.
- **Historical Context:** The timing of the manuscript's appearance aligns with a period of heightened interest in esoteric knowledge in Europe. This context suggests that creating a mysterious book would have been timely and potentially profitable.

- **The Absence of Authorship Claims:** Notably, there are no historical records of any individual or group claiming authorship or explaining the manuscript, which is unusual for a hoax. Most hoaxes are eventually confessed or exposed.
- **The Enduring Enigma**: The fact that the Voynich Manuscript continues to baffle experts adds to its legend. Whether it's a genuine repository of unknown knowledge or an elaborate medieval joke, it has secured its place in history.
- **A Subject of Ongoing Study:** The Voynich Manuscript continues to be an object of study in various fields, from linguistics to computer science. In recent years, artificial intelligence and advanced computational techniques have been applied in attempts to decode it.

Remember: **you may never need to know** the secrets hidden within the pages of the Voynich Manuscript, but its enduring mystery captivates the imagination, representing one of the most tantalizing puzzles in the world of historical cryptology.

45. The Enigma of the Zodiac Killer

The Zodiac Killer, a name that strikes chords of fear and mystery, emerged as a notorious figure in the late 1960s and early 1970s in Northern California. The killer's identity remains one of the most elusive puzzles in American criminal history. This unidentified assailant is believed to be responsible for a series of murders, claiming the lives of at least five individuals between 1968 and 1969, although in his cryptic communications, he boasted of killing as many as 37 people. The victims, often young couples found in secluded areas and a lone cab driver, were the tragic targets of his brutal spree.

What set the Zodiac Killer apart and propelled the case into a media frenzy was not just the heinous nature of the crimes but the killer's chilling interactions with the police and the public. The Zodiac took to sending letters to local newspapers and the police, some containing ciphers, which he claimed, once solved, would unveil his true identity. These letters, often beginning with the salutation "This is the Zodiac speaking," were marked with a distinctive symbol—a crosshair-like circle—which became an unnerving trademark of his communications.

The enigma deepened with the Zodiac's ciphers. Of the four cryptograms he sent, only one has been definitively cracked. This deciphered message was a macabre statement of the killer's enjoyment of murder, reading in part, "I like killing because it is so much fun." The other ciphers, including the notorious 340-character cryptogram, have remained unsolved, despite efforts from professional and amateur cryptographers alike. The unsolved nature of these codes has fueled endless theories and discussions, keeping the Zodiac Killer's menacing legacy alive in the public imagination.

Decades have passed since the Zodiac Killer's reign of terror, yet his identity continues to evade law enforcement and investigators. The case remains open, with technological advancements in forensic science offering a glimmer of hope in unearthing new leads.

The Zodiac Killer's story, shrouded in mystery and horror, continues to be a subject of fascination, inspiring numerous books, movies, and endless speculation, a testament to the enduring human intrigue with the unsolved and the unknown.

- **Cinematic Depiction:** The Zodiac Killer's story was vividly brought to life in David Fincher's 2007 film "Zodiac." The movie, based on Robert Graysmith's book, explores the obsessive quest to uncover the killer's identity and the impact it had on those involved in the case.
- **Literary Investigations:** Several books have delved into the Zodiac mystery, with Robert Graysmith's "Zodiac" (1986) being one of the most notable. Graysmith, who was a cartoonist at the San Francisco Chronicle when the Zodiac letters arrived, became deeply engrossed in solving the mystery, offering detailed accounts and theories.

- **The Arthur Leigh Allen Theory:** Of the numerous suspects, Arthur Leigh Allen remains a prominent figure in discussions about the Zodiac's identity. Allen became a suspect due to his proximity to the locations of the murders and some circumstantial evidence, including owning a Zodiac-brand watch and the same caliber gun used in one of the murders. However, he was never charged due to lack of concrete evidence, and DNA testing in 2002 did not match him to the Zodiac letters.

- **DNA and the Zodiac:** Advances in DNA technology have provided hope in uncovering the Zodiac's identity. In recent years, investigators have attempted to obtain a full DNA profile from the saliva on the stamps and envelopes of the Zodiac's letters.
- **The Cypher Theories:** Amateur and professional code-breakers continue to pour over the Zodiac's unsolved ciphers. In December 2020, a team of private citizens claimed to have cracked the 340-character cipher, which seemingly contained a taunting message from the killer but no revelation of his identity.
- **The Costume:** One of the most chilling aspects of the Zodiac Killer was his costume, described by survivors of an attack at Lake Berryessa. He wore a black hood with clip-on sunglasses over the eyeholes and a bib-like device on his chest that had the Zodiac symbol.

Zodiac Killer Copycats

The notoriety of the Zodiac Killer has unfortunately inspired a number of copycat crimes over the years, with various criminals emulating his modus operandi and the characteristic taunting nature.

- These instances demonstrate the dark influence that infamous criminal cases can have on certain individuals, leading them to replicate these notorious acts in their own twisted pursuits.

One such instance occurred in New York in the early 1990s. The "Zodiac Copycat Killer," Heriberto Seda, mimicked the

Zodiac Killer's methods by shooting and stabbing people from 1990 to 1993. Seda's fascination with the original Zodiac Killer was evident in the letters he sent to the police and media, taunting them just as the original Zodiac had done decades earlier. He used astrological signs to choose his victims, a chilling echo of the original Zodiac's cryptic communications and symbolisms.

In Japan, a series of murders and attacks in 1995 known as the "Zodiac murders" were also thought to be inspired by the Zodiac Killer. The perpetrator, who was never caught, sent letters to media outlets claiming responsibility for the murders and signed them with a symbol similar to that of the Zodiac Killer. The letters contained astrological references and threatened further violence, mirroring the original killer's penchant for media attention and psychological manipulation.

These grim echoes of the past serve as a stark reminder of the lasting impact high-profile criminal cases can have. The Zodiac Killer's legacy, marred by violence and enigma, not only remains a subject of public intrigue but also, regrettably, a source of inspiration for subsequent criminal acts. Remember: while the fascination with unsolved cases is a natural aspect of human curiosity, it can sometimes lead to unforeseen and tragic consequences when it crosses the line into the realm of emulation.

Remember: **you may never need to know** the intricate details of the Zodiac Killer's ciphers or the theories about his identity, but this case stands as a chilling reminder of the complexities and challenges of criminal investigations, as well as the enduring human fascination with the unknown and unsolved.

46. The Curious Case of the Cottingley Fairies

Step into the whimsical and controversial world of the Cottingley Fairies, a tale that captured the public's imagination and sparked a debate between belief and skepticism in the early 20th century. This story revolves around a series of photographs taken by two young cousins, Elsie Wright and Frances Griffiths, in Cottingley, England, which they claimed to be evidence of real fairies.

- **The Initial Photographs:** In 1917, Elsie, 16, and Frances, 9, used a camera to take photographs in the garden, which appeared to show fairies dancing around Frances. They claimed these were real creatures they had encountered. A second photograph soon followed, showing Elsie with a gnome-like figure.
- **Sir Arthur Conan Doyle's Involvement:** The story gained significant attention when Sir Arthur Conan Doyle, the creator of Sherlock Holmes and a spiritualist, became interested in the photographs. He used them in a 1920 article for "The Strand Magazine," presenting them as genuine evidence of supernatural entities, which gave the story widespread publicity.
- **Public and Scientific Reaction:** The photographs sparked a mixture of fascination and skepticism.

Some believed in their authenticity, seeing them as a magical glimpse into another world, while others dismissed them as clever fakes. Experts in photography and illusion, including those from the Kodak company, examined the prints but could not conclusively prove them as fakes or authenticate them.

- **Admission of a Hoax:** The mystery of the Cottingley Fairies persisted for decades. It wasn't until the 1980s that the truth came to light. Elsie and Frances, then elderly, confessed that the photographs were indeed a hoax. They had used cardboard cutouts of fairies copied from a popular children's book, attaching them to hatpins to create the illusion of dancing fairies.
- **Enduring Fascination:** Despite the confession, the Cottingley Fairies case continues to fascinate as an example of how easily and fervently people can be drawn to the magical and unexplained. It remains a curious footnote in the history of photography and a poignant story of childhood imagination.

The Cottingley Fairies case serves as a reminder of the thin line between fantasy and reality and how our desire to believe in the extraordinary can sometimes color our perception of the world. Remember: **you may never need to know**, the story of their brief flight in the public eye is a testament to the enduring allure of mystery and wonder in our lives.

47. The Phenomenon of Aurora Borealis

The Aurora Borealis, also known as the Northern Lights, presents one of nature's most spectacular and enchanting displays. This luminous phenomenon, with its mesmerizing swirls of green, purple, and pink, lights up the polar skies, capturing the imagination of anyone fortunate enough to witness it. Here's a glimpse into the science and lore behind this celestial spectacle.

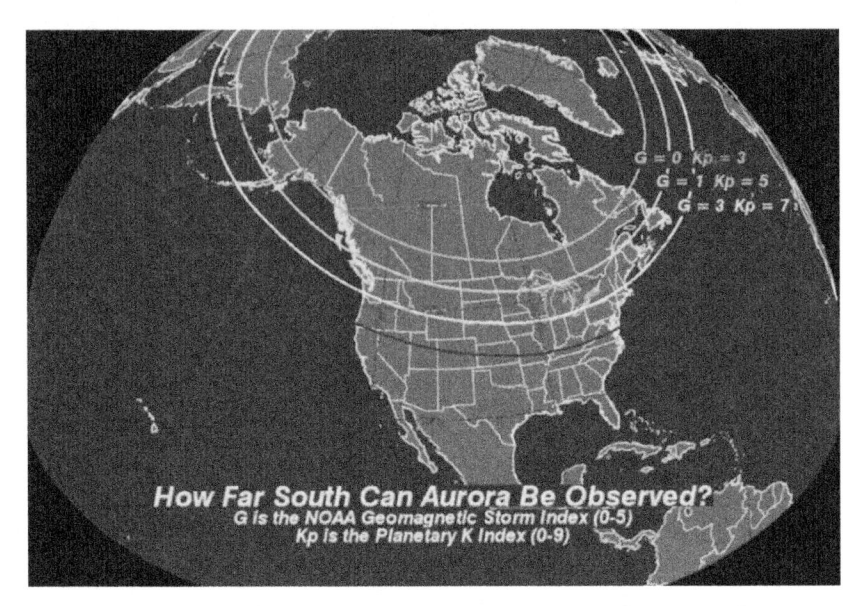

How Far South Can Aurora Be Observed?
G is the NOAA Geomagnetic Storm Index (0-5)
Kp is the Planetary K Index (0-9)

- The Aurora Borealis is a result of interactions between the Earth's atmosphere and charged particles from the sun. These particles are carried towards the poles by the Earth's magnetic field and collide with gases like oxygen and nitrogen in the atmosphere, creating the dazzling light show.
- The intensity and frequency of the Northern Lights are closely linked to solar activity. Solar flares and coronal mass ejections from the sun increase the number of charged particles interacting with the Earth's atmosphere, often leading to more vivid displays.
- The varying colors of the aurora are due to the type of gas particles involved in the collisions. Oxygen emits green and red light, while nitrogen produces blue and purple hues. The blending of these colors creates the aurora's signature ethereal glow.
- The Aurora Borealis, or Northern Lights, is a celestial spectacle that draws travelers to the far reaches of the northern hemisphere. Here's a guide to some of the best locations to witness this natural wonder and what you can do while you're there:

- **Tromsø, Norway:** Often called the 'Capital of the Arctic', Tromsø offers a high chance of Northern Lights sightings from September to April. Visitors can combine aurora hunting with dog sledding, snowshoeing, and visiting the iconic Arctic Cathedral.
- **Reykjavik, Iceland:** While you can catch the Northern Lights from the city, heading out to less urban areas like Thingvellir National Park increases your chances. Reykjavik also offers geothermal spas like the Blue Lagoon for a relaxing experience under the auroral glow.
- **Fairbanks, Alaska:** Positioned under the 'Auroral Oval', Fairbanks is an ideal spot for viewing the lights. The city offers guided aurora tours and the chance to explore the stunning Alaskan wilderness by day, including visits to Chena Hot Springs.
- **Yellowknife, Canada:** This city in Canada's Northwest Territories is known for its clear skies, making it perfect for Northern Lights viewing. Activities include ice fishing, snowmobiling, and learning about the indigenous cultures at the Prince of Wales Northern Heritage Centre.
- **Abisko, Sweden:** Located in the Swedish Lapland, Abisko is almost free from light pollution and cloud cover, providing excellent aurora viewing conditions. Visitors can also enjoy a trip on the Aurora Sky Station and explore the picturesque landscapes of the Abisko National Park.
- **Rovaniemi, Finland:** Known as the official hometown of Santa Claus, Rovaniemi offers a magical winter experience with aurora viewing. Enjoy reindeer sleigh rides, visit the Santa Claus Village, and stay in unique accommodations like glass igloos.
- **Luosto, Finland:** This small resort town is home to the Aurora Chalet, where you can receive 'Aurora Alarms' when the Northern Lights appear. During the day, explore the Amethyst Mine or enjoy skiing and snowboarding.

The Aurora Borealis, a stunning display of nature's grandeur, stands as a testament to the Earth's wonders. This ethereal light show, with its dazzling hues and mystical presence, not only captivates the eyes but also ignites the imagination, reminding us of the endless mysteries and beauties of our universe. Remember: you may never need to know the scientific intricacies behind this magnificent spectacle, but witnessing the Northern Lights, even if just once, can be a profound reminder of the awe-inspiring natural world that surrounds us, waiting to be explored and appreciated.

48. The Secrets of Stonehenge

Stonehenge, an iconic and ancient monument located in the English countryside, has stood as a silent witness to millennia of history. This prehistoric structure, composed of a ring of standing stones, has fascinated archaeologists, historians, and visitors alike with its enduring mysteries and secrets.

Stonehenge was constructed in several stages, with the earliest known structure dating back to about 5,000 years ago. The most recognizable part of Stonehenge, the outer ring of sarsen stones capped with lintels, was erected around 2500 BC.

The construction of Stonehenge is an architectural marvel, especially considering the time period in which it was built. Some of the stones, weighing as much as 25 tons, were transported from distances as far as 20 miles away. The precise manner in which the stones were shaped and erected demonstrates sophisticated engineering skills.

Cultural Significance

- **Mythical Associations:** Stonehenge has been romantically linked to Merlin, the fabled wizard of Arthurian legend. One medieval myth suggests Merlin magically transported the stones from Ireland, where giants had originally placed them.
- **Druidic Connections:** Despite popular belief, there's no definitive evidence linking Stonehenge to the Druids, as the structure predates their culture. However, it remains a focal point for modern Druidic and Pagan ceremonies, especially during solstices.
- **Literary Inspirations:** Stonehenge has appeared in literature and poetry for centuries, symbolizing endurance and mystery. Thomas Hardy famously used it as a setting in his novel "Tess of the D'Urbervilles," where it served as a place of refuge and solace.

Archaeological Discoveries

- **Neolithic Settlements:** Recent excavations near Stonehenge have uncovered evidence of Neolithic houses, pottery, tools, and burial mounds, suggesting a large, organized community with a rich cultural and religious life.
- **Bluestone Riddle:** The smaller bluestones, traced to the Preseli Hills in Wales, some 150 miles away, present an ongoing archaeological puzzle. How they were transported such a distance remains a subject of debate, with water transport and glacial movement being considered.
- **Human Remains:** Analysis of skeletal remains found near Stonehenge indicates that some of the individuals buried there might have come from as far away as Western Britain, hinting at the site's wide-reaching significance in the ancient world.

Mysterious Origins

- **Astronomical Precision:** Stonehenge's alignment with the solstices suggests it may have been used as an astronomical

observatory. On the summer solstice, the sun rises directly over the Heel Stone, creating a spectacular sight.
- **The Healing Theory:** Analysis of the human remains suggests that many had suffered from illness or injury, leading some to theorize that Stonehenge was a site of pilgrimage for healing, akin to a prehistoric Lourdes.
- **Varied Theories:** Over the years, theories about Stonehenge's purpose have ranged from it being a coronation place for Danish kings, a Druid temple, to a prehistoric calendar. Each theory reflects the era in which it was proposed, mirroring contemporary understandings and preoccupations.

Remember: **you may never need to know** all the secrets hidden beneath the stones of Stonehenge, but this monumental relic of the past serves as a compelling reminder of our ancestors' ingenuity and the enduring allure of ancient mysteries.

49. The Disappearance of Amelia Earhart

Embark on a journey into one of the 20th century's greatest mysteries: the disappearance of Amelia Earhart. A pioneering aviator and a symbol of courage and adventure, Earhart's fate has been the subject of speculation and intrigue since she vanished in 1937 while attempting to circumnavigate the globe.

- **A Pioneering Flight:** Amelia Earhart set out on her ambitious round-the-world flight in June 1937, accompanied by navigator Fred Noonan. Their plan was to fly a Lockheed Electra aircraft around the equator, a journey that would cover about 29,000 miles.
- **The Final Communication:** Earhart's last known communication was on July 2, 1937, near Howland Island in the Pacific Ocean. She reported running low on fuel and being unable to find the island, a crucial refueling stop. Shortly after, she and Noonan disappeared,

sparking one of the biggest air and sea searches in history, led by the United States Navy and Coast Guard.

- **Theories and Speculations:** Numerous theories have emerged regarding Earhart's fate. Some suggest she crash-landed in the ocean and perished at sea. Others speculate that she may have been captured by Japanese forces, as her disappearance occurred near Japanese-controlled islands during the lead-up to World War II.
- **Search for Wreckage:** Over the decades, several expeditions have been launched to find Earhart's plane, but none have conclusively identified any wreckage as belonging to her Lockheed Electra. The deep waters and vast expanse of the Pacific Ocean have complicated these efforts.
- **The Nikumaroro Hypothesis:** One prominent theory posits that Earhart and Noonan landed on Nikumaroro (formerly Gardner Island), surviving for a time as castaways. This theory is supported by artifacts found on the island and analysis of distress calls thought to have been sent from there after her disappearance.
- **Cultural Impact:** Earhart's disappearance transformed her into a legendary figure, symbolizing the spirit of exploration and the unresolved mysteries of the era of early aviation. Her life and mysterious fate continue to inspire books, films, and research.

- Ongoing Fascination: The enduring mystery of Amelia Earhart's disappearance continues to captivate the public's imagination, representing an unsolved puzzle in the annals of aviation history.

Remember: while you may think **you never need to know** the intricate details of Amelia Earhart's final flight, perhaps it's something you should. Her legacy as a trailblazer and adventurer stands as a profound testament to the resilience and daring spirit of exploration. It reminds us to courageously pursue our dreams and face the unknown, embodying the very essence of human curiosity and determination.

50. The Legend of Bigfoot

The legend of Bigfoot, also known as Sasquatch, is one of the most enduring mysteries of the North American wilderness.

This mythical creature, often depicted as a large, hairy, bipedal humanoid, has been a part of Native American folklore for centuries and has captured the modern public's imagination through numerous reported sightings, footprints, and anecdotes.

Pop Culture Tidbits:

- Film and Television: Bigfoot has been a popular subject in movies and TV shows, ranging from horror films like "The Legend of Boggy Creek" to family-friendly fare like "Harry and the Hendersons." The creature has also been featured in numerous documentaries and reality shows, including "Finding Bigfoot."
- Advertising Mascot: Bigfoot has been used in advertising, most famously as the mascot for Jack Link's Beef Jerky in the "Messin' with Sasquatch" ad campaign, showcasing the creature's blend of humor and mystery.

Expeditions and Research:

- Bigfoot Field Researchers Organization (BFRO): Perhaps the most prominent group dedicated to the pursuit of Bigfoot, the BFRO organizes regular expeditions, inviting both believers and skeptics. These excursions involve scouting locations with a history of sightings, setting up night watches, and using audio equipment to try and capture sounds attributed to Bigfoot.

- The Falcon Project: This ambitious initiative planned to use an unmanned aerial vehicle (UAV) equipped with thermal imaging cameras to search for Bigfoot from the skies, offering a new technological approach to the hunt.

- Lack of Physical Evidence: Mainstream science demands physical evidence for undisputed acceptance of a new species. In the case of Bigfoot, the absence of such evidence – like a body or bones – has led many scientists to dismiss the phenomenon.

- Alternative Explanations: Experts often suggest that purported Bigfoot sightings are either hoaxes or misidentifications of known animals, like bears. Additionally, the footprints, considered the most compelling physical evidence, are often explained as being misinterpretations or deliberate fakes.

- The Patterson-Gimlin Film (1967): One of the most famous pieces of evidence, this short film purports to show a Bigfoot walking through a clearing. It sparked widespread interest and led to numerous expeditions in the Bluff Creek area of California.

- Expedition Bigfoot (2019): This expedition, turned into a TV series, saw a team of experts using advanced data algorithms to pinpoint potential Bigfoot habitats. This modern approach combines technology with traditional field research.

- Numerous television programs have been dedicated to finding Bigfoot, involving everything from night-vision cameras to DNA analysis of hair and tissue samples supposedly from the creature.

Hiroo Onoda and Bigfoot:

- The Unexpected Encounter: Hiroo Onoda, a Japanese soldier who famously did not surrender until 1974, years after World War II had ended, reportedly encountered a Bigfoot researcher during his time hiding in the Philippines.
- A Curious Intersection: The researcher, reportedly searching for Bigfoot in the jungles where Onoda was hiding, came across the soldier, highlighting the wide-reaching and unexpected nature of Bigfoot lore.

- A Tale of Survival: Onoda's story, while not directly related to Bigfoot, became intertwined with the legend due to this bizarre and unlikely meeting.

The legend of Bigfoot, whether seen as a real creature or a cultural phenomenon, continues to inspire curiosity and adventure. Remember: while **you may never need to know** if Bigfoot truly roams the forests, the stories and expeditions in search of this legendary creature remind us of the enduring human fascination with the mysterious and the unknown.

51. Hiroo Onoda: No Surrender

So now that we have teased the Hiroo Onoda story, we may as well explore the remarkable tale further.

Hiroo Onoda's story is a remarkable tale of endurance, survival, and the complexities of war. Onoda, a Japanese Army intelligence officer, became famous for continuing to fight World War II for nearly three decades after the war had ended, unaware that Japan had surrendered.

- Initial Deployment: In December 1944, Onoda was sent to Lubang Island in the Philippines. His orders were to conduct guerrilla warfare during World War II and not to surrender or take his own life.
- End of the War: When the war ended in 1945, Onoda and a few companions who remained did not believe the news of Japan's surrender, suspecting it to be enemy propaganda.
- Years in Hiding: Onoda continued his campaign on Lubang, living in the mountains, surviving on stolen rice, coconuts, and bananas. He engaged in sporadic skirmishes with local residents and police.
- Refusing to Surrender: Over the years, various attempts were made to persuade Onoda and his remaining companion (the others had died or surrendered) that the war was over. Leaflets were dropped, and family members even spoke over loudspeakers, but they believed it all to be tricks.

<u>The Surrender:</u>

Encounter with Norio Suzuki: Norio Suzuki, a young Japanese adventurer intrigued by Onoda's story, arrived on Lubang Island in February 1974. Suzuki's unique quest was to find "Lieutenant Onoda, a panda, and the Abominable Snowman, in that order." Against all odds, Suzuki found Onoda in the jungle and befriended him. However, Onoda, still loyal to his original orders, refused to surrender unless his commanding officer ordered him to do so.

Verification of the War's End: Suzuki returned to Japan with photographic proof of his encounter, causing a sensation and prompting the Japanese government to track down Onoda's commanding officer, Major Yoshimi Taniguchi. Taniguchi had since become a bookseller after the war.

- **The Formal Surrender:** In a surreal and emotional encounter, Major Taniguchi flew to Lubang Island to formally relieve Onoda of his duties. On March 9, 1974, in a ceremony attended by Philippine and Japanese officials, Onoda handed over his sword, rifle, ammunition, and several grenades he had preserved from the war. He was pardoned by Philippine President Ferdinand Marcos for the skirmishes and conflicts he had been involved in during his years in hiding.

The Aftermath:

- Return to Japan: Onoda's return to Japan was met with a hero's welcome. His tale of survival and unwavering dedication captivated the nation and the world. He found a country vastly different from the one he had left, transformed by peace and modernization.

- **Life Reflections:** Onoda's adjustment to post-war life in modern Japan was challenging. He was a man out of time, struggling to reconcile the world he had left behind with the new realities of the 1970s. His story raised profound questions about duty, belief, and the lasting impacts of war.
- **Legacy:** Hiroo Onoda's story remains one of the most extraordinary tales of survival and loyalty. His decades-long holdout is a testament to the resilience of the human spirit and the profound effects of war on individual lives. His experience continues to be studied and discussed as a unique case in the annals of military history and psychology.

The tale of Hiroo Onoda is not just one of unwavering commitment and survival; it's also shrouded in controversy and moral complexities. His prolonged guerrilla campaign on Lubang Island had significant and tragic consequences.

- Impact on Local Population: During his 29 years on Lubang Island, Onoda's commitment to his military orders led to violent encounters with local residents. He and his companions were responsible for several shootings, resulting in the deaths and injuries of a number of islanders. These actions, while carried out under the belief that the war was ongoing, had lasting impacts on the local community.

- Refusal to Acknowledge Surrender: Onoda's refusal to surrender despite numerous efforts to convince him the war had ended also stoked controversy. Leaflets were dropped by airplanes declaring the war was over, and even Onoda's own brother visited the island, trying to persuade him to surrender. Onoda dismissed these as enemy tricks or propaganda, showcasing his deep-rooted commitment to his original orders but also raising questions about the extent of his adherence to reality.

- **Reaction in Japan and the Philippines:** Upon his return to Japan, Onoda was celebrated as a national hero by many, embodying the samurai spirit and loyalty. However, others viewed him with mixed feelings, considering the unnecessary violence and suffering caused. In the Philippines, while he was officially pardoned by President Marcos, the memories of his actions left a complex legacy among the locals on Lubang Island.

- **Psychological Interpretations:** Psychologists have found Onoda's story intriguing, often discussing it in terms of the human capacity for belief and survival in extreme conditions. His ability to maintain a wartime mindset for decades, isolated and with minimal resources, speaks to both the resilience and the potential pitfalls of human psychology in war.

Would you, as a reader, find yourself capable of such unwavering loyalty and commitment? Onoda's tale is not just a narrative of personal endurance; it reflects the broader cultural and historical context of Japan during the war era, highlighting the intense dedication and resilience ingrained in its soldiers.

Remember: while **you may never need to know** all the intricate details of Hiroo Onoda's long, solitary war, his story invites us to reflect on the complexities of loyalty, belief, and the human capacity to endure. It's a poignant reminder of the profound effects of war and the lengths to which individuals will go in adherence to their nation and principles.

52. Mary Celeste: Maritime Mystery

- The Mary Celeste remains a captivating maritime mystery, a ghostly vessel adrift with no souls aboard, discovered in the Atlantic near the Azores in December 1872. This brigantine set sail from New York to Genoa under Captain Benjamin Briggs, carrying his family and a crew of seven. When found, the ship was in good condition but hauntingly vacant; the lifeboat was missing, and the ship's log's last entry was made ten days before her discovery.

- The condition of the Mary Celeste only deepened the mystery. The crew's belongings and the cargo of alcohol were largely undisturbed. There were no signs of struggle or violence, suggesting a sudden, perhaps panicked, decision to abandon ship. Theories have ranged wildly from mutiny, piracy, and even supernatural phenomena to a more likely scenario involving an explosion of alcohol fumes causing fear and a hurried evacuation.

- Captain Briggs: A seasoned mariner, Briggs was known for his meticulousness and had a wife and daughter aboard, making theories of his intentional abandonment unlikely.

- The Ship's Origins: Originally named "Amazon," the ship had a troubled past, including a collision and various mishaps, before being renamed the Mary Celeste.

- The Dei Gratia: The ship that discovered the Mary Celeste, the Dei Gratia, found her in a disheveled but navigable state, adding to the enigma.

- The Salvage Hearings: The Dei Gratia's crew claimed salvage rights, leading to hearings that initially suspected foul play but found no evidence of it.

- Arthur Conan Doyle's Influence: Doyle, the creator of Sherlock Holmes, wrote a short story about the incident, fueling public interest and speculation.

- Captain Briggs: A seasoned mariner, Briggs was known for his meticulousness and had a wife and daughter aboard, making theories of his intentional abandonment unlikely.

- The Ship's Origins: Originally named "Amazon," the ship had a troubled past, including a collision and various mishaps, before being renamed the Mary Celeste.

- The Alcohol Cargo: The ship carried 1,701 barrels of denatured alcohol, a fact that has led to theories about fume-induced explosions.

- Insurance Fraud Theories: Some have speculated that the abandonment was part of an insurance fraud scheme, but investigations did not support this theory.

- The "Pirate" Theory: The theory of a pirate attack has been largely dismissed due to the undisturbed cargo and personal belongings.

- Meteorological Phenomena: Some theorists suggest that a waterspout might have scared the crew into abandoning the ship.

- Undersea Earthquakes: The theory of underwater seismic activity releasing gases has been proposed but remains speculative.

- Final Voyage of the Mary Celeste: The ship continued to sail under different ownership until 1885 when it was deliberately wrecked in an insurance fraud.

Modern scientific approaches

Modern scientific approaches to the Mary Celeste mystery have brought forward intriguing hypotheses, particularly focusing on the chemical properties of the ship's cargo, which consisted of a large amount of industrial alcohol.

One prominent theory suggests that a build-up of alcohol fumes might have caused panic among the crew. The cargo, denatured alcohol, could potentially release a significant amount of vapor. If the crew had opened the hold and encountered a rush of fumes, they might have feared an imminent explosion. This could explain their hurried departure from the ship in the lifeboat, intending to return once the fumes had dissipated. However, they might have been unable to relocate the ship after distancing themselves for safety.

Another scientific hypothesis revolves around the phenomenon known as a "seaquake," a type of underwater earthquake that can release gases from the seabed. Such an event might have caused the ship to shudder violently, leading the crew to believe an explosion was imminent. This, coupled with the possibility of alcohol fumes, might have prompted a swift evacuation. Scientists suggest that the crew, in their haste, failed to properly secure the lifeboat to the ship, resulting in their drift away into peril.

In addition to these theories, researchers have also considered the possibility of a freak wave or sudden water spout causing enough alarm to abandon the ship. While these natural phenomena wouldn't directly relate to the cargo's chemical properties, they could have contributed to a perfect storm of circumstances, leading to the crew's decision to leave the ship temporarily.

Despite these scientific endeavors to solve the mystery, the fate of the Mary Celeste's crew remains one of the maritime world's most enduring enigmas. The combination of scientific analysis and historical investigation continues to shed light on this intriguing case, yet the true story may forever lie in the depths of the past.

The tale of the Mary Celeste, drifting silently across the ocean's expanse, serves as a chilling reminder of the sea's mysteries. Remember: while you may never need to know the full truth behind this ghostly vessel's fate, its story sails on in the realm of maritime legend, a spectral narrative of the unfathomable deep.

53. The Lost Treasure of the San Miguel

Embark on a journey into one of history's most tantalizing tales of lost treasure – the story of the Spanish galleon San Miguel.

The San Miguel was part of the Spanish treasure fleet, a convoy of ships transporting vast amounts of precious metals and jewels from the New World to Spain. It's believed that the San Miguel sank in the early 18th century, laden with a fortune in gold, silver, and precious gems.

Part of the Treasure Fleet: The San Miguel was one of many ships tasked with transporting the riches of the Americas back to Spain. These fleets were often targeted by pirates and were vulnerable to the treacherous weather conditions of the Atlantic.
The Sinking: According to historical records, the San Miguel was lost in a severe storm off the coast of Florida. The exact location of the wreck has been a subject of speculation and numerous searches over the centuries.

The allure of its potential wealth, consisting of gold, silver, and precious jewels lost to the depths of the sea, has led to numerous expeditions aimed at uncovering its secrets. Despite significant advancements in underwater technology and extensive historical research, the exact location of the San Miguel's final resting place remains shrouded in mystery. Contemporary explorers, armed with sophisticated sonar equipment, submersibles, and historical maps, have scoured the seabed, particularly around the waters off the Florida coast where the ship is believed to have sunk. Yet, the elusive galleon continues to evade discovery, its treasure a tantalizing enigma that lies somewhere in the vast Atlantic.

The quest for the San Miguel's treasure is not without its complications. Salvage operations have frequently been embroiled in legal and ethical battles. These disputes often arise over ownership rights to any potential finds. The complexity of maritime law, which governs the rights to salvage in international waters, adds layers of legal contention between various parties. On one side are the treasure hunters and salvage companies, investing time and resources in the hope of uncovering the galleon's riches. On the other side are governments, particularly the Spanish government, which often lays claim to such wrecks as part of its national heritage.

Additionally, historical and archaeological societies voice concerns over the preservation of underwater cultural heritage, emphasizing the scientific and historical value of such wrecks over their monetary worth.

These legal and ethical challenges highlight the broader debate surrounding underwater treasure hunting. The hunt for the San Miguel's treasure is a microcosm of this global discussion, balancing the thrill of discovery and potential financial gain against the preservation of historical sites and respect for maritime heritage. The ongoing saga of the San Miguel, from its fateful voyage to its modern pursuit, continues to be an intriguing narrative of history, adventure, and the enduring allure of lost treasure.

The tale of the San Miguel and its lost treasure is a captivating chapter in maritime history, filled with the allure of undiscovered riches and the mysteries of the deep. Remember: whilst **you may never need to know** where the treasure is. The treasure of the San Miguel may never be found, its story continues to enchant and remind us of the ocean's untold secrets and the human quest for discovery and fortune.

54. The Curious Concept of Schrödinger's Cat

Schrödinger's Cat is a thought experiment in quantum mechanics, devised by Austrian physicist Erwin Schrödinger in 1935. This paradoxical experiment illustrates the complexity and counterintuitive nature of quantum mechanics, particularly the idea of superposition, where particles can exist in multiple states simultaneously until observed.

The Thought Experiment:
- **The Setup:** Imagine a cat placed in a sealed box with a radioactive atom, a Geiger counter, a hammer, and a vial of poison. The radioactive atom has an equal probability of decaying or not decaying. If it decays, the Geiger counter triggers the hammer to release the poison, killing the cat.
- **Quantum Superposition:** According to quantum theory, until the box is opened and the cat is observed, the cat is considered to be both alive and dead simultaneously. This state of being in multiple states at once is known as superposition.
- **Interpretation of Quantum Mechanics:** Schrödinger's Cat was not a serious proposal for a real experiment but rather a critique of the Copenhagen interpretation of quantum mechanics, which posits that a quantum system remains in superposition until it's observed, at which point it collapses into one state or another.

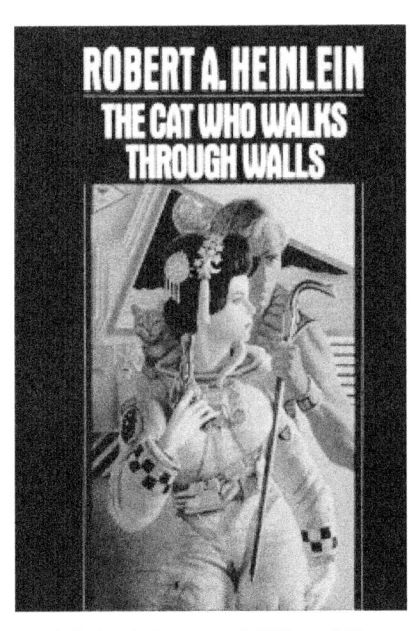

The experiment highlights the role of the observer in quantum mechanics. The act of observation affects the outcome, a concept that has profound philosophical implications regarding the nature of reality.

- **In Literature:** The concept has been explored in literary works such as "The Cat Who Walks Through Walls" by Robert A. Heinlein, where it's used to discuss the nature of reality.
- **Television and Film:** The paradox is often used in science fiction and fantasy genres. For example, in the TV series "The Big Bang Theory," the character Sheldon Cooper frequently uses Schrödinger's Cat to explain scientific and non-scientific concepts alike.

- **Educational Tool:** In education, Schrödinger's Cat is used to introduce students to the complex ideas of quantum mechanics and superposition, often serving as an engaging way to spark interest in physics.

The story of Schrödinger's Cat, far from being a mere theoretical construct, has become a part of our collective imagination, illustrating the often-bewildering world of quantum physics. It challenges our understanding of reality and the role of observation in shaping it. Remember: while **you may never need to know** the intricacies of quantum mechanics or the fate of the hypothetical cat, this thought experiment serves as a captivating gateway into the world of scientific wonder, blurring the lines between the known and the unknown, the seen and the unseen.

55. Munch, The Scream

"The Scream" by Edvard Munch is one of the most iconic and recognizable paintings in the world. Created by the Norwegian artist in 1893, this expressionist masterpiece has captivated and unnerved audiences for over a century.

Munch's Origin and The Scream's Genesis:

Edvard Munch: Born in 1863 in Norway, Munch grew up

- in a household marked by illness and death, which profoundly influenced his artistic themes of anxiety, emotional suffering, and human vulnerability.
- Inspiration for The Scream: The painting was inspired by a personal experience of Munch, where he felt an overwhelming sense of despair and anxiety, symbolized by the anguished figure

against a blood-red sky. Munch created several versions of "The Scream" in various media, including painting and lithography.

Why "The Scream" Resonates:

- Universal Themes: "The Scream" encapsulates universal themes of existential angst and the human condition, making it a timeless piece that resonates with diverse audiences.
- Visual Impact: Its stark, swirling colors and the haunting figure capture a moment of intense emotional experience, drawing viewers into its expression of inner turmoil.

Visiting "The Scream" and the Munch-Goya Connection:

- **Oslo, Norway:** "The Scream" is housed in the Munch Museum in Oslo, which holds the largest collection of Munch's works.

Munch and Goya: A visit to the museum offers a unique opportunity to explore the parallels between Munch and Francisco Goya, another master of expressing human angst and darkness. The museum often features exhibitions that draw connections between the two artists, showcasing how they both delved into the depths of human psyche and emotion.

- Munch was a pioneer in the Expressionist movement, influencing the development of German Expressionism in the early 20th century.
- Extensive Work: Munch was incredibly prolific, creating over 1,800 paintings, 4,000 drawings, and 15,000 prints in his lifetime.

- Artistic Evolution: His style evolved over the years, moving from naturalistic themes to more symbolic and expressive approaches.
- Munch's influence extends beyond painting, impacting photography, film, and modern art in general.

Illness and Mental Health Struggles

- **Early Life and Family Tragedy:** Munch's exposure to illness and death started early in his life. His mother died of tuberculosis when he was just five years old, and he later lost his favorite sister, Johanne Sophie, to the same disease. These early experiences with loss and grief had a profound impact on his psyche and his artistic themes.
- **Personal Health:** Munch himself was often ill during his childhood, a factor that contributed to his introspective and melancholic nature. He is known to have said, "Sickness, insanity and death were the angels that surrounded my cradle and they have followed me throughout my life."
- **Mental Health Struggles:** Munch's mental health was a constant struggle. He experienced bouts of depression and anxiety, which were exacerbated by his excessive drinking and a tumultuous romantic life. His famous series "The Frieze of Life" paintings, including "The Scream," delves into themes of love, fear, death, and melancholia, mirroring his inner turmoil.
- **Breakdown and Recovery:** In 1908, Munch's anxiety became overwhelming, leading to a nervous breakdown. He voluntarily entered a clinic in Copenhagen where he received therapy. This period marked a turning point in his life and art; post-treatment, his work became more optimistic and colorful, reflecting his improved mental state.
- **Art as Therapy:** Munch often used art as a means to cope with his mental anguish. He believed that his psychological state was integral to his work, saying, "My fear of life is necessary to me, as is my illness. Without anxiety and illness, I am a ship without a rudder... they are part of me and my art. They are indistinguishable from me, and their destruction would destroy

Remember: while you may never need to know the intricate details of Munch's brush strokes or the specific shades of color in "The Scream," understanding this masterpiece and its creator offers a profound glimpse into the human soul, transcending time and place. Visiting the Munch Museum, especially the exhibitions that intertwine Munch and Goya, is not just a journey through art history but an exploration of the depths and complexities of human emotion.

56. The Simpsons Predicts the Future

The Simpsons, the long-running animated sitcom created by Matt Groening, has gained a reputation for its uncanny ability to predict future events. Over its decades on air, the show has featured scenarios that eerily foresaw real-world developments, leading many fans to view "The Simpsons" as almost prophetic. Here are some notable examples:

- **President Donald Trump:** In a 2000 episode titled "Bart to the Future," the show depicted Donald Trump as a future U.S. President. This became reality in 2016, leaving audiences astounded by the show's prescience.

- **Smart Watches:** In a 1995 episode, "Lisa's Wedding," Lisa's fiancé is seen speaking to a phone on his wrist. The concept, which seemed futuristic at the time, is now a reality with the advent of smartwatches.
- **Disney Acquires 20th Century Fox:** In the 1998 episode "When You Dish Upon a Star," a sign outside the 20th Century Fox studio shows it as a "Division of Walt Disney Co." This prediction came true in 2019 when Disney acquired 21st Century Fox.
- **The Higgs Boson Equation:** In a 1998 episode, "The Wizard of Evergreen Terrace," Homer Simpson is seen standing in front of a blackboard with an equation that, in real life, would predict the mass of the Higgs Boson particle. This was more than a decade before physicists discovered the particle at the Large Hadron Collider.
- **FIFA Corruption Scandal:** In a 2014 episode titled "You Don't Have to Live Like a Referee," the show depicted a FIFA official being arrested for corruption. The following year, several FIFA officials were arrested on charges of corruption.
- **Greece's Economic Collapse:** In a 2012 episode, a news ticker reads "Europe puts Greece on eBay," a humorous nod that eerily foreshadowed Greece's economic crisis.

- **Ebola Outbreak:** In a 1997 episode, "Lisa's Sax," Marge offers a sick Bart a book titled "Curious George and the Ebola Virus." This was years before the Ebola virus became widely known for its outbreak in West Africa in 2014.
- **Lady Gaga's Super Bowl Performance:** In 2012, an episode titled "Lisa Goes Gaga" featured pop star Lady Gaga performing in a wire harness, flying over the audience — a spectacle that closely resembled her actual performance at the Super Bowl halftime show in 2017.

The phenomenon of "The Simpsons" predicting future events has sparked a great deal of debate and curiosity. Several factors contribute to this discussion, weighing whether these instances are mere coincidences, a reflection of the show's insightful writing, or something more.

- **Coincidence vs. Deliberate Prediction:** A major point of debate is whether these 'predictions' are just coincidences due to the show's long run. With over 30 years on air and a vast number of episodes, some argue that it's statistically probable for some scenarios to align with future events. Others, however, feel that the precision and specificity of some predictions go beyond mere coincidence.
- **Cultural and Social Commentary:** "The Simpsons" is renowned for its satirical take on society and culture. The show's writers are often lauded for their ability to tap into societal trends and extrapolate them into humorous scenarios. This foresight might not be prophecy but a keen observation of societal patterns and trajectories.

- **Self-Fulfilling Prophecy:** Some instances might be cases of life imitating art. The show's immense popularity and cultural impact could lead to real-world actions being influenced or inspired by its content. For example, Lady Gaga's Super Bowl performance might have been influenced by her portrayal in the show.
- **The Show's Broad Scope:** "The Simpsons" covers a wide range of topics and scenarios in its episodes. This broad scope increases the likelihood of some plots coinciding with future events. From politics to technology, the show has touched on nearly every aspect of modern life.
- **Selective Interpretation:** There is also the argument of confirmation bias, where people are more likely to notice and remember the predictions that come true, while ignoring the vast majority of content that does not correlate with future events.
- **The Writers' Perspectives:** Interviews with the show's writers and creators often downplay the idea of intentional predictions. They usually attribute these occurrences to the show's nature of exploring various "what if" scenarios and the law of large numbers.

In conclusion, while the debate continues, it's clear that "The Simpsons" has an uncanny knack for creating content that, intentionally or not, resonates with future realities. Whether these predictions are chalked up to coincidence, the show's perceptive writing, or its wide-ranging narrative scope, they certainly contribute to the show's enduring appeal and mystique. Remember: while **you may never need to know** whether "The Simpsons" can genuinely predict the future, the discussion it sparks is a testament to the show's enduring impact on popular culture.

57 - Crazy Laws of the Middle East

From sandcastle regulations to goldfish rights, the Middle East offers a fascinating glimpse into a diverse legal landscape, where ancient traditions mingle with modern realities. So, ditch the guidebooks and prepare for a hilarious (and surprisingly informative) journey through laws that will make you scratch your head and chuckle in equal measure.

Privacy Palaces and Public Polishing: In the United Arab Emirates, your car is your kingdom, but keep it spick and span! A dusty chariot earns frowns and fines, while the thought of using a VPN for a sneaky peek at Netflix? Forget it! Privacy comes at a hefty price tag, literally. But fear not, fellow adventurers, for Dubai offers its own brand of thrills. Just keep your shimmying and salsa steps confined to your living room during Ramadan, because public dancing, even in the privacy of your own four walls, can land you in hot water.

Melodies and Misdemeanors: Music lovers, take note! Iran frowns upon public displays of Western tunes, so keep your head-banging for heavy metal confined to your headphones. In Saudi Arabia, Valentine's Day is celebrated with a subtle whisper, not a booming proclamation. Ditch the red roses and heart-shaped balloons, because even a splash of scarlet in your shop window could earn you a stern reprimand.

Snacking and Snapping: Got a rumble in your tummy on the Qatari bus? Quell it with a silent prayer, because public munching is a major faux pas. In Kuwait, watch your vocabulary, even in the digital realm. A keyboard-fueled tirade on WhatsApp could lead to real-world consequences. And in Bahrain, remember, a picture is not always worth a thousand words. Respecting privacy is paramount, so capture the scenery, not the faces.

- **United Arab Emirates:** Planning to use a VPN in the UAE? Better think twice! It's not just about bypassing geo-blocks for your favorite show; you could be fined up to 2 million dirhams. That's a lot of money for a bit of extra browsing privacy! And about your car – keep it clean. A dusty car isn't just an eyesore; it's a ticket to finesville. Sandstorm or not, a dirty car is a no-go.

- **Dubai:** Curiosity killed the cat, and in Dubai, snooping on someone's phone could kill your bank account. If you're caught peeking at someone else's phone without permission, you could face a hefty fine or a six-month vacation behind bars. Also, during Ramadan, keep the volume down. Dancing in your living room? Only if you can do it silently!

- **Iran:** Feel like grooving to some Western tunes in Iran? You might want to stick to head-bopping in private. Public dancing, especially to Western music, could land you in more trouble than a bad dance move.

- **Saudi Arabia:** In Saudi Arabia, Valentine's Day is less about hearts and flowers and more about keeping it low-key. Selling anything red or heart-shaped can be a heartbreaker for shop owners, as it goes against cultural norms. So, if you're feeling romantic, maybe stick to chocolates and a nice dinner inside.

- **Kuwait:** In Kuwait, beware of bad language. Swearing on WhatsApp or other social media platforms isn't just rude, it's illegal. A digital slip of the tongue could land you in legal hot water.

- **Qatar:** Fancy a quick snack on public transport in Qatar? Better hold that thought. Eating or drinking on buses, trains, and metros is a strict no-no. Getting caught mid-bite or sip might cost you more than the price of your snack.

- **Bahrain:** In Bahrain, the personal is private, especially when it comes to photographs. Taking pictures of people without their explicit consent is not just a breach of social etiquette but a legal offense that can lead to serious consequences.

- **Oman:** In Oman, keep an eye on your car's cleanliness. Much like in the UAE, a car that's not kept clean is not just seen as untidy but as a public nuisance, and could see you fined.

- **Lebanon:** Love your pet fish in Lebanon? Make sure it's not a goldfish in a bowl. Oddly enough, keeping a goldfish in a bowl is considered animal cruelty due to the lack of space and stimulation.

- **Jordan:** Thinking of borrowing a library book in Jordan? Just make sure to return it on time. Not returning library books is taken seriously and could see you facing more than just a late fee.

- **Israel:** In Israel, picking up or collecting certain types of sea shells is prohibited, as they're considered a natural resource. So, beachcombers, look but don't take!

- **Turkey:** Feeling fancy? Save the feather boas for another occasion. In Turkey, wearing overly flamboyant clothing in religious sites is considered disrespectful. Pack your travel wardrobe with tasteful attire instead.

- **Egypt:** Craving a refreshing dip in the Red Sea? Remember, public nudity is strictly forbidden, even on secluded beaches. Opt for a swimsuit that keeps things covered for a swim without the worry.

- **Morocco:** Calling all photographers! While capturing the beauty of Morocco is encouraged, snapping pictures of locals without their permission can land you in hot water. Respect their privacy and ask for consent before clicking that shutter.

- **Abu Dhabi:** Got a sweet tooth? Think twice before chewing gum in Abu Dhabi. Importing, selling, or chewing gum is illegal for hygiene and environmental reasons. Stick to mints or candies instead.

- **Jordan:** Planning a road trip? Buckle up and keep your hands on the wheel. Eating or drinking while driving is a no-go in Jordan, and police take road safety seriously. Focus on the road and enjoy the scenery later.

- **Israel:** Feeling spontaneous? Resist the urge to climb ancient ruins. Touching and climbing historical structures in Israel is prohibited to prevent damage to these irreplaceable treasures. Appreciate them from afar.

- **Oman:** Feeling adventurous? Think twice before venturing into the desert alone. Hiring a licensed guide is mandatory for desert excursions in Oman, ensuring your safety and respecting the delicate ecosystem.

- **Qatar:** Love animals? Leave wild creatures alone. Feeding or approaching wild animals in Qatar, even with good intentions, can disrupt their natural behavior and potentially pose a danger. Observe them from a safe distance.

- **Saudi Arabia:** Planning a pilgrimage to Mecca? Remember, public displays of affection, even between spouses, are not permitted in holy sites. Respecting local customs and religious sensitivities is paramount.

- **Iran:** Feeling artistic? Public graffiti is a no-no in Iran. Expressing yourself creatively is encouraged, but stick to designated spaces and avoid defacing public property.

- **United Arab Emirates:** Don't let the glitz and glamour fool you. Public drunkenness is illegal in the UAE, and consequences can be severe. Celebrate responsibly and avoid any risky behavior.

- **Bahrain:** Feeling the need for speed? Keep your racing ambitions off the public roads. Street racing is strictly prohibited in Bahrain, and hefty fines await those who break the law.

- **Kuwait:** Need a power nap during your workday? Don't sleep on the job! Taking a nap at your workplace is frowned upon in Kuwait, so consider alternative ways to recharge during your lunch break.

58 - The Riddle of the Sphinx

The Riddle of the Sphinx is a classic element of Greek mythology, rich with symbolism and intrigue. It's best known through the story of Oedipus, the tragic hero of Theban legend who encounters the Sphinx on his journey.

In Greek mythology, the Sphinx was a creature with the head of a woman, the body of a lion, and the wings of a bird. She was sent by the gods to the city of Thebes as a punishment and posed a riddle to travelers to prevent them from entering the city.

The most famous riddle asked by the Sphinx was, "What walks on four feet in the morning, two in the afternoon, and three in the evening?" Those who failed to answer correctly were killed and eaten by the Sphinx.

Oedipus, the prince of Thebes, encountered the Sphinx and successfully answered the riddle: "Man — as an infant, he crawls on all fours; as an adult, he walks on two legs; and in old age, he uses a 'third leg' or a walking stick."

Upon hearing the correct answer, the Sphinx, defeated, either threw herself off a cliff or devoured herself, thus ending her reign of terror over Thebes.

Representation of Life Stages :

A Metaphor for Human Existence: The Sphinx's riddle is a profound metaphor for the human lifecycle. The answer, "Man," and its explanation − crawling as a baby, walking on two feet as an adult, and using a walking stick in old age − encapsulate the journey of human life from birth to death.

- Allegory of the Human Condition: This riddle serves as an allegory of the human condition, highlighting the inevitable transformations we undergo through different stages of life. It illustrates the physical changes humans experience and symbolizes the psychological and emotional growth accompanying each stage.

- Mortality and Wisdom: The riddle also reflects on the inevitability of aging and mortality. The Sphinx, by posing this riddle, forces those who encounter her to confront the reality of their human existence − a journey from helplessness to strength and back to dependency.

Psychological and Philosophical Meanings:

- **Symbol of the Human Psyche:** In psychological terms, the Sphinx is often viewed as a symbol of the mysteries and complexities of the human mind. Her enigmatic nature represents the unconscious, the realm of hidden knowledge, fears, and desires that lie beneath the surface of human awareness.
- **The Enigma of Existence:** Philosophically, the Sphinx stands as a representation of life's enigmas and the human quest for understanding and meaning. The challenge of her riddle goes beyond a mere intellectual puzzle; it's a contemplation of life's profound mysteries – our origin, purpose, and destiny.
- **The Quest for Knowledge:** The Sphinx's riddle, in its essence, is a quest for knowledge and understanding. It challenges individuals to look beyond the obvious, to delve into deeper insights about life and existence. This pursuit of knowledge is a fundamental aspect of the human experience, echoed in various philosophical traditions.

The Riddle of the Sphinx, with its deep symbolic roots and philosophical implications, remains one of the most intriguing and enduring elements of ancient mythology. Remember: while **you may never need to know** the answer to the Sphinx's riddle, its significance extends beyond a mere puzzle, representing the profound mysteries and stages of human life.

59. Reel vs Real: The Truth Behind Gangster Movies

Gangster movies have captivated audiences for decades, offering a gritty, often romanticized glimpse into the world of organized crime. But how accurate are these cinematic portrayals? Let's dive into some of the most famous gangster films and assess their fidelity to real mob life.

- **"The Godfather" (1972)**
  - Accuracy Rating: "Sleeps with the Fishes"
  - Based On: Fictional Corleone family, inspired by various real Mafia families.
  - Reality Check: While Vito Corleone's world is more opera than documentary, the portrayal of Mafia codes, family dynamics, and vendettas hits close to home. The film captures the essence, if not the day-to-day truth, of mob life. Just don't expect every Don to have Marlon Brando's charisma.
- **"Goodfellas" (1990)**
  - Accuracy Rating: "As Real As It Gets"
  - Based On: The life of Henry Hill and the Lucchese crime family.
  - Reality Check: Scorsese nails it with a gritty, unglamorous look into the life and times of Henry Hill. From heists to spaghetti sauce, "Goodfellas" paints a vivid picture of 1960s and '70s mobster life. Extra points for Joe Pesci making us laugh and then immediately terrifying us.
- **"Scarface" (1983)**
  - Accuracy Rating: "Say Hello to My Little Friend (Fiction)"
  - Based On: The rise and fall of a fictional drug lord, Tony Montana.
  - Reality Check: If you're looking for a documentary on drug trafficking, keep looking. "Scarface" is more about mountains of a certain white powder and less about the nuanced truth of organized crime. Plus, Al Pacino's Cuban accent? Fuhgeddaboudit!
- **"The Departed" (2006)**
  - Accuracy Rating: "Departed from Reality"
  - Based On: Fictionalized version of the Boston mob scene, inspired by the Winter Hill Gang.
  - Reality Check: Between Jack Nicholson's over-the-top mob boss and DiCaprio's undercover jitters, "The Departed" is a fun ride but takes more liberties than a mob accountant. It's a bit like expecting a history lesson from a barroom storyteller – entertaining but embellished.

- **"American Gangster" (2007)**
  - Accuracy Rating: "Frankly, Quite Accurate"
  - Based On: The life of Frank Lucas, a Harlem drug kingpin.
  - Reality Check: Denzel Washington's portrayal of Frank Lucas walking the tightrope between family man and heroin distributor is spot on. The movie sticks close to Lucas's narrative, though it might have added a little extra Hollywood shine for good measure.
- **"Casino" (1995)**
  - Accuracy Rating: "Jackpot for Realism"
  - Based On: The lives of Frank "Lefty" Rosenthal and Anthony Spilotro and their operation of the Stardust Casino in Las Vegas.
  - Reality Check: Scorsese hits the casino jackpot again with a film that's almost a documentary on the mob's Vegas operations. Robert De Niro's and Joe Pesci's portrayals of the casino kingpin and his enforcer buddy are spot-on, mirroring the glitz, glamor, and eventual downfall of the mob's hold on Sin City. Just remember, the house always wins, unless the FBI is playing.
- **"Donnie Brasco" (1997)**
  - Accuracy Rating: "Undercover Authenticity"
  - Based On: The true story of Joseph D. Pistone, an FBI agent who infiltrated the Bonanno crime family.
  - Reality Check: This film delves into the dangerous life of an undercover agent within the Mafia. Johnny Depp's portrayal of Brasco/Pistone's dual life brings out the emotional and moral complexities of deep undercover work. The film nails the tension and peril of infiltrating the mob, but maybe they glamorized the hair styles a bit too much.
- **"A Bronx Tale" (1993)**
  - Accuracy Rating: "Neighborhood Watch"
  - Based On: A semi-autobiographical story by Chazz Palminteri.
  - Reality Check: Less about the mob and more about life around it, "A Bronx Tale" captures the essence of growing up in a mob-influenced neighborhood.

These films, each in their own right, offer a window into different facets of mob life, from the glitzy casinos to the gritty streets. They blend reality with cinematic flair, giving us a taste of the mob life, sans the risk of wearing cement shoes. Remember: while **you may never need to know** the ins and outs of Mafia operations, these movies provide a front-row seat to the action, no FBI surveillance required.

60. Tom and Jerry: The Psychological Perspective

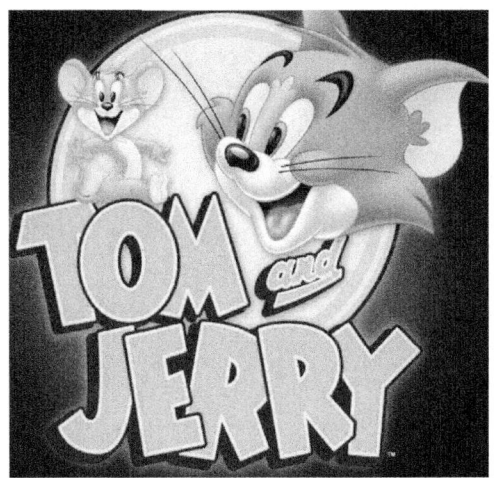

Meet Tom and Jerry, the iconic cat and mouse duo, who are more than just slapstick heroes – they're walking, well, running and chasing, personality tests! Let's delve into their antics to uncover some 'pawsitively' intriguing insights about human personalities.

Tom's 'Tail' of Traits – The Dark Triad with Whiskers:

- Narcissistic Needy Cat: Tom, with his endless plots to catch Jerry and be the hero, could give any narcissist a run for their money. He's got that 'look at me, I'm the cat's whiskers' vibe, often ending up with a face full of frying pan.
- Machiavellian Mastermind...or Not: He's got plans and traps that Machiavelli would be proud of, except they backfire. Every. Single. Time. It's like watching a mastermind with butter paws.
- Psychopathy, but Make It Cartoon: Chasing a mouse with a mallet? Classic cartoon psychopathy. But hey, no animals were harmed in the making of this show!

Jerry's Gentlemanly Gestures – The Light Triad in Tiny Form:

- Faith in Mouse-manity: Jerry might be small, but his heart is huge. He sees the good in everyone, even in a cat who's after his tail.
- Humanism in a Mouse: Kind, respectful, and always up for helping a fellow rodent in distress. Jerry is the tiny hero with a big heart.
- Kantianism with Cheese: He's honest, ethical, and won't use others for cheese gains... unless it's really good cheese.

Self-Reflection, Cartoon Style:

- Are You Team Tom or Team Jerry?: Do you plot like Tom but end up befriending everyone like Jerry? Or are you the master of your own cheese, living life one clever escape at a time?
- Growing Up Cartoon: Just like Tom and Jerry, we evolve. Maybe you started as a prankster Tom and grew into a wise Jerry. Or vice versa, because who doesn't love a good plot twist?

So, there you have it – a cartoon guide to understanding personalities. Next time you're feeling philosophical, ask yourself: Are you the cat chasing ambitious dreams (and occasionally your own tail), or the mouse outsmarting life's challenges with a smile and a cheeky cheese snack?

Remember: while **you may never need to know** if you're more Tom or Jerry in real life, it's a fun way to look at our personalities. Plus, it's a great excuse to rewatch some classic cartoons, all in the name of 'research,' of course!

61. The Legend of El Dorado

The legend of El Dorado, a land brimming with gold and jewels, has captured imaginations for centuries. Initially, El Dorado was not a place but a person – a mythical tribal chief covered in gold dust. The term "El Dorado" means "The Golden One" in Spanish.

According to the legend, this chief would cover himself in gold dust during a sacred ritual and then dive into Lake Guatavita, in present-day Colombia, washing off the gold. This ritual, witnessed by Spanish explorers, gave birth to tales of a land of unimaginable riches.

The Hunt for El Dorado:

A Magnet for Conquistadors: The legend fueled the greed of Spanish conquistadors and European adventurers who ventured into the South American jungles in search of this opulent kingdom.

A Wild Gold Chase: Expeditions and searches for El Dorado often ended in vain, with many explorers losing their lives or minds in the relentless pursuit. The dense jungles, harsh conditions, and the allure of gold created a perfect recipe for obsession and disaster.

Literature – "El Dorado" by Voltaire (1761):
- Voltaire's satirical novella "Candide" features the legendary city of El Dorado. In this story, El Dorado represents an ideal society, a utopia untouched by European greed and corruption, offering a critical reflection on contemporary European societies.

- **Film – "The Road to El Dorado" (2000):**
    - This animated musical adventure film by DreamWorks Animation reimagines the quest for El Dorado. The story follows two con artists who accidentally discover the mythical city of gold. The film portrays the city as a thriving, advanced civilization, highlighting aspects of indigenous culture and architecture.
- **Video Games – "Uncharted: Drake's Fortune" (2007):**
    - In this popular action-adventure video game, the protagonist, Nathan Drake, searches for the lost treasure of El Dorado. The game blends historical and mythical elements, allowing players to explore interpretations of ancient South American cultures and the enduring allure of the legend.
- **Art – Depictions in Maps and Historical Artworks:**
    - The legend of El Dorado inspired numerous historical maps and artistic representations, often depicting the golden king or the city itself. These works reflect the European fascination with the myth and the exoticization of the New World.
- **Historical Research – Anthropological Studies:**
    - The myth of El Dorado has prompted extensive historical and anthropological research into the indigenous cultures of South America, particularly those around Colombia's Lake Guatavita. Studies focus on understanding the ritualistic and societal significance of gold in these cultures, providing a deeper insight into their belief systems and ways of life.

Reality Check – Spoiler Alert!

No Gold, But Rich in Culture: Despite the exhaustive searches, the legendary city of gold was never found. What was discovered, however, were rich and diverse indigenous cultures and civilizations with their own real treasures - not in gold, but in heritage and history.

So, while **you may never need to know** the exact location of El Dorado (because, spoiler alert, it doesn't exist), the legend itself is a golden tale of human ambition, imagination, and the timeless allure of a good old-fashioned treasure hunt. It reminds us that sometimes, the real treasure isn't gold, but the stories and cultures we uncover along the way.

62. The Mystery of the Loch Ness Monster

The Loch Ness Monster, or "Nessie," is a creature said to inhabit Loch Ness, a deep freshwater loch in the Scottish Highlands. The legend dates back to the 6th century, with the first reported sighting by St. Columba, but it gained widespread attention in the 20th century.

The most famous evidence of Nessie's existence came from a 1934 photograph, known as the "Surgeon's Photograph," which purportedly showed the monster's head and neck. Despite later being exposed as a hoax, it cemented Nessie's image in public consciousness.

Over the years, numerous scientific expeditions have attempted to uncover the truth behind the Loch Ness Monster. These have included sonar searches and DNA sampling of the loch's waters to identify unusual species.

Explanations for Nessie sightings range from misidentified animals (like giant eels or sturgeons) and floating logs to seismic activity causing ripples and waves on the loch's surface.

Many skeptics believe that the Loch Ness Monster is a mix of hoaxes, wishful thinking, and misinterpretations of natural phenomena. espite the lack of concrete evidence, the legend persists, with enthusiasts and cryptozoologists continuing to search for proof of Nessie's existence.

Tourism in the Scottish Highlands

In the heart of the Scottish Highlands, Loch Ness is not just a body of water; it's a beacon for mystery enthusiasts and curious travelers from around the world. The allure of possibly spotting the elusive Nessie has turned this serene loch into a bustling tourist hotspot. But there's more to this legendary location than just monster hunting.

Let's face it, the chance to potentially snap a selfie with a legendary monster is too tempting to pass up. Visitors come with binoculars in hand and hopes high, ready to catch a glimpse of something extraordinary. It's like a wildlife safari, but instead of lions or elephants, you're on the lookout for a prehistoric sea creature. It's the ultimate 'Ness-sessary' adventure.

But Loch Ness isn't just about Nessie. It's a gateway to the enchanting Scottish Highlands, with its rugged landscapes, historic castles, and tranquil beauty. After a day of monster spotting, tourists often find themselves exploring the nearby Urquhart Castle ruins or taking scenic drives through the glens. It's a place where nature and legend intertwine, offering visitors a chance to step into a storybook setting.

The Loch Ness Monster remains one of the world's most enduring mysteries. It embodies our fascination with the unknown and the allure of ancient legends. Whether Nessie is real or not, the tale captures our imagination, reminding us of the mysteries that still lie hidden in the depths of our planet's lakes and oceans. Remember: while **you may never need to know** if Nessie truly lurks in the depths of Loch Ness, the legend itself continues to ripple through our collective fascination with the mysterious and the unexplained.

63. The Curse of Tutankhamun's Tomb

In 1922, archaeologist Howard Carter made a groundbreaking discovery in Egypt's Valley of the Kings – the nearly intact tomb of Tutankhamun, a pharaoh of the 18th dynasty. This discovery was a significant archaeological achievement, shedding light on ancient Egyptian culture and burial practices.

The curse supposedly associated with Tutankhamun's tomb emerged in the wake of the discovery. Media sensationalized the deaths of several people connected to the tomb's opening, attributing them to a curse inscribed on the pharaoh's sarcophagus. However, no such inscription has ever been found.

The most famous death linked to the curse is that of Lord Carnarvon, the financial backer of the excavation. He died in Cairo shortly after the tomb's opening, leading to widespread speculation about the curse's authenticity.

Several other individuals associated with the tomb died in the years following its opening. While many of these deaths can be attributed to natural causes, the timing and nature of these fatalities fueled rumors of a supernatural curse.

The curse is largely considered a media creation. The fascination with ancient Egypt and the mysterious allure of curses made for compelling stories that captivated the public's imagination during the 1920s.

The curse of Tutankhamun's tomb has indeed inspired a variety of creative works, each exploring the conspiracy in unique ways. Here are three notable examples:

"The Mummy" (1999) - Film

This blockbuster film, directed by Stephen Sommers, is a loose adaptation that blends the curse of Tutankhamun with other Egyptian myths. It presents the curse as an ancient, powerful force unleashed when the tomb is disturbed. The movie uses the curse as a central plot device, bringing to life a vengeful mummy with supernatural powers.

While the film takes significant creative liberties with historical accuracy, it played a crucial role in reigniting popular interest in ancient Egyptian mythology and the concept of archaeological curses.

"Tutankhamun: The Truth Uncovered" (2014) - Documentary

This BBC documentary takes a more scientific approach to the story of Tutankhamun, including the alleged curse. It delves into the details of the pharaoh's life and death, using modern forensic techniques to explore the facts behind the tomb's discovery.

Modern analysis suggests that the deaths were coincidental. Studies have shown that the majority of people who entered the tomb lived long and healthy lives. Some theories propose that ancient molds or bacteria in the tomb might have caused illnesses, but these have not been conclusively proven.

By focusing on scientific evidence and expert analysis, the documentary demystifies many aspects of the curse, presenting it more as a media sensation than a factual occurrence.

In conclusion, while the curse of Tutankhamun's tomb makes for a gripping tale, its roots lie more in sensational journalism and human fascination with the mysterious than in ancient Egyptian reality. Remember: while **you may never need to know** if a pharaoh's curse could strike you down, the tale of Tutankhamun and his tomb continues to captivate and educate, showing us the timeless allure of ancient mysteries.

64. The Mysterious Disappearance of the Roanoke Colony

In the late 1500s, the age of exploration was in full swing, with European powers vying to colonize the New World. England, under Queen Elizabeth I, was eager to establish its own permanent settlement in North America, both for economic gain and as a base to harass Spanish fleets.

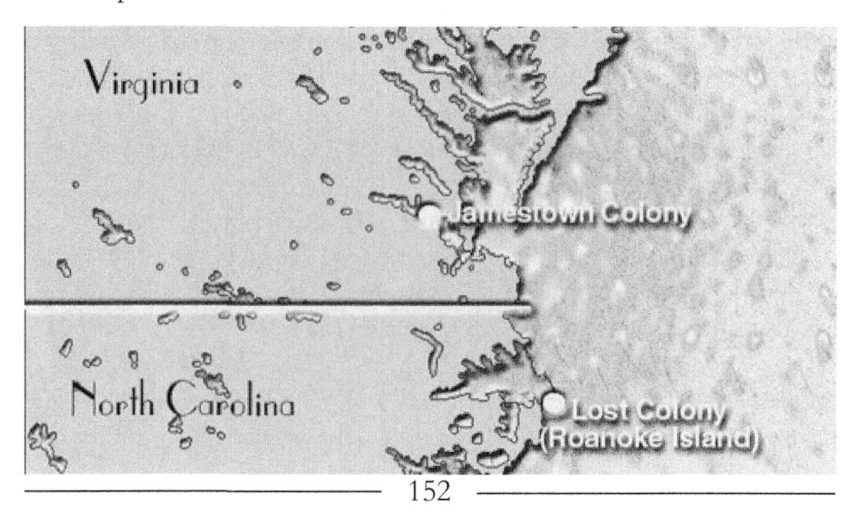

Roanoke Island, located off the coast of present-day North Carolina, was chosen as the site for this new English colony. It was considered strategic for its location and resources.

The First Attempt at Settlement

- Initial Expedition (1584): The first English reconnaissance expedition arrived at Roanoke in 1584, led by explorers Philip Amadas and Arthur Barlowe. They established friendly relations with the local Native American tribes, the Secotans and the Croatoans.
- Sir Walter Raleigh's Charter: Sir Walter Raleigh, granted a charter by Queen Elizabeth, orchestrated the expedition to establish the colony. Though he never visited Roanoke himself, he was instrumental in organizing and funding the endeavor.

The Lost Colony of Roanoke:

- Second Expedition (1585-1586): The first colony was established in 1585 under the leadership of Sir Richard Grenville. Due to food shortages, difficulties with local tribes, and other hardships, the colonists abandoned Roanoke, returning to England with Sir Francis Drake in 1586.
- The Final Group (1587): A third group, led by John White, arrived in 1587. This group included men, women, and children, intended to establish a permanent settlement. John White, appointed as the governor, left for England later that year to gather more supplies.

The Mystery Unfolds....

John White's Delayed Return:
- <u>A Delayed Rescue Mission:</u> John White's return to Roanoke was significantly delayed by an overarching conflict: the Anglo-Spanish War. England and Spain were embroiled in a series of naval battles for supremacy on the seas, a conflict that had escalated by the late 1580s. White found himself trapped in England, unable to secure a ship for his return journey due to the war's demands on English naval resources. His attempts to return were further hampered by the priority given to military needs over colonial resupply missions.
- <u>Personal Anguish:</u> For John White, this delay was not just a logistical frustration; it was a personal anguish. His family, including his daughter Eleanor and his granddaughter Virginia Dare, the first English child born in the Americas, were among the colonists he had left behind. The three-year delay was agonizing for White, who was desperate to reunite with his family and ensure the colony's survival.

The Deserted Colony:
- <u>A Haunting Discovery:</u> When White finally returned to Roanoke on August 18, 1590, he encountered a haunting scene. The colony he had left bustling with life was now eerily deserted. There were no signs of a struggle or battle; the houses had been dismantled, suggesting an organized departure rather than a hasty escape. The only clue to the colonists' fate was the word "CROATOAN" carved into a fence post and the letters "CRO" on a tree. These enigmatic clues suggested a possible move to Croatoan Island, known today as Hatteras Island, where the Croatoan people, a friendly Native American tribe, resided.
- <u>A Mystery Left Unsolved:</u> White attempted to search for the colonists on Croatoan Island but was prevented by a series of misfortunes, including bad weather and lost anchors. His search was ultimately abandoned, and he returned to England without discovering the fate of his family or the other settlers. This abandonment left the mystery of Roanoke unsolved, with the lost colonists' fate becoming the subject of speculation and folklore.

Theories
- Assimilation with Native Tribes: One of the prevailing theories is that the Roanoke colonists assimilated with local Native American tribes. This theory is supported by reports from subsequent explorers and settlers of encountering Native Americans with European features and artifacts in the years following the colony's disappearance.
- Move to a New Location: Another theory suggests that the colonists, facing harsh conditions and possible shortages, moved inland or to another location along the coast, such as Chesapeake Bay, in search of better resources and living conditions.
- Starvation or Disease: The colonists might have suffered from starvation, disease, or environmental hardships. The lack of food and proper shelter could have led to their demise, especially if they were unable to establish friendly relations with local tribes for support and sustenance.
- Destruction by Hostile Forces: There is also the possibility that the colonists fell victim to hostilities, either from rival Native American tribes or from other unforeseen dangers. However, the absence of any evidence of violence at the abandoned site makes this theory less likely.

The disappearance of the Roanoke colony remains an enduring mystery, a historical puzzle that continues to intrigue scholars and the public alike.

Remember: while you may never need to know what truly happened to the Roanoke settlers, their story is a captivating chapter in the early history of American colonization, a reminder of the perils faced by those who ventured into unchartered territories.

65. The Legend of the Jersey Devil

The legend of the Jersey Devil is rooted in the Pine Barrens, a vast and dense forest in Southern New Jersey. The area's isolation and its eerie landscape have fueled many folktales, but none as famous as that of the Jersey Devil.

The story dates back to the 18th century and centers around the Leeds family. As folklore goes, Mother Leeds, burdened with twelve children, cursed her thirteenth child while it was still in the womb, declaring it to be the Devil.

According to legend, the child was born as a normal baby but then transformed into a creature with hooves, a goat's head, bat wings, and a forked tail. It let out a blood-curdling scream before flying up the chimney and disappearing into the Pine Barrens.

Trivia Tidbits

- Early References: The earliest references to the Leeds Devil, or the Jersey Devil, are found in 18th-century Quaker writings, which mention the Leeds family and their supposed demonic offspring.
- Leeds Family Crest: Some believe the legend is linked to the Leeds family crest, which features dragons, and was interpreted as a sign of allegiance to the occult.
- The Name 'Jersey Devil': The name "Jersey Devil" wasn't widely used until the 20th century. Before that, it was commonly known as the Leeds Devil.
- The 1909 Panic: A major event in the Jersey Devil lore occurred in January 1909 when a series of strange footprints appeared across South Jersey, causing widespread panic and reported sightings.

- Newspaper Sensation: The 1909 sightings were sensationalized by newspapers, leading to schools and businesses being temporarily shut down.
- Publicity Stunts: Over the years, various hoaxes and publicity stunts have been carried out, claiming to have captured or sighted the Jersey Devil.
- Cultural Impact: The legend has inspired numerous books, movies, TV shows, and even a professional sports team name – the New Jersey Devils.
- Scientific Explanations: Explanations for sightings range from misidentified wildlife (like sandhill cranes) to mass hysteria and folklore perpetuation.
- Tourist Attraction: The legend has become a part of New Jersey's tourist attractions, with tours and events centered around the Jersey Devil.

The Jersey Devil's influence on popular culture extends across various media, capturing the imagination of audiences far beyond the Pine Barrens of New Jersey.

Television - "The X-Files":

Episode: In the "The Jersey Devil" episode of "The X-Files" (Season 1, Episode 5), FBI agents Fox Mulder and Dana Scully investigate a series of murders in Atlantic City that appear to be linked to the Jersey Devil legend.

Video Games:

"Jersey Devil" (PlayStation): A platform game released in 1997 where players control a protagonist named Jersey Devil, navigating through various levels to stop the evil Dr. Knarf and his mutant plants.

Comic Books:

- Appearance in Comics: The Jersey Devil has been featured in several comic book stories, including titles like "The Pineys" and "Weird NJ."
- Cultural Relevance: These appearances often reimagine the legend, blending it with other mythologies or using it as a backdrop for horror and fantasy narratives.
- Movies:
- "The Last Broadcast" (1998): This horror film incorporates the Jersey Devil legend into its story, involving a documentary crew searching for the creature in the Pine Barrens.
- Significance: The movie adds a modern twist to the legend, using the found footage style that would later become popular in horror cinema.

Music:

- Bruce Springsteen's Reference: The Jersey Devil has been mentioned in Bruce Springsteen's music, including in the song "A Night with the Jersey Devil."
- Local Influence: As a native of New Jersey, Springsteen's reference to the legend in his music underscores its cultural significance in the region.

These examples demonstrate the Jersey Devil's lasting impact on popular culture. The legend has transcended its local folklore origins to become a versatile and enduring figure in various forms of entertainment. Remember: while **you may never need to know** every pop culture reference to the Jersey Devil, its presence across media underscores our enduring fascination with myths and legends.

66. Pepsi vs. Coca-Cola: The Cola Wars

Coca-Cola's Early Start:

- Creation by Dr. John S. Pemberton: Coca-Cola's journey began when Dr. John Stith Pemberton, a pharmacist in Atlanta, Georgia, created a distinctive syrup in 1886. Pemberton, initially concocting a coca wine, switched to a non-alcoholic version due to local prohibition laws.

- First Sales at Jacobs' Pharmacy: Pemberton's bookkeeper, Frank M. Robinson, is credited with naming the beverage "Coca-Cola," reflecting its two key ingredients at the time: coca leaves and kola nuts. Robinson also penned the distinctive script that became the famous logo. The first servings of Coca-Cola were sold for five cents a glass at Jacobs' Pharmacy in Atlanta.
    - **Medicinal Beginnings:** Initially marketed as a "brain tonic" and "temperance drink," Coca-Cola was advertised as a remedy for headaches and as a stimulant. The early versions of Coca-Cola contained traces of cocaine, derived from coca leaf extract, though this ingredient was phased out by 1929.

- **Rapid Growth and Bottling:** Asa Candler, a businessman, acquired the rights to Coca-Cola in the late 1880s and aggressively marketed the drink. The introduction of bottled Coca-Cola in 1894 allowed for wider distribution, and by 1895, Coca-Cola was being sold across the United States.

Pepsi's Emergence:

- Caleb Bradham's Invention: Pepsi-Cola was created by Caleb Bradham, a pharmacist in New Bern, North Carolina. Bradham concocted the drink in his drugstore in 1893, originally calling it "Brad's Drink." It was a mixture of sugar, water, caramel, lemon oil, nutmeg, and other natural additives.
- **Renaming to Pepsi-Cola:** In 1898, Bradham renamed his beverage "Pepsi-Cola," believed to be derived from the digestive enzyme pepsin and kola nuts used in the recipe. He marketed it as a drink that aided digestion and boosted energy.
- **Trademark and Expansion:** Bradham trademarked the Pepsi-Cola name in 1903 and moved the bottling of Pepsi-Cola from his drugstore to a rented warehouse. That year, he sold over 7,800 gallons of syrup, demonstrating the drink's growing popularity.
- **The Great Depression and Beyond:** Pepsi faced bankruptcy in 1923 due to sugar price fluctuations. It was reorganized and revitalized under new ownership. In the 1930s, Pepsi gained popularity with its innovative marketing strategy of selling 12-ounce bottles for the same five-cent price as Coca-Cola's six-ounce bottle.
- **The Pepsi Challenge:** In the 1970s, Pepsi launched the Pepsi Challenge, a blind taste test where consumers preferred Pepsi over Coca-Cola, putting pressure on Coca-Cola and gaining market share.

New Coke Debacle: In 1985, Coca-Cola attempted to reformulate its original recipe to compete with Pepsi's sweeter taste, leading to the New Coke controversy. The public backlash was swift, and Coca-Cola soon reverted to its original formula, termed "Coca-Cola Classic."

Both brands have become deeply ingrained in global culture, with their logos, slogans, and imagery recognized worldwide.

Pepsi and Coca-Cola have used celebrity endorsements to strengthen their brand appeal, with stars like Michael Jackson, Britney Spears, and Santa Claus (for Coca-Cola's Christmas advertising).

Both Coca-Cola and Pepsi are global giants, with products sold in virtually every country. Coca-Cola often holds a larger market share globally, but PepsiCo's broader range of products, including snacks, makes it a formidable competitor.

In recent years, both companies have faced challenges due to the growing health-consciousness of consumers, leading to innovations in low-sugar and zero-calorie products.

The battle between Pepsi and Coca-Cola is more than just about soda; it's a story of two companies continuously adapting and competing in a dynamic market. Remember: while **you may never need to know** the intricate details of the cola wars, understanding this rivalry offers insights into marketing strategies, consumer preferences, and the power of branding in shaping global beverage industries.

67. The Original Formula of Coca-Cola

Coca Leaf Extract: The Secret Ingredient
- 1886: A Coca-Cola Odyssey Begins: Imagine a time when your soda break was more... exhilarating. The original Coca-Cola, a brainchild of Dr. John S. Pemberton, wasn't just your average thirst quencher. Infused with coca leaf extract, it was like having a mini energy boost in a glass – a 'legal' pick-me-up, if you will.

Cocaine Content: A Modest Dose of Buzz
- Cocaine: The Wonder Additive: Back in the day, cocaine was the 'aspirin' of the times. Found in the coca leaf extract, it turned Coca-Cola into a 'miracle tonic' that could pep you up. With about 9 milligrams of cocaine per serving, it was less "Open Happiness," more "Open Alertness."

Public Perception and Legal Cha-Cha-Cha
- Changing Times, Changing Minds: Fast forward to the early 1900s, and suddenly, cocaine in your soda isn't looking so chic. People started realizing that maybe, just maybe, this wonder drug had a darker side. Enter the Pure Food and Drug Act of 1906, raining on the cocaine parade.

Removal of Cocaine: Keeping the Kick, Losing the Con
- Coca-Cola Goes to Rehab: By 1904, Coca-Cola was on a path to reinvention. The company began using "spent" coca leaves – essentially, coca leaves that had their 'naughty' side removed. The taste stayed, but the cocaine high waved goodbye.

Coca-Cola Today: A Story of Adaptation
- Coca-Cola: Evolved and Cocaine-Free: Today's Coca-Cola keeps it 100% family-friendly. The cocaine is completely removed and repurposed for medical use (because why waste good stuff?). The coca leaf extract still adds that secret flavor, but without any of the jittery side effects.

The story of Coca-Cola's original formula is like a trip down an old-school pharmacy aisle, where sodas came with a side of 'whoa.' But as times changed, so did Coca-Cola, proving that even the most iconic brands can ditch their wild past for a more refined present. Remember: while **you may never need to know** about Coca-Cola's 'coke' days, it's a fizzy reminder of how times, tastes, and recipes evolve. After all, who needs cocaine when you've got caffeine?

68. The Origin of Football (Soccer): A Game of Many Fathers

Ancient Ancestors: A Ball and Some Rules

Worldwide Kick-Off: The history of football, or soccer as it's known in some countries, is a tale of many cultures. Think ancient China with 'cuju,' a game where players kicked a ball into a small net. Or the Greeks and Romans with their ball games, each adding a touch of civilization to the art of kicking.

Not-So-Friendly Medieval Matches: In medieval England, football wasn't the gentleman's sport we know today.

Picture entire villages clashing in chaotic matches, with goals miles apart and rules... well, what rules?

Codification: Turning Chaos into a Sport

- The Cambridge Rules (1848): Imagine a group of British school chaps saying, "Let's make this game less wild." The Cambridge Rules were a first attempt to bring some order to the football chaos. It laid down the foundation but didn't quite seal the deal.
- Sheffield Rules (1857): Enter Sheffield FC, the world's oldest football club. They brought their own set of rules, adding throw-ins and corner kicks to the mix. Football was getting closer to its modern form, but the plot was still thickening.

The FA Takes the Field

The Football Association (FA) Formation (1863): The real game-changer came with the formation of the Football Association in England. A gathering of clubs in London said, "Enough of this confusion!" and drafted the first official rules of football. This was it – the birth of football as we know it.

The Great Divide - Soccer and Rugby: Not everyone was happy with the new rules. A split occurred, with some clubs favoring a game where handling the ball was allowed, leading to the birth of rugby. Those who stuck to kicking formed what we now know as football, or soccer in some circles.

Global Spread

The British Influence: Kicking Off Around the Globe
- Colonial Kick-Start: As the British Empire expanded its horizons, so did football. British sailors, soldiers, and traders brought the game to far-off lands, turning it into an international pastime.
- **Early Adopters:** The first international football match was between Scotland and England in 1872. But it didn't stop there – countries like Argentina and Uruguay had clubs established by British expats as early as the late 1800s.
- **Europe Catches On:** In mainland Europe, football quickly became a staple. Countries like Italy, Spain, and Germany saw the formation of their first clubs in the late 19th and early 20th centuries, each adapting the game to their unique cultural styles.

FIFA and the World Cup: Uniting Nations Through Football

- **Formation of FIFA:** The Fédération Internationale de Football Association (FIFA) was established in Paris in 1904, with founding members from France, Belgium, Denmark, the Netherlands, Spain, Sweden, and Switzerland. FIFA's goal was to oversee football across nations, transcending political and cultural boundaries.
- **The Inaugural World Cup (1930):** The first FIFA World Cup was held in Uruguay in 1930, marking a significant milestone in the sport's history. Only 13 teams participated then, but it set the stage for what would become the world's most watched sporting event.
- **Statistics and Reach:** Today, FIFA boasts over 200 member nations – more than the United Nations! The 2018 World Cup in Russia had over half of the global population (3.572 billion viewers) tune in at some point, with 1.12 billion watching the final match.

Football's Cultural and Social Impact
- **Beyond the Game:** Football is more than just a sport; it's a cultural phenomenon. It reflects and influences social and political narratives in countries around the world. For instance, in Brazil, football is intertwined with national identity, while in Africa, it's a tool for social empowerment and unity.

- **Grassroots and Youth Development:** Worldwide, grassroots football programs nurture young talent and foster community spirit. It's a sport that transcends socio-economic barriers, offering a common language for people of diverse backgrounds.

Football's journey from the British Isles to a global phenomenon is a testament to its universal appeal and the power of sport to unite people. From the alleys of Buenos Aires to the fields of rural Africa, football resonates with a spirit of camaraderie and competition. Remember: while **you may never need to know** every goal scored in World Cup history, the story of football's global spread is a narrative of cultural exchange, unity, and the sheer joy of playing and watching the beautiful game.

69. Castro's Exploding Cigar

The Plot: More Than Just Smoke

- A Spy Movie Script, but Real: Imagine a scene straight out of a James Bond film – a cigar, a world leader, and a covert assassination plan. This was the reality during the height of Cold War tensions between the United States and Cuba.
- The Target – Fidel Castro: Fidel Castro, the charismatic and controversial leader of Cuba, was known for his love of cigars. This habit caught the attention of the CIA, which was actively seeking ways to remove him from power.

The CIA's Covert Operations

- Operation Mongoose: As part of the broader effort called Operation Mongoose, the CIA explored various methods to undermine or eliminate Castro. Ideas ranged from the bizarre to the deadly, reflecting the urgency and desperation of the times.

- The Exploding Cigar: Among the many plans was the idea to provide Castro with a box of cigars rigged to explode upon lighting. This plan, however, never went past the drawing board. The feasibility and practicality of such an assassination method were questionable.

The Bigger Picture: Wild Schemes

Other Assassination Attempts: The exploding cigar was just one of many plots to assassinate Castro. Other ideas included a contaminated diving suit, poisoned pills, and even efforts to undermine his charismatic image by making his beard fall out.

Failed Attempts: Despite numerous attempts and plans, all efforts to assassinate Castro or diminish his power ultimately failed. Castro famously joked about surviving over 600 assassination plots, a testament to his survival skills and perhaps to the outlandish nature of some of the CIA's plans.

- CIA's Project A-12: Castro's exploding cigar plot was part of the CIA's larger anti-Castro initiative, Project A-12, which involved various schemes to undermine his regime.

- 1967: The Year of the Plot: The exploding cigar plot came to light in 1967 when a former CIA operative divulged details about the agency's assassination attempts against Castro.

- Deliverance Dilemma: The biggest challenge was delivering the lethal cigar to Castro, a task that proved too risky and impractical for actual execution.

- New York Police Department Involvement: The NYPD's Intelligence Division was once approached by the CIA to assist in delivering the exploding cigar to Castro during his 1960 visit to the United Nations.
- Declassified Documents: The exploding cigar plot was confirmed in the 1990s when declassified CIA documents revealed various assassination attempts against Castro.
- Castro's Awareness: Fidel Castro was aware of the numerous assassination attempts against him, including the exploding cigar plot, often joking about the CIA's creativity.
- No Direct Orders: Despite the various plots, there is no documented evidence that a U.S. President directly ordered Castro's assassination.
- 600+ Assassination Attempts: Castro claimed to have survived over 600 assassination attempts, a figure that includes both serious plots and more fanciful plans like the exploding cigar.
- Legacy in Media: The exploding cigar plot has been depicted in films and books, often cited as an example of the extreme lengths of Cold War espionage efforts.

The Stuff of Legends

The story of Castro's exploding cigar has become a part of Cold War lore, illustrating the lengths to which governments went during this period of global tension. It's a blend of historical fact and legend, showcasing a time when truth was often stranger than fiction.

Remember: while **you may never need to know** the intricate details of espionage tactics used against Fidel Castro, the tale of the exploding cigar is a quirky footnote in the annals of history, serving as a reminder of the surreal and shadowy world of Cold War spy games.

70. Left- and Right-Hand Traffic: A Tale of Directional Diversity

The origin of driving on different sides of the road dates back to horseback riders. In most countries, right-handed riders preferred to keep to the left to have their right arm free for greetings or... sword fighting. Talk about a medieval road rage solution!

The shift to right-hand traffic in many parts of the world is often attributed to Napoleon. The theory goes that because Napoleon was left-handed, he preferred his armies to march on the right, spreading this practice across his conquered lands.

Rules of the Road: Left vs. Right

Left-Handed Legacy: Countries like the UK, Australia, and India drive on the left, a practice inherited from British rule. It's like keeping a bit of the old empire's charm, but with more traffic.
Right-Handed Majority: About 65% of the world's population drives on the right. From the US to Russia and China, right-hand driving is the norm, making cross-border road trips a bit of a mind-bender for the uninitiated.

- Sweden's Big Switch: Sweden switched from left to right-hand driving in 1967. On Dagen H (H Day), all traffic in Sweden stopped for a few hours before switching sides. It was less of a traffic dance and more of a careful shuffle.
- Samoa's Recent Swap: Samoa changed from right to left-hand driving in 2009 to align with other South Pacific nations, causing a national stir and making car imports from neighbors like Australia easier.
- The Horse and the Cart: In countries with left-hand traffic, horse-drawn vehicles have the whip mounted on the right. So, if you ever time travel, remember where to sit to avoid a whip in the face.

The choice of left or right-hand traffic is a blend of history, habit, and sometimes, the hand you hold your sword in. While driving on different sides might seem like a recipe for chaos, it's a fascinating example of how historical choices shape modern life.

Remember: while you may never need to know the exact reasons why some countries prefer to drive on the left or right, this quirky piece of trivia is a reminder of how diverse and oddly practical our world can be. Just make sure to look both ways before crossing – you never know which side the car's coming from!

71. Starbucks in Italy

In 2018, Starbucks made a daring foray into Italy, the land that practically invented espresso. Opening its first store in Milan, the birthplace of espresso culture, was like bringing ice to the Arctic!
The Inspiration Behind the Green Siren

- From Seattle to Milan: Starbucks' journey to Italy traces back to its very roots. Howard Schultz, the man who transformed Starbucks into the global giant it is today, first found his inspiration after a trip to Milan in the 1980s. He was captivated by the vibrant Italian coffee culture – the intimate espresso bars, the art of coffee-making, and the role of cafes as a social gathering spot.
- Bringing the Italian Espresso Home: Schultz's vision was to bring the Italian espresso bar experience to America, blending the quality of Italian coffee with the convenience of American service. This vision birthed the Starbucks we know today, with its wide array of coffees and iconic, relaxed atmosphere.

The Italian Challenge: Will Espresso Meet Frappuccino?

When Starbucks decided to enter Italy, it faced a cultural conundrum. Italian coffee culture is steeped in tradition, where coffee is more than a drink; it's a ritual. Espresso is consumed quickly, often standing at the bar, and always freshly brewed. Would Italians embrace a foreign coffee chain known for its frappuccinos and lounge-style seating?

Many Italians were skeptical. In their view, Starbucks represented a commercialization of their cherished coffee traditions. Yet, there was also curiosity about what this global coffee phenomenon could offer to the Italian espresso experience.

In 2018, Starbucks opened its first Italian store in Milan with a nod to Italian traditions. The Milan Roastery wasn't just another coffee shop; it was a luxurious homage to coffee, right in the heart of the city that inspired Schultz decades ago.

The Roastery's design pays tribute to Italian elegance, set in a renovated historic building. The menu offers classic Italian coffee alongside Starbucks' signature drinks, but with a respectful twist – traditional Italian pastries and no 'venti' sizes.

- Italian Baristas: Starbucks trained its Italian baristas extensively, ensuring they match the skill and speed of their local counterparts.
- Local Ingredients: Embracing localism, the Milan Starbucks sources its pastries and snacks from local Italian bakeries.
- Cultural Fusion: The store is a fusion of American and Italian coffee cultures, offering a unique experience that blends the familiar Starbucks model with traditional Italian elements.

Starbucks' entry into Italy is more than just a business expansion; it's a full-circle moment from inspiration to homage. While some Italians might view it as a commercial intrusion, others see it as a respectful tribute to their coffee culture.

Remember: while **you may never need to know** every detail of how Starbucks brewed its way into Italy, this story is a testament to how global and local cultures can blend, creating a new, shared coffee experience. It's a tale of how one man's Italian espresso epiphany turned into a global coffee revolution.

72 - Crazy Laws of the United States

Buckle up, because we're diving into the gloriously wacky world of American laws! It's true, the USA has a legal landscape as vast and diverse as the Grand Canyon itself. From coast to coast, state to state, there's a whole smorgasbord of rules and regulations, some sensible, some downright strange. Why is it like this? Well, grab your metaphorical cowboy hat and mosey on over, partner, because I'm about to lasso the reasons why American laws are such a tangled mess of fascinating contradictions.

Firstly, gotta remember the whole "50 independent states" thing. Each state is like its own miniature country, with its own history, culture, and, yes, you guessed it, laws. It's like a patchwork quilt sewn together with legal thread, each state adding its own unique squares of regulations. Want to sing karaoke before noon in Massachusetts? Nope, sorry, gotta wait till the afternoon sun shines. But head over to Nevada, and you can belt out your ballads before breakfast (just don't do it in your pajamas!).

Then there's the layer cake of federal law on top. Uncle Sam, bless his bureaucratic heart, has his own set of rules that apply to the whole shebang. Think taxes, national parks, and those fancy interstate highways you zoom down. So, sometimes state laws and federal laws play nice together, like two kids sharing a sandbox. But other times, they clash like cowboys over a water hole. Imagine California's love for environmental regulations bumping heads with Texas' oil industry. Sparks fly, legal battles ensue, and everyone gets a headache.

Another reason for the legal hodgepodge is the good ol' American spirit of innovation. We're a nation of pioneers, always pushing the boundaries, even when it comes to laws. Remember the Wild West days? Laws were practically scribbled on saloon napkins back then. As society evolved, so did the rules, leading to a sometimes messy, always interesting patchwork of legal precedents. Think of it like a legal jazz solo, improvised on the fly, with each judge adding their own riff.

And let's not forget the influence of special interests and lobbyists. They're like the backroom dealers of the legal world, whispering sweet nothings (and maybe a few bucks) into the ears of politicians. This can lead to some pretty peculiar laws, like the one in Alabama that makes it illegal to sell peanuts after sundown (seriously, no late-night peanut cravings allowed!).

So, there you have it, folks. The reasons for America's vast and varied legal landscape are as complex and colorful as the country itself. It's a crazy quilt of history, culture, and good ol' American ingenuity, all stitched together with legal thread. And hey, even if it makes your head spin sometimes, there's no denying it's one heck of a ride. Now, go forth and explore the weird and wonderful world of American laws, partner. Just remember, don't wear pajamas while gambling in Nevada, and don't throw snowballs at cops in Missouri. You wouldn't want to end up on the wrong side of a legal hootenanny, now would you?

- **Wyoming:** Skiers, think twice before hitting the slopes after a few drinks. It's illegal to ski while intoxicated in Wyoming, a law that makes perfect sense when you consider the safety aspects.

- **Louisiana:** Love crawfish? In Louisiana, stealing these little crustaceans is a serious offense, with potential jail time for those who pinch too many.

- **Rockville, Maryland:** Mind your language in Rockville. Public swearing can hit your wallet with a fine, keeping the streets family-friendly.

- **Gainesville, Georgia:** Fried chicken enthusiasts, remember: in Gainesville, this poultry delight must be eaten with your hands. Using utensils is not just frowned upon, it's against the law!

- **Florida:** Thinking of donning a mask for a midnight stroll? Not so fast. In Florida, adults roaming the streets masked can face legal repercussions, unless it's a holiday or a drill.

- **Rehoboth Beach, Delaware:** If you're in church in Rehoboth Beach, keep those whispers to a minimum. Even a hushed conversation can be considered a disturbance and might attract a fine.

- **Hawaii:** Here's an odd one – putting coins in your ears is a no-no in Hawaii. This law dates back to a time when the local currency was being destroyed, and people got creative with hiding their money.

- **Alabama:** Driving blindfolded in Alabama? That's a definite no. Visibility is key when you're behind the wheel, and this law ensures drivers keep their eyes on the road.

- **Louisiana:** Think sending a surprise pizza is a harmless prank? In Louisiana, it's considered harassment, and you might end up paying more than just for the pizza.

- **North Carolina:** Bingo lovers, take note. In North Carolina, keep your bingo games under five hours, and stay sober while playing – both are the law.

- **Arkansas:** Love your late-night snacks? Be careful in Arkansas, where it's illegal to honk your horn near a sandwich shop after 9 p.m. This law was likely enacted to prevent disturbances in dining areas.

- **Alabama:** In Alabama, opening an umbrella on the street is prohibited. This unusual law might have been intended to prevent accidents or obstructions on crowded walkways.

- **Colorado:** In Colorado, collecting rainwater is illegal. This law is likely tied to water rights and the allocation of natural resources.

- **Connecticut:** A pickle must bounce to officially be considered a pickle in Connecticut. This peculiar standard was likely established to ensure the quality and texture of this popular snack.

- **Florida:** Skateboarding without a license is prohibited in certain parts of Florida, reflecting an attempt to regulate this activity and ensure safety.

- **Georgia:** In Quitman, Georgia, chickens are not permitted to cross the road. This law is likely a humorous take on ensuring livestock and poultry are kept under control.

- **Hawaii:** It's against the law in Hawaii to place a coin behind your ear. This unique regulation dates back to early 20th-century efforts to control local currency.

- **Indiana:** In Indiana, pi is legally 4, not 3.1415. This bizarre law appears to be a misunderstood attempt to simplify mathematics.

- **Kansas:** It's illegal to catch a fish with bare hands in Kansas. This law might be aimed at protecting fish populations or ensuring fair sportsmanship in fishing.

- **Alabama:** Selling peanuts after sundown is a no-go in some Alabama towns. This curious law may stem from concerns about food spoilage or sanitation in the pre-refrigeration era.

- **Arizona:** It's illegal to hunt camels in Arizona, a seemingly unnecessary rule considering the rarity of wild camels in the state. This law likely arose from a failed experiment of using camels for transportation in the 19th century.

- **Colorado:** If you're a dog owner in Denver, Colorado, don't expect to stroll through the park with more than two furry companions. This leash law limits the number of dogs one person can walk at a time.

- **Florida**: In Key West, it's illegal to feed pigeons in public. This rule likely aims to control the pigeon population and keep beaches and tourist spots clean.

- **Illinois:** In Chicago, wearing slippers while driving is forbidden. While the reason may seem unclear, it might be related to safety concerns regarding footwear that could potentially hinder proper control of the vehicle.

- **Maine:** Forget using fireworks to celebrate, as they're generally illegal in most Maine towns and cities. This regulation aims to prevent fires and injuries associated with personal fireworks displays.

- **Nevada:** In Elko County, Nevada, brothels are required to post a prominent sign with the words "No Loitering" clearly visible. This odd directive seems like a tongue-in-cheek attempt to maintain some semblance of decorum outside these establishments.

- **New Jersey:** In Salem County, New Jersey, it's illegal to sing on Sundays except in church or at home. This antiquated law likely reflects strict religious observance of the Sabbath in past eras.

- **New York:** Public swimming pools in New York City must have at least one lifeguard who can speak Yiddish. This requirement ensures the safety of Yiddish-speaking residents who may not understand English instructions during emergencies.

- **Oregon:** In Baker County, Oregon, it's illegal to sell or purchase a live octopus. This rule is likely aimed at protecting octopus populations and preventing cruelty to these intelligent creatures.

- **Alabama:** No fortune telling allowed except for entertainment purposes. So, predicting your future is okay for fun, but not if you're serious about it.

- **California:** Unlawful to sell a baby doll without eyelashes within the state. Apparently, bald-eyed dolls are too creepy for Californians.

- **Florida**: Live Oak trees are considered the State Tree, and it's illegal to kill or damage them without a permit. Guess Florida prefers leafy giants over sprawl.

- **Georgia**: While masks are generally frowned upon, it's legal to wear one while riding a motorcycle... just to protect your face from bugs, of course.

- **Idaho**: Throwing a brick at a highway is a big no-no, even if you have the world's strongest arm.

- **Illinois**: If you're a barber in Chicago, don't even think about cutting hair on Sundays. Those locks will have to wait until Monday.

- **Kentucky**: Dueling is technically legal, but only if both parties are registered blood donors and the fight takes place within 20 feet of a courthouse. Talk about a morbid twist on conflict resolution.

- **Louisiana**: Throwing a banana peel in front of someone can land you in hot water. Seems slipping on potassium is considered assault in the Bayou State.

- **Massachusetts**: In Nantucket, singing karaoke before noon is prohibited. So, save your belting for the afternoon crowds.

- **Michigan**: Want to name your kid something wacky like "Strawberry Shortcake"? Prepare to get creative, as unusual names require court approval.

- **Minnesota**: It's illegal to fish while sitting on a horse. Apparently, Minnesota prefers two-legged anglers.

- **Mississippi**: Sunday shopping is a no-go in some counties, forcing residents to plan their purchases well in advance.

- **Missouri**: Throwing snowballs at police officers is considered disorderly conduct. Even in a snowball fight, respect the blue.

- **Montana**: Don't even think about selling used mattresses unless they're properly disinfected. No one wants to inherit someone else's nightmares (or bed bugs).

- **Nevada**: While gambling is legal in Vegas, it's illegal to play slot machines while you're wearing pajamas. Dress code applies even to one-armed bandits.

- **New Hampshire**: Don't try to bribe Santa Claus in New Hampshire. It's a misdemeanor, and who wants to be on the naughty list?

- **New Jersey:** It's illegal to pump your own gas. So, sit back, relax, and let the professionals handle it.

- **New Mexico:** Want to ride a camel? Head to New Mexico, where it's perfectly legal (unlike in neighboring Arizona).

- **New York:** In New York City, it's illegal to shake a dust mop out your window. Imagine the chaos if everyone went on a spontaneous dusting spree!

- **Ohio**: Selling goldfish in bowls smaller than one gallon is forbidden. Goldfish deserve some swimming space, even in the Buckeye State.

Remember, while **you may never need to know** that in parts of the United States, it's illegal to sing off-key, these laws are snapshots of the American spirit - sometimes serious, often amusing, but always intriguing.

73. The Mysterious Shroud of Turin

perplexing and debated relics of Christian history – the Shroud of Turin. This long piece of linen cloth, imprinted with the faint, brownish image of a man with wounds akin to crucifixion, has captivated believers, skeptics, and scientists alike.

The Shroud's documented history begins in the 14th century in France, where it was revered as the burial shroud of Jesus Christ. However, its sudden appearance and the lack of clear historical records from earlier periods fueled skepticism and controversy. The local bishop of Lirey, where it was first displayed, even declared it a fake, leading to its brief confiscation.

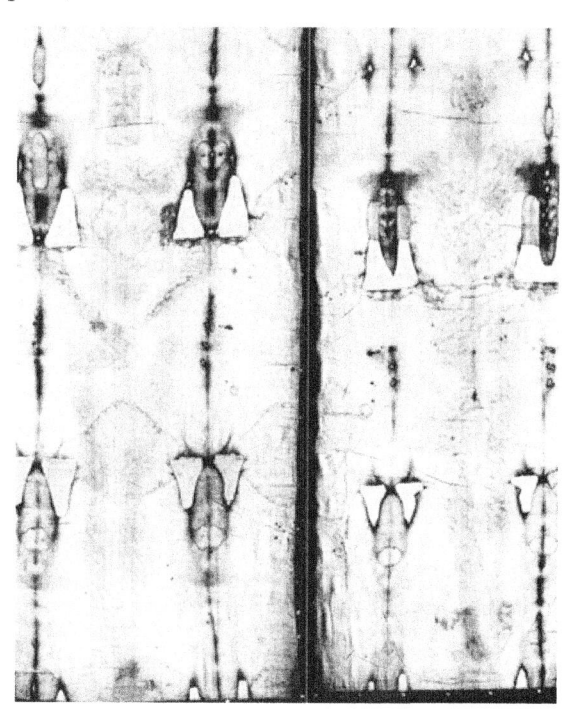

The debate took a scientific turn in 1988 when radiocarbon dating tests were conducted. These tests dated the shroud to the medieval period, between 1260 and 1390, suggesting it was not old enough to have been Christ's burial cloth. This conclusion, however, was not universally accepted. Critics argued that the sample might have been contaminated or taken from a section of the shroud repaired in the Middle Ages, skewing the dating results.

Pollen particles found on the shroud hinted at its presence in the Middle East, adding another layer to the mystery.

Furthermore, the shroud's image, detailed and with a three-dimensional quality when rendered in negative, defied explanation. Traditional medieval artistic methods seemed incapable of producing such an image, leading some to propose supernatural origins.

- **Invisible Reweaving:** Some experts have suggested that skilled reweaving of the shroud in the past might have affected the carbon dating results.
- **Bloodstain Analysis:** Detailed studies of the bloodstains on the shroud align with wounds typical of crucifixion, adding to its authenticity claims.
- **Photographic Enigma:** The discovery that the shroud's image becomes clearer in photographic negatives has further mystified its origins and method of creation.
- **Rare Public Viewings:** Despite its fragile state, the shroud has been displayed publicly on rare occasions, each drawing millions of curious and faithful visitors from around the globe.

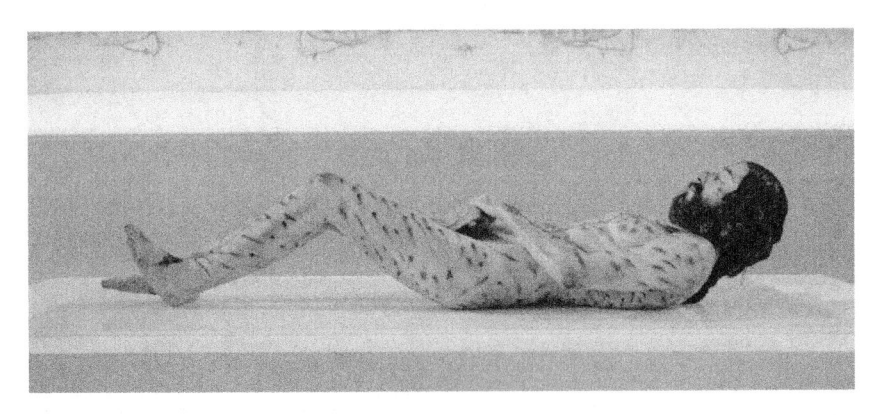

Today, the Shroud of Turin remains an object of deep veneration for many, a subject of intense scientific scrutiny, and a puzzle for the curious. Its blend of historical, religious, and scientific elements has made it a symbol of the eternal human quest for understanding.

The Shroud of Turin, whether a medieval creation or a relic of ancient history, stands as a testament to the enduring interplay of faith, science, and the human fascination with the unknown.

Remember: **you may never need to know** all the answers the Shroud of Turin holds, but its mystery invites us to ponder the deeper questions of belief, history, and the limits of our knowledge.

74. The Riddle of the Hanging Gardens of Babylon

In the annals of ancient wonders, few are as shrouded in mystery as the Hanging Gardens of Babylon. Said to be an astonishing feat of engineering and beauty, these gardens have captivated historians and travelers for centuries, yet their existence and true location remain one of history's tantalizing enigmas.

- The Hanging Gardens are believed to have been constructed in the ancient city of Babylon, near present-day Baghdad in Iraq. According to legend, they were built by King Nebuchadnezzar II around 600 BC, a gift to his homesick wife, Amytis of Media, who longed for the green hills and valleys of her homeland.

- Despite their fame, the Hanging Gardens are not mentioned in any surviving Babylonian texts, and their actual existence has been a topic of debate among historians. Some suggest they were purely mythical, or perhaps confused with another garden in the ancient world.

Descriptions from Antiquity

The most detailed descriptions of the gardens come from Greek historians like Strabo and Philo of Byzantium, who wrote about them centuries after their supposed existence. They described a garden that defied the typical visual concept of a garden: a series of terraces with lush vegetation, resembling a green mountain, complete with a complex irrigation system.

These accounts paint a picture of an engineering marvel, with plants supposedly irrigated using water from the Euphrates River, raised using a chain pump mechanism.

The Mystery Deepens

Archaeological efforts to locate the Hanging Gardens have been met with limited success. Excavations in Babylon have failed to uncover definitive evidence of the gardens, leading some scholars to propose alternative locations, such as the Assyrian city of Nineveh.

The lack of concrete evidence has fueled various theories. Some historians now believe that the gardens were purely legendary, an embellished tale passed down through generations. Others hold onto the possibility that they did exist but were destroyed by earthquakes and time.

Intriguing Trivia: Unraveling Babylon's Puzzle

- **Architectural Wonder:** If they did exist, the Hanging Gardens would have been an architectural and engineering marvel, especially considering the technological limitations of the time.

- **A Lost Wonder:** The Hanging Gardens are the only one of the Seven Wonders of the Ancient World for which the location has never been definitively established.
- **Symbol of Love:** The romantic story of Nebuchadnezzar creating the gardens for his wife adds a layer of intrigue and romance to the legend.
- **Advanced Irrigation:** The described irrigation system of the gardens, if true, would have been a remarkable achievement, showcasing the advanced understanding of hydraulics in the ancient world.
- **A Blend of Cultures:** The gardens, if they existed, would have been a fusion of Persian and Babylonian cultural influences, reflecting the diverse nature of Nebuchadnezzar's empire.

A Garden of Questions

The Hanging Gardens of Babylon, whether real or imagined, represent the human capacity for wonder and the desire to create beauty. Their story is a blend of history, myth, and a testament to the enduring allure of ancient civilizations. **Remember:** while **you may never need to know** whether the Hanging Gardens truly existed, their story invites us to imagine and marvel at the possibilities of the ancient world.

75. The Legend of the Kraken

In the realm of maritime lore, few creatures have captured the imagination quite like the Kraken. This legendary sea monster, said to dwell off the coasts of Norway and Greenland, has been a source of fear and fascination for sailors and storytellers for centuries.

Origins of the Myth

The earliest mentions of the Kraken come from Norse mythology and Scandinavian folklore, where it was described as a gigantic, octopus-like creature capable of engulfing ships and whales with its massive tentacles.

Tales of the Kraken often depict it as an enormous beast, lurking beneath the waves, with descriptions varying from a giant squid to something more monstrous and mythical.

The Kraken has been immortalized in poems, paintings, and stories. Alfred Tennyson's famous poem "The Kraken" and the Norwegian artwork "Den Store Søslange" ("The Great Sea Serpent") by Theodor Kittelsen are prime examples.

- **A Symbol of Nature's Power:** The Kraken, in folklore, represents the unpredictable and often dangerous nature of the sea, embodying the fears of those who venture into its depths.
- **Scientific Speculation:** Marine biologists have speculated that the giant squid, which can reach over 40 feet in length, might be the real creature behind Kraken legends.
- **A Navigator's Nightmare:** In old maritime maps, the Kraken was sometimes depicted as a warning for uncharted or dangerous waters.
- **Tentacles in Pop Culture:** The Kraken has made appearances in numerous films, such as "Pirates of the Caribbean," where it is portrayed as a monstrous servant of the sea.
- **A Metaphor for the Unknown:** Beyond its physical description, the Kraken has often been used metaphorically to represent the fears and unknowns of exploration and adventure

Seafarers' Tales and Exaggerations

Throughout the ages, the vast and mysterious oceans have been a source of awe and terror for those who navigate their waters. Among the many legends born from the sea, the Kraken stands out as a particularly formidable figure in maritime folklore. Sailors' accounts of encounters with this fearsome creature have both captivated and horrified listeners for centuries.

These tales, often passed down through generations of seafarers, paint a picture of a monster of colossal size and strength. The Kraken, as described by these mariners, was capable of enveloping entire ships with its massive tentacles, dragging them down to the ocean's depths.

Sailors spoke of turbulent waters, strange whirlpools, and sudden, unexplained disappearances of ships and crew, attributing these phenomena to the Kraken's mighty presence.

However, the line between fact and fiction in these stories is often blurred. Historians and marine scientists have speculated that the origins of the Kraken legend may lie in real encounters with giant squids. These deep-sea creatures, rarely seen but known to exist, can grow to formidable sizes, with the largest recorded specimen measuring over 40 feet. Such an encounter, especially under challenging and frightening conditions at sea, could easily be embellished into a tale of a monstrous beast by sailors eager to share their extraordinary experiences.

The embellishments and exaggerations typical in sailors' tales served various purposes. For some, these stories were a way to explain the unexplainable, giving a face, or in this case, tentacles, to the unknown dangers of the sea.

For others, these tales added a sense of adventure and mystery to the life of a sailor, a welcome diversion from the daily routines and hardships of maritime life. They also served as cautionary tales, warning of the perils of the sea, and in some cases, were used to deter others from venturing into certain dangerous or uncharted waters.

Intriguingly, the Kraken's legend also reflects the human tendency to personify nature's forces. Just as ancient civilizations attributed natural phenomena to gods and mythical creatures, sailors attributed the ocean's unpredictable and often destructive power to the Kraken. This personification of the sea's dangers into a single, formidable entity speaks to the human need to make sense of and give narrative to the natural world, especially in an age when the ocean was a vast, unexplored frontier.

Remember: while **you may never need to know** the depths of truth behind these maritime myths, they offer a captivating glimpse into the ocean's enduring mystery and the human spirit's quest to unravel it.

76. Oswald's, Soviet Adventure

Lee Harvey Oswald, infamously known for assassinating President John F. Kennedy in 1963, had a lesser-known chapter in his life that's often overshadowed by his notorious crime. Before he became a figure etched in tragic American history, Oswald had an intriguing and somewhat bewildering stint in the Soviet Union.

Lee Harvey Oswald, infamously known for assassinating President John F. Kennedy in 1963, had a lesser-known chapter in his life that's often overshadowed by his notorious crime. Before he became a figure etched in tragic American history, Oswald had an intriguing and somewhat bewildering stint in the Soviet Union.

From Marine to Defector

- Oswald, a former Marine, made a dramatic life choice in 1959, at the age of 19. In a move that stunned many, he defected to the Soviet Union, renouncing his American citizenship. This decision was rooted in his growing disillusionment with the West and his fascination with communism.
- After arriving in Moscow, Oswald pleaded with Soviet authorities for citizenship. Initially, his request was denied, and he even attempted suicide over the refusal. The Soviets, reconsidering their stance, allowed him to stay and assigned him a job in Minsk at a radio and television factory.

Lee Harvey Oswald's life in the Soviet Union, which he had hoped would be a fresh start in a communist paradise, turned out to be more mundane and frustrating than he had anticipated. His journey and experiences in the USSR provide a fascinating glimpse into the life of an American defector during the height of the Cold War.

Ordinary Job, Extraordinary Circumstances: Oswald landed a job at the Gorizont Electronics Factory in Minsk, where he worked assembling televisions. Far from the ideological work he might have envisioned, his job was routine and unremarkable, a stark contrast to his grandiose expectations of contributing to the communist cause.

COMMISSION EXHIBIT No. 1392

- **Modest Living under Scrutiny:** Oswald's life in Minsk was a far cry from the glamour or intrigue one might associate with a defector's life. He lived in a simple, government-provided apartment

However, this apparent normalcy was underscored by constant surveillance. The KGB kept a close eye on him, monitoring his interactions and movements—a common practice for foreigners in the Soviet Union, especially defectors.

- **Cultural and Social Challenges:** Adjusting to life in the Soviet Union was not smooth sailing for Oswald. He struggled with the language barrier, cultural differences, and the general dreariness of Soviet life. Oswald often found himself isolated, unable to fully integrate into Soviet society or find like-minded individuals.

- **Disillusionment Sets In:** The reality of living in the Soviet Union soon clashed with Oswald's idealistic views. He became increasingly disenchanted with the monotonous lifestyle, the lack of personal freedoms, and the pervasive bureaucracy of the Soviet system. The utopia he had imagined was nowhere to be found.

- **A Love Story in the Cold War:** Amidst this backdrop, Oswald met Marina Prusakova, a pharmacy worker, at a dance hall. Their courtship was swift, and they married within six weeks of meeting. Their relationship offered a personal dimension to Oswald's life in the USSR, a humanizing contrast to his political disillusionment.

- **The Mundane and the Absurd:** Oswald's life was filled with the everyday mundanity of work, home life, and occasional interactions with neighbors and colleagues. However, this ordinariness was punctuated by moments of absurdity, such as his awkward attempts to discuss Marxism with factory workers or his naive efforts to navigate the complexities of Soviet life.

In essence, Oswald's time in the Soviet Union was a chapter of unfulfilled expectations and growing disenchantment, wrapped in the irony of an American seeking a communist haven only to find himself longing for home. This paradoxical experience adds a layer of tragicomedy to the narrative of a man who would later return to the United States and become a central figure in one of its most tragic events. Remember: while you may never need to know the minutiae of Oswald's Soviet sojourn, his tale serves as a curious anecdote in the mosaic of Cold War history, illustrating the complexities and sometimes absurdities of life behind the Iron Curtain.

Return to the United States

- In a twist of fate, Oswald's fascination with the Soviet lifestyle waned, and he sought to return to the United States. In 1961, he came back to America with his Soviet wife, Marina, and their daughter.
- His return raised eyebrows and questions, but he managed to slip back into American life relatively unnoticed until that fateful day in Dallas in 1963.

In conclusion, Lee Harvey Oswald's Soviet adventure stands as a unique and bizarre chapter in the annals of Cold War history. His journey from an American Marine to a Soviet defector, and back to a notorious figure in American history, is a path few, if any, have ever taken or would even consider. His experiences in the USSR, marked by disillusionment and the stark reality of life under a regime he once idealized, highlight the complexities of seeking utopia in a fundamentally different world.

Oswald's story is a vivid reminder of the unpredictable courses our lives can take, and the sometimes vast gulf between our dreams and reality. It serves as a peculiar footnote in history, a testament to the lengths individuals will go in search of their ideals, only to find themselves confronting a very different truth. Remember: while **you may never need to know** the intricate details of Oswald's life in the Soviet Union, his unusual journey offers a unique perspective on the human quest for belonging and the often unexpected outcomes of our most fervent pursuits.

77. The Ha Giang Loop

Nestled in the remote northern reaches of Vietnam, the Ha Giang Loop is a breathtaking journey through a landscape that seems to defy reality. This route, winding through the Ha Giang province, is more than just a road trip; it's an adventure into the heart of Vietnam's natural beauty and cultural richness.

Riding Through the Clouds

A Motorcyclist's Dream: The Ha Giang Loop is renowned among motorbike enthusiasts. The route, approximately 350 kilometers long, offers a thrilling ride with hairpin bends, steep inclines, and awe-inspiring vistas. It's a journey that tests skills and rewards with unparalleled scenic beauty.

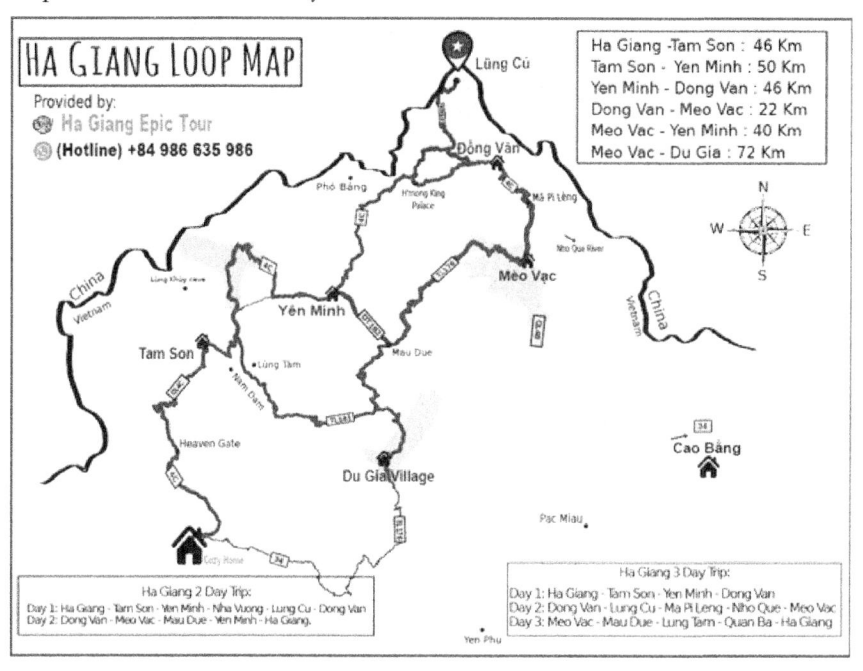

Travelers are treated to a visual feast: towering limestone karsts, deep canyons, verdant rice terraces, and rivers cutting through valleys. Each turn presents a view more spectacular than the last, often shrouded in mist, adding to the mystique.

What to Expect and How to Dodge the Grim Reaper

- Ha Giang is like a live exhibit of Vietnam's cultural tapestry. You'll encounter the Hmong, known for their vibrant clothing and indomitable spirit; the Tay, with their stilt houses and rice wine; and the Dao, whose red headscarves could give any fashionista a run for their money.

- Picture yourself in a local village, where the roosters are your wake-up call and life moves at the pace of a leisurely stroll. Here, Wi-Fi is replaced by real connections with locals, offering a crash course in cultural diversity – no textbook needed!
- Imagine bunking in a traditional house, where the only Netflix is the live performance of local dances and the only 'chill' comes from the mountain air. It's like camping, but with actual beds and way more cultural immersion.
- The local markets are a carnival of colors and smells. You'll find everything from handcrafted souvenirs to mysterious local delicacies that challenge your culinary bravery. It's like a treasure hunt, except the treasure might just be an exotic fruit or a hand-woven scarf.
- The loop's roads are not your average highways. They come with hairpin bends and jaw-dropping cliffs. It's like a rollercoaster, except you're the driver, and there's no safety harness. Tip: Honk on blind corners to alert your fellow road adventurers – it's like a secret handshake but louder.
- The weather can be as unpredictable as a plot twist in a telenovela. One moment it's sunshine and rainbows, the next it's a downpour. Packing a raincoat is like bringing an umbrella to a water fight – not entirely effective, but it's the thought that counts.

The Ha Giang Loop is a rollercoaster of cultural wonders and adrenaline-pumping roads. It's a journey that will test your mettle, broaden your horizons, and maybe even make you a pro at dodging chickens on a motorbike. Just remember, as you soak in the sights and sounds of this vibrant region, stay alert, embrace the unexpected, and always travel responsibly.

After all, while you may never need to know how to navigate a hairpin bend while a herd of goats crosses the road, isn't it a thrilling story to share? Remember: **you may never need to know** all the quirks and challenges of the Ha Giang Loop, but conquering it could be one of your most memorable adventures. PS. You can hire your own driver, this may just save your life!

78. The Puzzle of the Antikythera Mechanism

Dive deep into the world of ancient mysteries with the Antikythera Mechanism, a device that has baffled historians and scientists alike. This intricate contraption, unearthed from a shipwreck off the Greek island of Antikythera, is like a puzzle box crafted by time itself.

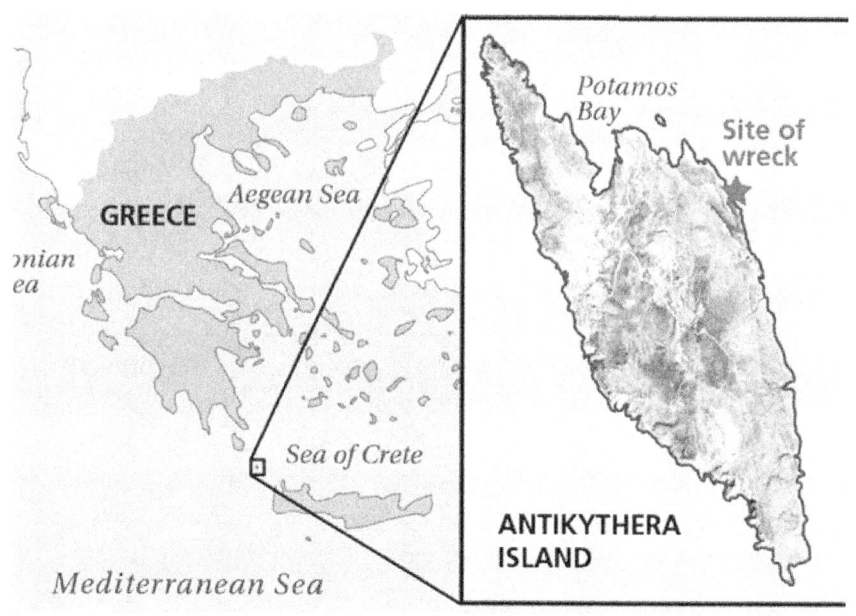

An Ancient Greek Enigma

Picture this – it's 1901, and divers off the coast of Antikythera stumble upon a shipwreck. Among the treasures, they find a corroded chunk of metal that turns out to be the world's first analog computer. Yes, the Greeks had tech support!

A Clockwork Orange, but Older: The mechanism, dating back to around 100 BC, is a complex assembly of gears and inscriptions. It's like finding a MacBook in Ancient Rome – mind-blowing and a tad confusing.

This ancient gadget could predict eclipses, track the paths of planets, and even tell your horoscope – all without needing to update its software.

- **The Google Calendar of Antiquity:** The mechanism was used to mark significant events like the Olympics. It was essentially a calendar, but with more gears and less syncing issues.
- The sophistication of the Antikythera Mechanism suggests that ancient Greek technology was way ahead of its time. It's like finding out your great-grandfather was coding apps in the 1920s.
- Some theorize that such technology was not uncommon in the ancient world, but much of this knowledge was lost over time. It's like history had a hard drive failure, and the Antikythera Mechanism is one of the few files that wasn't corrupted.

The Antikythera Mechanism continues to be a source of fascination and curiosity. It's a reminder of the ingenuity of our ancestors and a testament to the mysteries that still lie buried in the depths of history. And while **you may never need to know** the inner workings of this ancient Greek puzzle, it certainly adds a bit of intrigue to the narrative of human innovation. After all, who needs time travel when you've got relics like the Antikythera Mechanism unveiling the past's secrets?

79. Tupac in Puerto Rico

The idea of Tupac Shakur hiding out in Puerto Rico is one of the many conspiracy theories that have emerged since his untimely death in 1996. Tupac, a legendary rapper and a central figure in the East Coast-West Coast hip hop rivalry, was tragically killed in a drive-by shooting in Las Vegas. His murder has remained unsolved, fueling endless speculation and rumors about the circumstances surrounding his death.

The Conspiracy: Some Tupac fans refuse to believe that he actually died. Instead, they speculate that he faked his own death to escape the spotlight and his enemies, and subsequently fled to Puerto Rico. Why Puerto Rico? Perhaps because it's a beautiful island that's a bit off the radar yet still under U.S. jurisdiction.

- Sightings and Rumors: Over the years, there have been numerous alleged sightings of Tupac in Puerto Rico. These reports often come with blurry photos or vague anecdotes, none of which have been substantiated.

Tupac wasn't just a rapper; he was a poet, an actor, and a vocal social commentator. His lyrics, often laced with the harsh realities of life, police brutality, racial inequality, and his own personal struggles, resonated with a generation.

He was seen as a spokesperson for the disenfranchised, giving a voice to those who felt unheard. His songs like "Changes" and "Keep Ya Head Up" continue to inspire and influence not just musicians but activists and individuals seeking change.

The Death That Echoed

- **End of an Era:** Tupac's death, under the neon lights of Las Vegas, marked the end of an era in hip hop and ignited widespread debate and theories. It was a death that seemed almost cinematic, yet tragically real.
- **Unsolved Mystery:** The lack of resolution in his murder case has only added to his mystique and the plethora of conspiracy theories that have emerged, including the Puerto Rico theory.

Why Puerto Rico is a Popular Choice for Celebrity Hideouts: Island of the Stars

Puerto Rico, with its blend of tropical allure, cultural richness, and unique status, has become a speculative haven for celebrities seeking to escape the limelight or for those rumored to be in hiding. But why Puerto Rico? Let's explore some fascinating reasons and facts that make this island a popular choice for such celebrity theories.

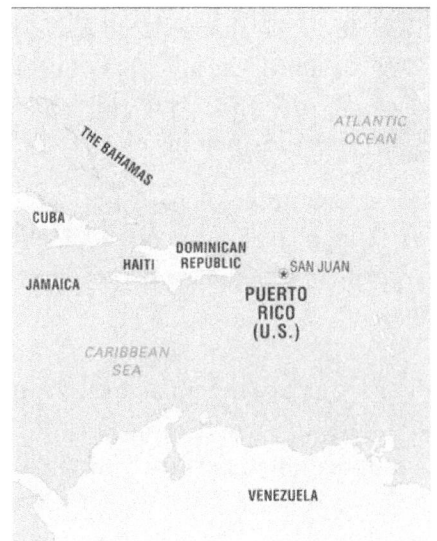

U.S. Territory with a Twist:
- **No Passport Needed:** As a U.S. territory, American celebrities can travel to and from Puerto Rico without a passport. It offers an escape without the hassle of international travel.
- **Privacy Laws:** Puerto Rico has stringent privacy laws, making it an appealing destination for those seeking to avoid paparazzi and public scrutiny.

The Perfect Blend of Isolation and Connectivity:
- Island Seclusion: The island's geography offers seclusion and the possibility of living away from the public eye, perfect for those seeking privacy.

A Vibrant Yet Laid-back Lifestyle:
- Cultural Richness: Puerto Rico is known for its rich culture, lively music, delicious cuisine, and friendly locals – a welcoming environment for anyone.
- Relaxed Pace: The island's laid-back lifestyle is a stark contrast to the fast-paced life many celebrities are accustomed to in places like Los Angeles or New York.

The Tax Haven Advantage:
- Tax Incentives: Puerto Rico offers significant tax incentives, particularly for U.S. citizens who become residents of the territory, making it financially attractive.

Beautiful Scenery and Luxury Living:
- Natural Beauty: With its stunning beaches, lush rainforests, and charming colonial architecture, Puerto Rico is an idyllic backdrop for relaxation and rejuvenation.
- Luxury Accommodations: The island boasts high-end resorts and private villas that cater to the rich and famous, offering luxury and exclusivity.

The Reality Check

- Despite the intrigue and the plethora of theories, there is no concrete evidence to support the claim that Tupac is alive and kicking it in Puerto Rico. The rumors are just that – rumors.
- Tupac's impact on music and culture is undeniable, and his legacy continues to influence artists and fans alike. Perhaps it's this profound impact that makes some fans cling to the hope that he's still out there.

Continuing Legacy

- Posthumous Releases: Tupac's legacy continued to grow after his death, with the release of several albums that he had recorded before his passing. These posthumous releases have kept his voice and message alive in the world of hip hop and beyond.

- **Inspirational Figure:** Tupac's influence extends beyond music. He has been the subject of documentaries, movies, and academic studies, examining his impact on culture, music, and the African American experience.

The theory of Tupac living a low-key life in Puerto Rico is a testament to his enduring legacy and the difficulty many have in accepting his death. While it's a captivating narrative, it remains in the realm of urban legends and hip hop folklore. Remember: you may never need to know the truth behind every Tupac conspiracy theory, but his music and influence continue to resonate, proving that legends never really die.

80. From Trenches to Middle-earth: J.R.R. Tolkien's Journey

J.R.R. Tolkien's "The Hobbit" is not just a cornerstone of modern fantasy literature; it's a window into the author's soul, shaped by the harrowing experiences of his youth. This section explores how the horrors of World War I influenced Tolkien's creation of Middle-earth, weaving his real-life battles into a timeless tale of adventure and resilience.

"The Hobbit" tells the story of Bilbo Baggins, a reluctant hero drawn into a quest to reclaim a lost dwarf kingdom from the fearsome dragon Smaug. Alongside a band of dwarves and the wizard Gandalf, Bilbo's journey is one of self-discovery, courage, and the forging of unlikely friendships.

This novel laid the groundwork for Tolkien's subsequent epic, "The Lord of the Rings". It captivated readers with its richly crafted world, leading to a successful franchise of movies that brought Middle-earth to life for a new generation.

J.R.R. Tolkien: The Man Behind the Myth

- **Early Life and Love of Language:** Born in 1892, Tolkien's early fascination with languages and myths set the stage for his future creations. His academic prowess in philology, the study of languages, deeply influenced his writing.
- **The Scars of War:** Tolkien's participation in the Battle of the Somme during World War I was a turning point. The brutality and loss he witnessed profoundly impacted him, stripping away his youthful innocence and bringing a somber depth to his view of the world.
- **Echoes of the Trenches:** In the muddy trenches of the Somme, amidst the chaos and despair, Tolkien began crafting the mythology of Middle-earth. The themes of friendship, sacrifice, and the struggle against overwhelming darkness in "The Hobbit" and "The Lord of the Rings" are reflective of his war experiences.
- **From Despair to Hope:** Tolkien's works transcend mere escapism. They represent a journey from the depths of despair to the possibility of hope and redemption, mirroring his own journey from the battlefields back to the tranquility of academic life.

This novel laid the groundwork for Tolkien's subsequent epic, "The Lord of the Rings". It captivated readers with its richly crafted world, leading to a successful franchise of movies that brought Middle-earth to life for a new generation.

- **Oxford Scholar:** Tolkien's academic career was rooted in Oxford, where he studied and later became a professor. His love for languages, particularly Old English and Finnish, influenced the creation of the Elvish languages in his books.
- **Inklings Group:** Tolkien was a member of the Inklings, an informal Oxford literary group. This group, which included C.S. Lewis, provided a supportive environment for discussing their works, including early versions of "The Lord of the Rings."
- **Enlistment and Service:** Tolkien voluntarily enlisted in the British Army in 1915. He served as a lieutenant in the Lancashire Fusiliers and was eventually dispatched to the Western Front.
- **The Battle of the Somme:** Tolkien's participation in the Battle of the Somme, one of the war's bloodiest conflicts, deeply affected him. The loss of close friends and the horrors of war significantly influenced his perspective on life and death, themes heavily explored in his writings.
- **Hospitalization and Writing:** Contracting trench fever, Tolkien was sent back to England in 1916. During his recovery, he began working on what would become the foundational texts of his Middle-earth legendarium.
- **Return to Academia:** After the war, Tolkien returned to academia. His scholarly work, especially in mythology and philology, continued to influence his writing.

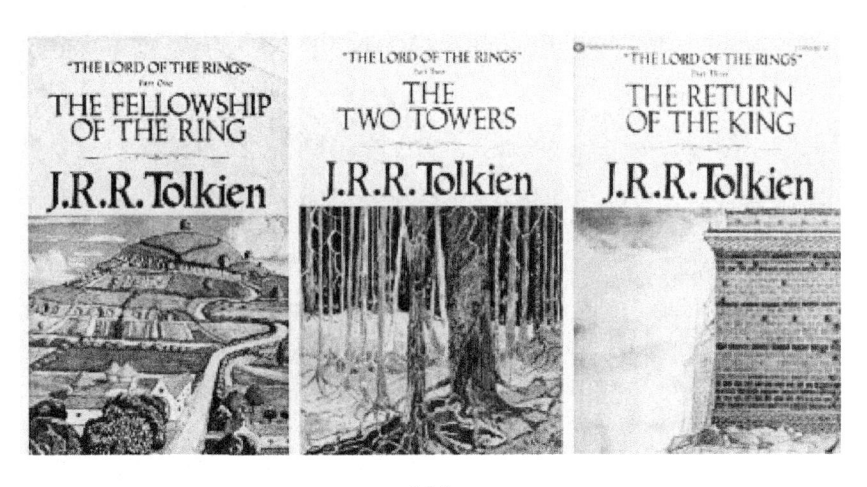

- **Creation of Middle-earth:** The mythology of Middle-earth was a project that spanned Tolkien's entire life. He began constructing its elaborate history, languages, and mythology as early as 1917.
- **"The Hobbit" and "The Lord of the Rings":** "The Hobbit," published in 1937, was initially written as a story for his children. Its success led to the writing of "The Lord of the Rings," which was published in three volumes between 1954 and 1955. These works revolutionized the fantasy genre and are considered some of the best-selling books ever written.
- **Family Man:** Tolkien was a devoted family man. He married Edith Bratt in 1916, and they had four children. His deep affection for Edith inspired the characters of Beren and Lúthien, a love story woven into the fabric of Middle-earth.
- **Lasting Impact:** Tolkien's influence on literature, popular culture, and even language studies is immense. His works have spawned movies, video games, and a vast array of merchandise, ensuring his legacy endures.

The Lasting Legacy of Tolkien's War

While **you may never need to know** the intricate details of Tolkien's life or the horrors of World War I, understanding this backdrop adds a layer of depth to the world of Middle-earth. Tolkien's personal battles gave birth to a world that continues to inspire and resonate with readers and viewers alike, offering a powerful testament to the human spirit's capacity for creativity in the face of darkness.

81. We Didn't Start the Fire

Billy Joel's "We Didn't Start the Fire" is more than just a catchy tune; it's a historical journey set to music. Released in 1989, the song remains a unique piece of cultural commentary, encapsulating the tumultuous journey of the latter half of the 20th century. Here's a deeper look into the song, its impact, and the inspiration behind its creation.

Decades of History: The song's lyrics are a rapid-fire enumeration of notable events, figures, and cultural phenomena from 1949 (Joel's birth year) to 1989. It covers a wide range of topics from the Cold War, civil rights movements, space exploration, to pop culture icons.

Surprisingly, "We Didn't Start the Fire" has been used in educational settings as a novel way to teach post-World War II history, encouraging students to explore the events mentioned in the song.

The song resonated with listeners who had lived through the decades it covered, serving as a reminder of how much had occurred in just 40 years.

While the song was a commercial success, critics were divided. Some praised its catchiness and historical references, while others critiqued it for its rapid pacing and surface-level treatment of complex events.

The song resonated with listeners who had lived through the decades it covered, serving as a reminder of how much had occurred in just 40 years.

While the song was a commercial success, critics were divided. Some praised its catchiness and historical references, while others critiqued it for its rapid pacing and surface-level treatment of complex events.

Billy Joel was inspired to write the song after a conversation with a younger person who was unaware of many historical events. Joel realized the breadth of change he had witnessed in his lifetime and decided to condense it into a song.

Crafting the lyrics was a challenge due to the vast amount of history Joel wanted to include. The song's structure required fitting these events into a rhythmic and rhyming format without losing their essence.

- **"Harry Truman, Doris Day, Red China, Johnnie Ray"**: This line from the beginning of the song mentions U.S. President Harry Truman, singer-actress Doris Day, the rise of Communist China under Mao Zedong (referred to as "Red China"), and popular 50s singer Johnnie Ray.
- **"Joe McCarthy, Richard Nixon, Studebaker, television"**: This snippet refers to Senator Joseph McCarthy, known for his anti-communist pursuits, U.S. President Richard Nixon, the Studebaker automobile company, and the emergence of television as a mass medium.
- **"North Korea, South Korea, Marilyn Monroe"**: These lyrics touch upon the Korean War that resulted in the division of Korea into North and South, and the iconic status of actress Marilyn Monroe.
- **"Einstein, James Dean, Brooklyn's got a winning team"**: Albert Einstein, iconic actor James Dean, and a nod to the Brooklyn Dodgers' success in baseball are covered here.
- **"Hemingway, Eichmann, Stranger in a Strange Land"**: References to author Ernest Hemingway, Nazi war criminal Adolf Eichmann, and Robert A. Heinlein's science fiction novel "Stranger in a Strange Land."

Song's Legacy

Enduring Popularity: "We Didn't Start the Fire" remains popular, often played on radio and in pop culture references. It's seen as a snapshot of an era, capturing the spirit of the late 20th century.

A Launchpad for Discussion: The song continues to spark conversations about history and the events that shape our world. It encourages listeners to reflect on how these events are interconnected and how they've shaped the current socio-political landscape.

These excerpts provide a glimpse into how the song weaves together diverse strands of history, culture, and politics, capturing the essence of several decades in a compact, musical format. Remember, while **you may never need to know** all the cultural and historical references in "We Didn't Start the Fire," the song remains a fascinating time capsule of the mid-20th century.

82. Belgians in the Congo

One of the many historical references in Billy Joel's song "We Didn't Start the Fire" is "Belgians in the Congo," which alludes to a significant and dark period in African and European colonial history. This phrase encapsulates the complex and often brutal relationship between Belgium and the Congo, a Central African region.

Colonial Rule and Exploitation:

The Congo Free State was established in the late 19th century by King Leopold II of Belgium. Initially portrayed as a humanitarian project, it quickly turned into a brutal regime of exploitation.

- The primary motive for colonization was the extraction of resources, particularly rubber, which became highly valuable with the rise of the automobile industry. Congolese laborers were forced to harvest rubber under inhumane conditions.
- King Leopold II of Belgium, driven by a desire for wealth and international prestige, sought to establish a personal empire. Unlike other European colonies in Africa, the Congo Free State was the private property of King Leopold, not the state of Belgium.
- Leopold initially portrayed his venture as a philanthropic and civilizing mission, part of the broader European rhetoric of the "White Man's Burden." This facade, however, thinly veiled his true intentions of economic exploitation.
- Scramble for Africa: The late 19th century was the height of the "Scramble for Africa," where European powers were rapidly colonizing African territories. Belgium, relatively smaller and less powerful, saw an opportunity in the Congo to establish its presence on the global stage.

- Berlin Conference: The Congo Free State was formally recognized at the Berlin Conference (1884-1885), a meeting where European powers divided Africa among themselves with little regard for indigenous populations.
- Rubber Boom: The global demand for rubber, fueled by the burgeoning automobile industry and the need for rubber tires, made the Congo's natural rubber resources extremely valuable.
- Forced Labor and Quotas: Congolese natives were forced into labor to extract rubber. Leopold's regime set up a brutal system of quotas and forced collection, leading to widespread abuse and suffering.
- Autocratic Control: King Leopold ruled the Congo Free State as an autocrat, with direct control over the administration and economic activities.
- Use of Force: The Force Publique, a military force in the Congo, was used to enforce labor policies, suppress resistance, and punish those who failed to meet rubber quotas.
- **Human Rights Abuses:** The exploitation led to horrific human rights abuses - including killings, mutilations, and destruction of villages.
- **Population Decline:** It is estimated that millions of Congolese people died due to disease, famine, and violence during this period.

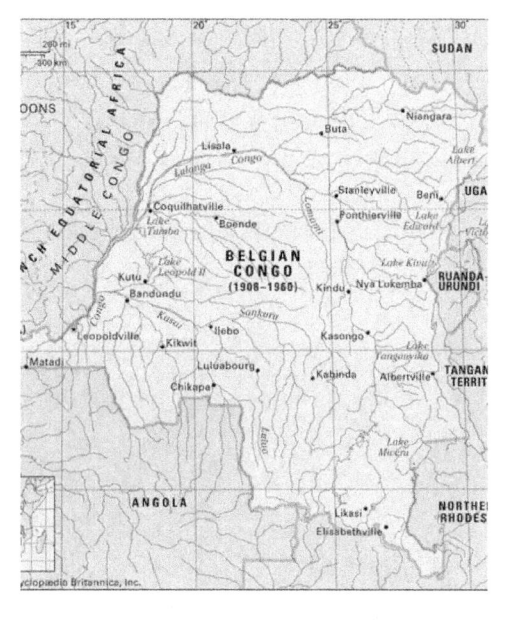

International Criticism and the End of Leopold's Rule: The Fall of the Congo Free State

As the atrocities in the Congo Free State began to surface, international criticism mounted, leading to a significant shift in the fate of the colony. The unraveling of King Leopold II's control over the Congo was a complex process influenced by global politics, humanitarian outcry, and the shifting tides of the early 20th century.

The Whistleblowers:

- **Reports from Missionaries and Insiders:** The initial reports of the brutal exploitation and inhuman treatment of the Congolese people were brought to light by missionaries and former officials working in the Congo. These individuals, appalled by the horrors they witnessed, began to document and report the abuses.

- **E.D. Morel's Role:** One of the most significant figures in exposing the reality of the Congo Free State was E.D. Morel, a British journalist and shipping clerk. Morel noticed a disturbing pattern in the cargo ships traveling between the Congo and Belgium: they arrived in Africa loaded with military equipment and returned filled with valuable rubber and ivory, but no trade goods exchanged. This led him to conclude that the only explanation was the exploitation of the Congolese people as forced labor.

The International Response:

- Rising Humanitarian Outcry: As Morel and others began to publicize the situation, a global humanitarian campaign emerged. This movement gained traction in Europe and the United States, putting pressure on the Belgian government and King Leopold II. The movement attracted a wide range of supporters, from political figures to famous authors like Sir Arthur Conan Doyle, who wrote "The Crime of the Congo" in 1909.

The Casement Report: In 1904, the British government commissioned Roger Casement, the British consul in the Congo, to investigate the situation. His report, published in 1905, detailed the brutal exploitation, forced labor, and rampant abuse in the colony. The Casement Report was instrumental in galvanizing public opinion against the Congo Free State.

The End of Leopold's Rule:

Forced Transfer of Power: The international pressure and mounting evidence of atrocities eventually forced King Leopold II to relinquish control of the Congo Free State. In 1908, the Belgian parliament, responding to both the international outcry and the moral implications of the reports, annexed the territory, turning it into a Belgian colony. This marked the end of Leopold's personal rule, though the legacy of his brutal regime would continue to affect the region for decades to come.

The transition from the Congo Free State to a Belgian colony did not immediately end the suffering of the Congolese people, but it did bring a close to one of the most egregious episodes of colonial exploitation.

CIA Involvement in the Congo during the Cold War

The story of the Congo after its transition from a personal fiefdom to a Belgian colony takes another intriguing turn with the involvement of the CIA during the Cold War era. This period marked a new chapter in the Congo's history, intertwined with global politics and espionage.

After gaining independence from Belgium in 1960, the Congo plunged into a period of political instability and conflict, known as the Congo Crisis. This period was characterized by regional conflicts, a struggle for power, and the involvement of various foreign powers, including the United States and the Soviet Union.

Patrice Lumumba's Rise and Assassination: One of the central figures during this period was Patrice Lumumba, the first democratically elected Prime Minister of the Congo. Lumumba's socialist leanings and perceived pro-Soviet stance alarmed the United States, which was deeply entrenched in the Cold War with the Soviet Union. His advocacy for complete independence and control over the country's resources was seen as a threat to Western interests.

The CIA's Covert Operations: The CIA, under the directive of the Eisenhower administration, became actively involved in the political landscape of the Congo.

Documents declassified years later revealed that the CIA had a hand in the plotting and execution of Lumumba's assassination in 1961, fearing that a Lumumba-led Congo would align with the Soviet bloc.

Supporting Mobutu Sese Seko: Following Lumumba's assassination, the CIA threw its support behind Mobutu Sese Seko, who would later become the military dictator of the country. Mobutu's anti-communist stance made him a favorable ally for the United States in the region.

Long-Term Impact: The CIA's involvement in the Congo set the stage for decades of dictatorship under Mobutu, who ruled the country (renamed Zaire) with an iron fist until 1997. The legacy of this intervention has had lasting impacts on the political and social fabric of the Congo, contributing to ongoing instability and conflict.

Remember, while **you may never need to know** the intricate details of this transition, the events that led to the end of Leopold's rule in the Congo highlight the power of international advocacy and the importance of ethical responsibility in global affairs.

83. The Enigma of the Toynbee Tiles

Delving into one of the urban landscape's most mystifying puzzles, the Toynbee Tiles are a phenomenon as enigmatic as they are fascinating. Scattered across more than two dozen cities in the United States and several South American countries, these peculiar tiles embed cryptic messages into the very fabric of the streets.

The first appearance of a Toynbee Tile dates back to the early 1980s, marking the beginning of one of the most intriguing urban mysteries. These tiles, often embedded into street asphalt, caught the public's eye not just for their unexpected placement but for their peculiar messages.

Inscribed with phrases like **"TOYNBEE IDEA IN MOVIE '2001 RESURRECT DEAD ON PLANET JUPITER,"** these tiles were initially met with curiosity and confusion. They seemed to pop up overnight, embedding themselves into the daily landscape of city dwellers.

A Widespread Phenomenon:

The tiles were not confined to a single location. Over time, their presence was noted in various major cities, turning a local oddity into a widespread phenomenon. Notable urban centers where the tiles were found include:

- **Philadelphia**: Often considered the epicenter of the Toynbee Tiles, Philadelphia's streets have housed numerous tiles, each varying slightly in wording and design. The city's residents and local media were among the first to notice and report on these mysterious installations.

- **New York City:** The bustling streets of New York City also became a canvas for the Toynbee message. Here, the tiles were found in busy intersections, often leading to public intrigue and media coverage, as pedestrians and commuters pondered their origin and meaning.
- **International Reach:** The phenomenon wasn't just an American curiosity. Far-flung cities like Buenos Aires and Rio de Janeiro reported sightings of these cryptic tiles, indicating a reach that extended beyond the United States. In these international locales, the tiles sparked conversations about global art movements and cross-cultural mysteries.

Public Reaction and Interpretations

For many city residents and visitors, the tiles were a source of intrigue and speculation. People would often stop to read and discuss the inscriptions, pondering their possible meanings.

- The cryptic nature of the message led to numerous theories. Some speculated a connection to historian Arnold Toynbee and Stanley Kubrick's "2001: A Space Odyssey," interpreting the message as a call for human resurrection on Jupiter.

- In the art and academic communities, the tiles were sometimes discussed in the context of guerrilla art and urban expression. They were seen as a unique form of street art, provoking discussions about the boundaries of public art and the use of urban spaces as mediums for expression.

The Human Resurrection on Jupiter

- The intriguing link between the Toynbee Tiles and the historian Arnold Toynbee, alongside Stanley Kubrick's iconic film "2001: A Space Odyssey," forms a key part of the tiles' enigma. To understand this connection, one needs to delve into the works of Toynbee and the thematic elements of Kubrick's film.
- Arnold Toynbee, a British historian, was renowned for his 12-volume analysis of the rise and fall of civilizations, titled "A Study of History." Toynbee's work explored the patterns of growth, decay, and renewal within civilizations, providing a comprehensive look at human history and its cyclical nature. One of his central ideas was the concept of "challenge and response," where a civilization's ability to respond to challenges determined its success or failure. Toynbee's work also touched upon the spiritual and philosophical aspects of human life, pondering the potential of human achievement and transformation.

Stanley Kubrick's "2001: A Space Odyssey," released in 1968, is a cinematic masterpiece that explores themes of human evolution, technology, and extraterrestrial life. The film is famous for its enigmatic narrative and groundbreaking visual effects. It begins with the dawn of man and follows the journey of humanity from the discovery of a mysterious monolith that seems to trigger a leap in human evolution. The film culminates in a journey to Jupiter, where the protagonist experiences a transformative odyssey through time and space, leading to a rebirth-like conclusion.

The connection between the Toynbee Tiles and these two cultural artifacts lies in their shared exploration of human evolution and potential. The phrase on the tiles, **"TOYNBEE IDEA IN MOVIE `2001 RESURRECT DEAD ON PLANET JUPITER,"** appears to combine Toynbee's theories of civilization cycles and spiritual evolution with the transcendent themes of Kubrick's film. It suggests a belief or hope in the potential for human rebirth or resurrection, perhaps on a cosmic scale, as implied in "2001: A Space Odyssey."

This fusion of Toynbee's historical and philosophical ideas with the sci-fi elements of Kubrick's film creates a unique and compelling narrative. The tiles may be interpreted as a call to humanity, urging a collective evolution or transformation akin to the leaps depicted in both Toynbee's work and Kubrick's film. The specific reference to Jupiter in both the movie and the tiles further deepens this connection, implying a cosmic dimension to this proposed human resurrection or rebirth.

Remember: while **you may never need to know** the exact purpose or creator of the Toynbee Tiles, their presence invites us to consider the larger mysteries of our world and the ways in which they manifest in our everyday surroundings.

84. The Legend of the Mothman: A Tale from West Virginia

In the annals of American folklore, few creatures are as enigmatic and spine-tingling as the Mothman, a legendary entity that has captured imaginations and fueled nightmares. This winged, red-eyed figure first made its presence known in the small town of Point Pleasant, West Virginia, and since then, it has become a cryptid of considerable intrigue and speculation.

The First Sightings

The Mothman saga began in November 1966. According to reports, a group of gravediggers working near Clendenin, West Virginia, were the first to witness this bizarre creature. They described a man-like figure gliding low over their heads, silent and swift.

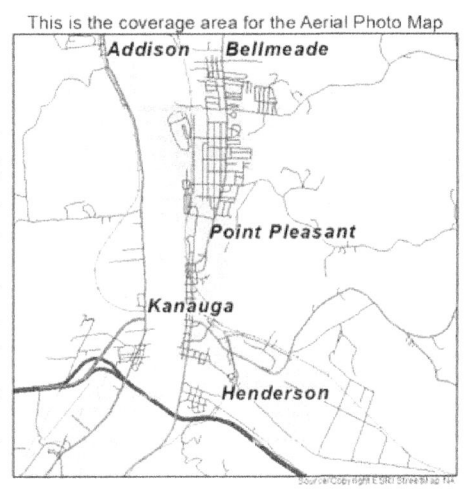

But it was in Point Pleasant where the Mothman legend truly took flight. Over the next year, more than a hundred sightings were reported in the area, describing a large, humanoid creature with massive wings and glowing red eyes.

The Silver Bridge Collapse

Adding to the Mothman's mystique is its association with the tragic collapse of the Silver Bridge on December 15, 1967. The bridge, connecting Point Pleasant to Ohio, suddenly gave way during rush hour, plunging vehicles and passengers into the icy river below, resulting in the loss of 46 lives. This catastrophe, occurring just over a year after the first Mothman sighting, led to speculation that the creature was either an omen or directly linked to the disaster.

The Mothman Festival: A Celebration of the Cryptid and Community

Nestled in the heart of Point Pleasant, West Virginia, the Mothman Festival has become an annual event that not only commemorates the legendary Mothman sightings but also celebrates the unique culture and history of the town. This festival, which started modestly, has grown into a significant event, drawing enthusiasts of the paranormal, folklore, and cryptozoology, as well as those simply seeking an unusual and entertaining experience.

The Mothman Festival was first organized in 2002, largely inspired by the growing interest in the Mothman legend following the release of "The Mothman Prophecies" film. The festival began as a small, community-focused event but quickly gained traction, attracting visitors from across the country and even overseas. What started as a one-day event has expanded into a weekend-long celebration, usually held in the third weekend of September.

The festival offers a range of activities that cater to all ages and interests. Highlights include guest speakers and authors who delve into the mysteries of the Mothman and other paranormal phenomena. Guided bus tours take visitors to notable locations from the Mothman legend, including the TNT area, the site of the former munitions plant where many of the initial sightings occurred. Vendors line the streets, selling a wide array of Mothman merchandise, from T-shirts and posters to more unique handmade crafts.

A centerpiece of the festival is the Mothman Museum, which houses an extensive collection of memorabilia, newspaper clippings, and artifacts related to the Mothman sightings and the Silver Bridge disaster. The museum not only provides a historical context to the legend but also offers an immersive experience for those keen to learn more about this enigmatic figure.

Beyond the lure of the supernatural, the Mothman Festival has become an important event for the community of Point Pleasant. It has helped to revitalize the town, bringing in tourism revenue and fostering a sense of pride and identity among the residents. For many in Point Pleasant, the festival is more than just a celebration of a local legend; it's a testament to the town's resilience and ability to find creative ways to tell its story and engage with visitors from around the world.

The Mothman's story reached a wider audience with the 2002 release of "The Mothman Prophecies," a film loosely based on the 1975 book of the same name by John Keel. The film, starring Richard Gere, brought the legend into the living rooms of millions, further cementing the Mothman's place in popular culture.

Despite its mythical status, skeptics and scientists have offered more earthly explanations for the Mothman sightings. Some suggest that the figure was actually a large bird, such as a sandhill crane or an owl, misidentified in the low light conditions. Others propose that mass hysteria played a role in the spread of the Mothman legend.

The Mothman remains a compelling figure in the world of cryptozoology and American folklore. Whether as a misunderstood animal, a supernatural harbinger, or a product of collective imagination, the Mothman continues to fascinate and haunt those who delve into its story. Remember, while **you may never need to know** the truth behind the Mothman, its legend offers a fascinating glimpse into the mysteries that can capture and hold our collective attention.

85. The Mysterious Hum of Taos, New Mexico

In the tranquil and artistic town of Taos, New Mexico, a peculiar mystery has resonated for years. It's known as the "Taos Hum," a low-frequency sound heard by a small percentage of the town's residents, creating intrigue and bafflement among locals and scientists alike.

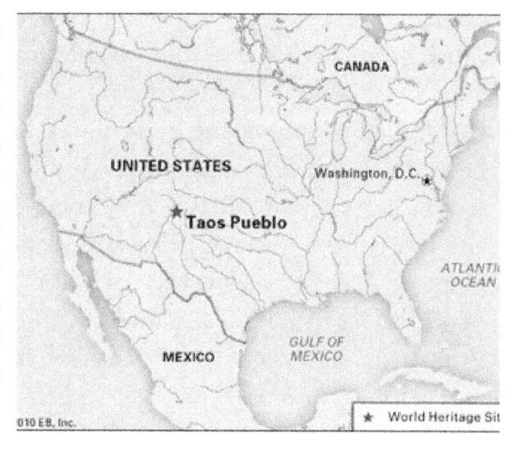

An Elusive and Enigmatic Sound

The Taos Hum first caught public attention in the early 1990s when residents began reporting a persistent and unexplainable low-frequency humming noise. Unlike typical environmental sounds, this hum seemed selective, heard only by a fraction of the population, a phenomenon known as "sensory gating."

Those who can hear the Taos Hum describe it as a distant, low-pitched drone, akin to the sound of a diesel engine idling in the distance. For many, it's just a minor nuisance, but for some, it becomes an overwhelming presence, affecting their quality of life and leading to frustration and discomfort.

Scientific Investigations and Theories

Intrigued by this auditory enigma, researchers have conducted numerous studies to uncover its origin. Explanations range from mundane to the extraordinary - from industrial equipment and electrical power lines to more esoteric theories involving underground UFO bases or secret government experiments. However, despite various investigations, including those by Sandia National Laboratories and the University of New Mexico, the source of the Taos Hum remains a mystery.

The Taos Hum has become part of the local lore, adding to the town's mystical allure. Taos, known for its artistic community and spiritual retreats, has embraced this enigma, seeing it as yet another layer to its cultural and historical tapestry. The Hum has inspired artworks, documentaries, and even music compositions, as artists attempt to capture and interpret this auditory mystery.

While the Taos Hum is one of the most famous, it's just a piece of a global puzzle of unexplained low-frequency noises. These mysterious sounds, often referred to as "hums," have been reported in various places around the world, each with its unique characteristics and local lore.

The Bristol Hum, UK

- Origins: First reported in the 1970s, the Bristol Hum plagued residents of this English city with a relentless low-frequency noise.
- Characteristics: Described as a continuous drone or throbbing sound, it led to widespread discomfort and speculation.
- Public Reaction: The phenomenon garnered significant media attention and scientific interest, yet, like the Taos Hum, its origin remained elusive.

The Largs Hum, Scotland

- Discovery: Residents of Largs, a town in Scotland, have also reported a mysterious humming sound.
- Investigations: Despite various theories and investigations, no definitive source has been identified.
- Community Impact: The Largs Hum has been a subject of local interest, with community meetings and discussions about its possible causes and solutions.
-

Similar Cases Worldwide

- Worldwide Reports: Other locations reporting similar phenomena include Auckland (New Zealand), Windsor (Canada), and Kokomo (USA).
- Common Features: In many of these cases, only a small percentage of the population can hear the sound, and its source often remains unexplained despite investigations.

Community Bonding: In many cases, the hums have brought communities together in a shared experience, leading to collective efforts to understand and address the issue.

Remember, while you may never need to know every detail about these global hums, they represent a curious intersection of science, psychology, and community dynamics, echoing our innate desire to explain and connect with the mysterious aspects of our world.

86. The Enigmatic Life of Kaspar Hauser

Kaspar Hauser's story is a curious blend of mystery, tragedy, and intrigue, a riddle from the annals of 19th-century Europe. Found wandering the streets of Nuremberg in 1828, Hauser's origins and early life were shrouded in mystery and controversy, sparking widespread public fascination.

First Appearance: Hauser appeared in Nuremberg in 1828, a teenager with limited speech and a childlike demeanor.

His Claim: He claimed to have spent his entire life confined in a dark cell, with minimal human contact and understanding of the world.

When Kaspar Hauser stumbled into Nuremberg's town square, he captured the public's imagination like a character from a Gothic novel. His bizarre appearance and limited communication skills piqued curiosity and sympathy.

The tale of his alleged confinement in a darkened cell since childhood circulated rapidly, making him a subject of fascination and a symbol of innocence corrupted by cruelty.

Hauser's journey from an almost feral state to a more civilized existence was closely observed by the public. Under the care of kind-hearted individuals, he gradually acquired language and social skills.

His progress was seen as both a triumph of human resilience and a fascinating psychological case study, shedding light on the nature versus nurture debate that was gaining traction in scientific circles at the time.

Doubts and Debates: Hauser's narrative was not without its skeptics. Some observers noted discrepancies in his stories and questioned his motives. Was he a cunning impostor seeking fame and fortune, or a genuine victim of unimaginable cruelty? This debate split public opinion and added an element of intrigue to his already mysterious persona.

Noble Connections: The most sensational theory about Hauser's origins involved royal intrigue. Some speculated that he might be the rightful heir to the throne of Baden, hidden away to alter the line of succession. This theory gave his story a romantic and tragic hue, linking his fate to the high-stakes world of European nobility.

Contemporary interpretations of Hauser's behavior suggest possible psychological conditions. Was his story a fabrication stemming from a pathological need for attention, or were his odd behaviors the result of lifelong isolation and trauma? Psychologists today might view his case through the lens of mental health, considering conditions like dissociative disorders or the effects of severe social deprivation.

Untimely Death and Legacy

Hauser's life came to a tragic and abrupt end when he was found with a fatal stab wound. The circumstances of his death were as mysterious as his life, fueling further speculation and conspiracy theories. Did he die at the hands of those who sought to silence him, or was it a self-inflicted wound, a final act in a series of deceptions?

Kaspar Hauser's enigmatic story has resonated through the years, influencing various aspects of popular culture. One notable example is the 1974 film "The Enigma of Kaspar Hauser," directed by Werner Herzog.

This German film, also known as "Jeder für sich und Gott gegen alle" (Every Man for Himself and God Against All), is a poignant portrayal of Hauser's life. It delves into the mysteries surrounding him and presents a deeply humanistic view of his struggle to adapt to society after a life of isolation.

Herzog's film is considered a classic of world cinema, praised for its exploration of themes like identity, humanity, and the fine line between sanity and madness. The portrayal of Kaspar Hauser by actor Bruno S., himself a person with a troubled past, adds an additional layer of authenticity and emotional depth to the film. It's a must-watch for those interested in Hauser's story and its enduring impact on culture and art.

In the end, while **you may never need to know** the full truth about Kaspar Hauser, his story remains a captivating glimpse into the complexities of human nature and the enduring allure of a good mystery.

87. Churchill's Greatest Quotes

Winston Churchill, the British Prime Minister during World War II, is renowned not only for his leadership during one of the darkest periods in history but also for his powerful and inspiring rhetoric. Here are some of his most famous and impactful quotes:

- **"We shall fight on the beaches"**:

Is a phrase etched in history, immortalized by Winston Churchill in one of his most rousing and memorable speeches. Delivered on June 4, 1940, to the House of Commons, this speech came at a critical moment in World War II. The British Expeditionary Force, along with allied troops, had just been evacuated from Dunkirk in a miraculous operation.

Despite the successful evacuation, Britain faced the grim prospect of a German invasion, with much of Europe already under Nazi control.

Churchill's speech was a masterstroke of oratory, designed not only to prepare the British public for the looming threat but also to inspire resilience and defiance. The phrase "We shall fight on the beaches" was part of a series of scenarios Churchill laid out, depicting the unyielding resistance Britain would put up against an invasion. He spoke of fighting on the beaches, landing grounds, fields, streets, and hills, thereby covering every conceivable terrain where the enemy might attempt to gain a foothold. This speech wasn't just about rallying the British people; it was a clear message to the world, and particularly to Nazi Germany, that Britain would never surrender. The speech encapsulated the spirit of the British resistance during the war – a determination to fight against overwhelming odds.

- **"Success is not final, failure is not fatal: It is the courage to continue that counts."**: This quote reflects Churchill's unwavering resilience and is often cited to inspire perseverance and determination.

- "Never in the field of human conflict was so much owed by so many to so few.": This quote is from a speech Churchill gave on August 20, 1940, praising the efforts of the Royal Air Force during the Battle of Britain.

- "You have enemies? Good. That means you've stood up for something, sometime in your life.": This quote encapsulates Churchill's bold and principled stand on various issues throughout his political career.

Adolf Hitler and Nazi Germany: Arguably the most significant and formidable enemy Churchill faced was Adolf Hitler and the Nazi regime. During World War II, Churchill's leadership was pivotal in opposing Nazi aggression. His refusal to consider peace talks with Hitler, even when Britain stood virtually alone against Germany in 1940, was a defining moment of his premiership. His speeches and broadcasts during the war years were instrumental in boosting British morale and resistance against the Nazis.

Neville Chamberlain and Appeasement Policy Advocates: Before World War II, Churchill was a vocal critic of the British government's policy of appeasement towards Nazi Germany, led by Prime Minister Neville Chamberlain. Churchill's stance on the Munich Agreement of 1938, which allowed Hitler to annex parts of Czechoslovakia, put him at odds with much of the British political establishment.

He believed that appeasing Hitler would only lead to further aggression.

Trade Unions and Labour Movement Leaders: Domestically, Churchill often found himself in opposition to the trade unions and leaders of the Labour movement. His views on socialism and labour unions were usually conservative. For instance, during the General Strike of 1926, as Chancellor of the Exchequer, Churchill took a hard stance against the striking workers, viewing the strike as a threat to the national economy and stability.

Each of these "enemies" represented different challenges and ideological standpoints that Churchill confronted throughout his career. His ability to stand firm in his beliefs, regardless of opposition or popularity, is a significant aspect of his legacy.

"Democracy is the worst form of government, except for all the others.": This quote, highlighting the flaws yet indispensability of democracy, is often brought up in discussions about political systems.

This statement was made in the context of a post-World War II world, during a period of significant political change and uncertainty. The quote, often cited in discussions on political theory, captures Churchill's wry acknowledgment of democracy's imperfections alongside a firm belief in its superiority over other forms of government.

Churchill, who had witnessed the catastrophic consequences of totalitarian regimes during World War II, understood the inherent challenges and messiness of democratic systems. Yet, he firmly believed that democracy, despite its flaws, offered the best mechanism for ensuring freedom and justice.

His experience leading Britain through the war had reinforced his conviction that democratic governments, capable of being held accountable by their citizens, were vital for a stable and just society. This period was marked by the rise and fall of fascist regimes, the beginning of the Cold War, and the struggle for power between democratic and communist ideologies. Churchill's observations on democracy came at a time when the world was grappling with the question of how best to govern nations in a way that promoted peace and stability.

It was delivered during a period of rebuilding and introspection when the world's powers were considering how to prevent the horrors of another global conflict. Churchill's words were a candid acknowledgment of democracy's shortcomings - it can be slow, inefficient, and frustrating. However, he saw these weaknesses as preferable to the alternatives, such as authoritarianism or totalitarianism, which had led to oppression and conflict. Churchill's quote, therefore, serves as a reminder of the importance of preserving and improving democratic systems, recognizing that while they are not perfect, they are the best hope for maintaining a free and fair society.

- "To improve is to change; to be perfect is to change often.": Churchill's perspective on change and progress is encapsulated in this quote, emphasizing the importance of adaptability.

- "If you're going through hell, keep going.": A powerful statement encouraging perseverance through the toughest of times.

- "History will be kind to me for I intend to write it.": This quote reflects Churchill's keen sense of history, not just as a participant but also as an author of his own and Britain's story.

- "Courage is what it takes to stand up and speak; courage is also what it takes to sit down and listen.": Here, Churchill highlights the dual nature of courage in both action and reflection.

Churchill's view of courage as a dual concept also extends beyond the realm of leadership into everyday life, where standing up for one's beliefs is as important as being open to new ideas and perspectives. In today's world, where polarizing opinions and rapid communication often dominate public discourse, this quote remains remarkably relevant. It serves as a reminder that true courage involves not only asserting one's stance but also being open to dialogue and understanding. In essence, Churchill's words encourage a balance between conviction and empathy, asserting that both are essential components of not just effective leadership, but also a compassionate and progressive society.

- "We make a living by what we get, but we make a life by what we give.": This quote reflects Churchill's views on the importance of service and philanthropy.

Remember, while **you may never need to know** these quotes verbatim, they offer timeless wisdom and insight into the character and leadership style of one of the 20th century's most significant figures.

88. The Secret Society of the Freemasons

The Freemasons, often shrouded in mystery and intrigue, are one of the world's oldest and most famous fraternal organizations. With roots tracing back to the local fraternities of stonemasons in the late medieval period, the Freemasons evolved over centuries into a more symbolic and philosophical society.

The Freemasons initially emerged from the guilds of stonemasons and builders who constructed Europe's cathedrals and castles. These guilds had secrets of the trade, rites, and signs for recognizing each other's legitimacy and skill.

By the 17th century, the organization began accepting members not involved in the stonemasonry trade, transforming into a more esoteric and philosophical society.

The square and compasses are the most identifiable symbols of Freemasonry, often accompanied by the letter "G," which stands for both God and geometry.

Freemasonry is known for its secretive meetings, rituals, and modes of communication. While it insists it's not a secret society but a society with secrets, the clandestine nature of its internal operations has been a subject of fascination.

- Founding Date Unclear: The exact origins of Freemasonry are unknown, with some theories dating it back to the construction of King Solomon's Temple.
- Grand Lodges: The first Grand Lodge, the governing body of Freemasonry, was established in England in 1717.
- Women Freemasons: Traditionally, Freemasonry has been male-only, but there are now women's lodges and co-masonic lodges where both men and women are members.
- Masonic Temples: Masonic temples, where meetings occur, are filled with symbolic architecture and art.
- Three Degrees: The three basic degrees in Freemasonry are Entered Apprentice, Fellowcraft, and Master Mason.
- Famous Masonic Authors: Writers like Mark Twain and Sir Arthur Conan Doyle were Freemasons.
- Charitable Work: Freemasons are known for their charitable efforts, including funding scholarships and hospitals.
- Presidential Masons: Several U.S. Presidents were Masons, including George Washington and Theodore Roosevelt.
- The All-Seeing Eye: This symbol, often associated with Freemasonry, represents the all-seeing eye of God.

- Mozart's Masonic Music: Wolfgang Amadeus Mozart composed Masonic music, including the opera "The Magic Flute" with Masonic themes.
- Masonic Rituals: Rituals are a core part of meetings, often including allegorical plays.
- Lewis and Clark Expedition: Both Lewis and Clark were Freemasons, and some say their expedition had Masonic influences.
- The Shriners: A branch of Freemasonry, known for their distinctive red fez hats and philanthropy, especially children's hospitals.
- Masonic Cipher: A special cipher is used in some Masonic documents.
- Aprons: Masons wear aprons during their rituals, symbolic of the aprons worn by stonemasons.
- Freemason Astronauts: Several NASA astronauts were Freemasons, including Buzz Aldrin.
- Largest Masonic Temple: The Detroit Masonic Temple is the largest in the world.
- Masonic Bible: While not a different version, many Masons have a personal Masonic Bible.

The world of the Freemasons, shrouded in secrecy and ritual, has been a fertile ground for conspiracy theories.

These theories range from the somewhat plausible to the utterly outlandish, often fueled by the organization's preference for privacy and its influential membership.

Influence and Power: One of the most common threads in Masonic conspiracy theories is the belief that Freemasons wield excessive control over governments and financial institutions. Theorists often cite the high number of Masons who have been influential politicians, business leaders, and other powerful figures. They suggest that Masonic lodges are places where covert decisions affecting national and global policies are made. This theory plays into the narrative of a shadowy elite guiding the course of history from behind closed doors.

Symbols and Architecture: Another area ripe with conspiracy theories is Masonic symbols, which are found in architecture, currency, and art. Theorists often claim that these symbols reveal the hidden influence of Freemasons in society. For example, the presence of the all-seeing eye and the pyramid on the U.S. dollar bill is frequently cited as evidence of Masonic control over the U.S. financial system. Additionally, conspiracy theorists sometimes argue that certain buildings, like the U.S. Capitol or the streets of Washington, D.C., are designed with Masonic symbolism in mind, reflecting a secret agenda.

Historical Events: Some conspiracy theories go as far as to link Freemasons with pivotal historical events. One popular theory suggests that Freemasons were behind the French Revolution, using it as a means to spread Enlightenment ideals and diminish the power of the church and monarchy. Another theory ties the organization to the assassination of public figures, claiming that these acts were part of a Masonic agenda to reshape political landscapes.

While these theories are often dismissed by historians and researchers as fanciful or paranoid, they continue to captivate the public imagination. The blend of secrecy, power, and ritual inherent to the Freemasons provides an almost irresistible canvas for conspiracy theorists.

Remember, while you may never need to know the ins and outs of these Masonic conspiracy theories, they offer a fascinating glimpse into how secrecy can breed speculation and myth in the public psyche.

89 - Bob Dylan's Unconventional Charm

Bob Dylan, an enigmatic figure in the world of music and poetry, has always danced to the beat of his own drum. His unique blend of musical genius and quirkiness has left many pondering, "Why is Bob Dylan so weird?" But in this weirdness lies his charm—a symphony in eccentricity that has resonated with generations.

Dylan's career is marked by constant reinvention. From folk to rock, gospel to blues, his refusal to be pigeonholed into one genre or expectation is legendary. This constant evolution, often defying fans' and critics' expectations, has been both baffling and mesmerizing.

Contrarian Spirit

At the heart of Dylan's perceived weirdness is his contrarian spirit. He often goes against the grain, whether in his musical choices or public appearances. This defiance of norms and expectations has been a constant in his career, making him unpredictable and, to some, odd.

Nonconformist Performances

Dylan's live performances often deviate from the recorded versions of his songs, which can be disorienting for audiences expecting a familiar sound. He has a reputation for rearranging his music so drastically that it becomes almost unrecognizable, a trait that some find weird but others see as artistic freedom.

Voice of the Voiceless

Dylan's lyrics often delve into themes of social justice, war, and love, but in a way that's abstract and open to interpretation. His songwriting doesn't follow the conventional storytelling format, which can seem strange to those accustomed to more straightforward lyrics.

- **Nobel Prize in Literature:** In 2016, Dylan was awarded the Nobel Prize in Literature, a rare achievement for a musician. His selection sparked debate, but it underscored his profound impact on the literary aspects of music.
- **Changing His Name:** Born Robert Zimmerman, he changed his name to Bob Dylan, reportedly after the Welsh poet Dylan Thomas. This was one of his first steps in crafting his unique identity.
- **The Electric Controversy:** At the 1965 Newport Folk Festival, Dylan went electric, playing with a rock band. This move was seen as a betrayal by folk purists, but it marked a pivotal moment in rock history.
- **The "Voice of a Generation" Tag:** Dylan has often been labeled the "voice of a generation," but he's always resisted this title. He's famously private and elusive, rarely giving straight answers in interviews.
- **The Never-Ending Tour:** Since the late 1980s, Dylan has been on what's called the "Never-Ending Tour," performing all over the world without a break. This relentless touring highlights his dedication to his craft.

- **Artistic Ventures Beyond Music:** Dylan is also an accomplished painter and author. His artwork has been exhibited in major galleries, and his book, "Chronicles: Volume One," received critical acclaim.
- **Film Appearances:** Dylan has dabbled in acting, with roles in films like "Pat Garrett and Billy the Kid." His mysterious persona has translated intriguingly to the screen.
- **A Rolling Stone Top Artist:** Rolling Stone magazine ranked him No. 2 in their list of the "Greatest Artists of All Time," just behind The Beatles.
- **Presidential Medal of Freedom:** In 2012, Dylan was awarded the Presidential Medal of Freedom, the highest civilian award in the United States, highlighting his influence on American culture.
- **Dylan's "Alias" Period:** During the 1970s, he adopted the alias "Jack Frost" for some of his production work, adding another layer to his enigmatic personality.

Bob Dylan's journey through the realms of music, literature, and art has been as unconventional as it has been influential. Remember, while **you may never need to know** every quirk and twist of Bob Dylan's career, his legacy stands as a testament to the power of embracing one's individuality and charting an unorthodox course through the world of art and fame.

90. The Legend of the Chupacabra

In the annals of cryptozoology, few creatures have captured the imagination as vividly as the Chupacabra. This legendary creature, whose name literally means "goat-sucker" in Spanish, is said to roam the Americas, preying on livestock and sparking fear and fascination.

First Sightings: The legend of the Chupacabra gained traction in the 1990s in Puerto Rico. Reports of livestock, particularly goats, found drained of blood and with peculiar puncture wounds, gave rise to the myth of a bloodthirsty creature lurking in the shadows.

Descriptions of the Chupacabra vary, but it is often depicted as a reptile-like creature with leathery or scaly greenish-gray skin and sharp spines running down its back. Some reports describe it as more dog-like, with a pronounced spinal ridge, pronounced eye sockets, fangs, and claws.

While the legend originated in Puerto Rico, similar reports have emerged from Mexico, the United States, and as far south as Chile, suggesting a widespread myth or phenomenon.

Media Frenzy and Global Attention

Viral Before Viral Was a Thing: In the pre-internet era of the 1990s, the Chupacabra phenomenon spread rapidly through word-of-mouth and sensationalist news reports, capturing imaginations across continents.

Numerous television programs and documentaries have dedicated episodes to the Chupacabra, often blending eyewitness accounts with expert commentary, further cementing its place in popular culture.
Despite its mythical status, the Chupacabra has been the subject of serious study by cryptozoologists, who seek to validate its existence through field research and analysis of reported encounters.

Mainstream scientists, while largely dismissive of the creature's existence, have used the Chupacabra as a case study in understanding how myths and urban legends can take hold in modern societies.
The majority of supposed Chupacabra sightings have been attributed to wild animals, particularly canines like dogs and coyotes, afflicted with mange, a condition that causes severe hair loss and skin lesions, giving them an eerie appearance.

The reports of livestock killings, often attributed to the Chupacabra, are frequently found upon investigation to be the work of known predators such as wild dogs or coyotes.

In some cases, the fear and fascination with the Chupacabra have led to instances of mass hysteria, where people are more susceptible to believing and spreading rumors about sightings and attacks.

- Role-Playing Games (RPGs): In the realm of video games, the Chupacabra often appears in RPGs as a monster or enemy character. Gamers may find themselves tracking or battling this elusive creature in various game environments, from dark forests to hidden dungeons.

- Adventure and Horror Games: The creature is also a popular choice in adventure and horror-themed games, where players may encounter it as part of a larger narrative involving mystery and supernatural elements.

In essence, while the Chupacabra remains a mythical creature in the eyes of science, its cultural impact is undeniable. It serves as a mirror to our collective psyche, reflecting our innate curiosity about the unknown and our propensity for storytelling. Remember: you may never need to know the detailed lore of the Chupacabra, but its story is a fascinating glimpse into the human fascination with the mysterious and the macabre.

91. The Unexplained Sounds of the Bloop

The Bloop is one of the most mysterious and captivating underwater sounds ever recorded. Detected in 1997 by the U.S. National Oceanic and Atmospheric Administration (NOAA), this ultra-low frequency and extremely powerful underwater sound was unlike anything ever recorded.

The Bloop was detected by underwater microphones placed thousands of miles apart, indicating its colossal volume.

The sound originated from a remote point in the South Pacific Ocean, a vast and largely unexplored region, adding to the intrigue. Initially, some speculated that the Bloop might have been produced by an enormous, unknown aquatic creature, given the sound's volume and organic quality.

Scientists also considered geological explanations, such as underwater volcanoes or icequakes—events where large icebergs crack and fracture.

NOAA scientists

The Bloop was detected in 1997 by NOAA's Equatorial Pacific Ocean autonomous hydrophone array. Scientists scrutinized the recording for several years. The sound was unique due to its duration, loudness, and frequency range. Researchers compared the Bloop's acoustic signature with sounds produced by icequakes – events involving cracking and fracturing of icebergs and sea ice. This comparison was crucial in drawing conclusions.

NOAA officially announced their conclusion regarding the Bloop in 2005. They stated that the sound matched the audio profile of an icequake.

The Bloop remains a fascinating example of the mysteries hidden in the Earth's oceans. While the scientific explanation points to natural causes, the allure of the unknown continues to captivate the public imagination. Remember: you may never need to know the intricacies of underwater acoustics or the specifics of the Bloop, but it serves as a reminder of the vast, unexplored wonders beneath the sea's surface.

- Documentary - "The Unexplained": The History Channel's series "The Unexplained" featured an episode on the Bloop, exploring its mysterious nature and the various theories surrounding it.
- "Stuff You Should Know" Podcast: The popular podcast "Stuff You Should Know" discussed the Bloop in an episode, attracting a large audience with their engaging and informative storytelling style.
- Sci-Fi Novel - "The Kraken Wakes": The Bloop inspired elements in John Wyndham's science fiction novel "The Kraken Wakes," where deep-sea noises signal the presence of extraterrestrial beings.
- TV Show Reference - "The X-Files": In an episode of "The X-Files," the Bloop is used as a plot device, hinting at the existence of unknown creatures in the ocean depths.
- Horror Game - "Subnautica": The video game "Subnautica," known for its underwater exploration and survival elements, features eerie sounds inspired by the Bloop, adding to the game's mysterious atmosphere.

- Educational Feature - "NOVA": PBS's "NOVA" science series aired an episode that included the Bloop, offering a scientific perspective on this unexplained phenomenon.
- YouTube Analysis - Vsauce: The popular science and education channel Vsauce discussed the Bloop in one of their videos, which garnered millions of views and sparked further public interest.
- Ambient Music Album - "Bloop's Wake": An ambient music album titled "Bloop's Wake" by artist Sferro incorporates the Bloop sound, creating a thematic exploration of underwater mysteries.
- Reddit Discussions: On Reddit, particularly in subreddits like r/UnresolvedMysteries, the Bloop has been a topic of extensive discussion, with threads attracting thousands of comments and upvotes.
- Cryptozoology Reference in "Cryptid Hunters": The novel "Cryptid Hunters" by Roland Smith references the Bloop as potential evidence of cryptids, intriguing readers interested in cryptozoology

92. The Mystery of the Devil's Kettle Falls

In the rugged terrain of Minnesota's North Shore, there lies a geological enigma that has puzzled hikers, geologists, and curious minds alike. Welcome to the Devil's Kettle Falls, a part of the Brule River where water takes a plunge into the unknown. This natural oddity, located in Judge C.R. Magney State Park, splits the river into two, with one side flowing on as expected, and the other disappearing into a deep pothole, seemingly vanishing from the face of the earth.

As the Brule River approaches the falls, it splits around a massive rock formation. Half of the river continues downstream, while the other half pours into a hole in the rock, and that's where the mystery deepens. The water that dives into this kettle doesn't reappear — at least not visibly. Where does it go? Does it join an underground river, feed into an aquifer, or journey to the center of the earth? These questions have baffled observers for years.

Over time, numerous theories and experiments have been conducted to uncover the kettle's secret. Scientists, amateur sleuths, and the simply curious have thrown in various objects, including GPS trackers, dye, and even ping pong balls, hoping they would reemerge downstream or somewhere nearby. But the kettle kept its secret, swallowing everything thrown into it without a trace.

Recent geological studies suggest a less dramatic but equally fascinating explanation. It's believed that the water reenters the river further downstream, but under the surface. The underground geological formations might be guiding the water back to the river without any visible signs of its journey. While this explanation might lack the allure of a mysterious underground passage, it does provide a more scientific understanding of this peculiar phenomenon.

The Devil's Kettle Falls has become a popular destination for hikers and nature enthusiasts, drawn by both its natural beauty and the allure of its mystery. It's a place where nature's wonders and mysteries meet, offering a unique and intriguing outdoor adventure.

The area around Devil's Kettle showcases a rich geological history, featuring ancient rock formations, basalt cliffs, and evidence of volcanic activity from millions of years ago.

The Devil's Kettle, with its enigmatic disappearance of half a river, has naturally become the subject of various local myths and folklore. These stories, often passed down through generations, add a mystical layer to the already intriguing geological phenomenon.

- **Supernatural Vortex:** One popular legend suggests that the kettle acts as a supernatural vortex or portal to another dimension. This theory plays into the mystery of why objects thrown into the kettle seemingly vanish without a trace.
- **Mythical Creatures:** Some tales talk about mythical creatures residing in the depths of the kettle. These range from benign water spirits to more malevolent entities guarding the secrets of the deep. Such stories likely stem from an attempt to personify or explain the unknown aspects of this natural feature.

- **Gateway to the Underworld:** In a more ominous interpretation, the kettle is sometimes depicted as a gateway to the underworld. This concept ties into broader mythological themes found across cultures, where certain natural formations are believed to be passages to other realms.
- **Cursed Waters:** Another thread of local lore posits that the waters of the Devil's Kettle are cursed. This belief could originate from the inexplicable loss of objects thrown into the kettle, fostering a sense of unease or superstition about its true nature.
- **Tales of Lost Travelers:** Some stories revolve around travelers or explorers who dared to explore the kettle and were never seen again. These tales serve as cautionary fables, warning of the dangers of venturing too close to the mysterious pothole.

Remember: While **you may never need to know** the precise mechanics of how the Devil's Kettle swallows half a river, this natural mystery serves as a humbling reminder of the many wonders our planet holds, some of which continue to elude even the most determined efforts to understand them.

93. The Phantom Time Hypothesis

The Phantom Time Hypothesis is a historical conspiracy theory that suggests a period of history, specifically the Early Middle Ages (614-911 AD), was fabricated or altered by historical figures. This hypothesis, proposed by German historian Heribert Illig in 1991, claims that about 297 years were added to the historical record, essentially creating a "phantom time" in history.

Illig's Argument: Illig proposed that the years between 614 and 911 AD never happened. He suggested that this period was either falsified or misinterpreted by historians.

Motivation Behind the Fabrication: The hypothesis asserts that Holy Roman Emperor Otto III, Pope Sylvester II, and possibly Byzantine Emperor Constantine VII, conspired to alter the calendar to place them in the year 1000 AD, believed to have significance due to the millennium.

Calendar Discrepancies: Illig used discrepancies in the Gregorian calendar reform of 1582, which adjusted for a 10-day discrepancy rather than a 13-day one as his basis, suggesting that the intervening period had been invented.

Challenges to the Hypothesis:

Lack of Evidence: There is a substantial amount of historical, archaeological, and astronomical evidence from various cultures that contradicts the Phantom Time Hypothesis. Documents, records, and artifacts from the period in question exist and align with the accepted historical timeline.

Astronomical Records: Astronomical events recorded during this "phantom time," such as solar eclipses and Halley's Comet sightings, align with current historical and astronomical calculations, further debunking the theory.

Global Implications: The hypothesis largely ignores non-European history. The proposed phantom time would have had to be coordinated across different civilizations worldwide, many of which were disconnected and had their own calendars and historical records.

The Phantom Time Hypothesis has been largely dismissed by mainstream historians and academics but remains a popular topic in alternative history circles. It has inspired discussions and debates about the reliability of historical records and the methods used in historical research.

Remember: While the Phantom Time Hypothesis presents an intriguing "what if" scenario, it's important to approach such theories with a critical mind. The vast array of evidence supporting the current historical timeline makes the hypothesis more of a curiosity than a credible theory. **You may never need to know** the intricacies of this hypothesis, but it's an interesting footnote in the annals of historical speculation.

94. The Mysterious Stone Spheres of Costa Rica

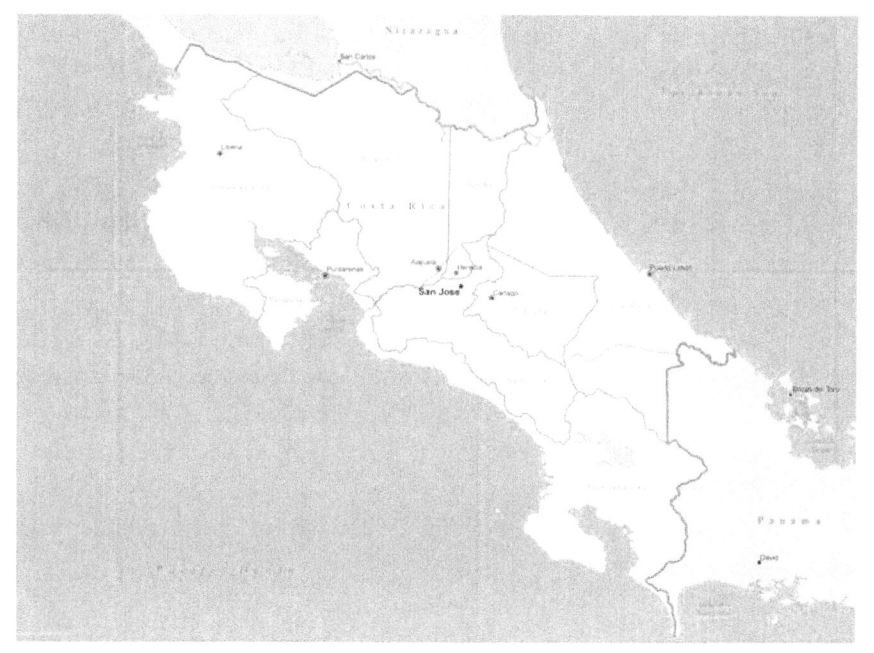

The Mysterious Stone Spheres of Costa Rica, also known as the Diquís Spheres, are a collection of over 300 petrospheres located primarily in the Diquís Delta in southern Costa Rica. These intriguing artifacts have puzzled archaeologists, historians, and visitors for decades due to their size, number, and the precision with which they were made.

Pre-Columbian Artifacts: The spheres date back to the Aguas Buenas period (300–800 AD) and the Chiriquí period (800–1550 AD), crafted by the pre-Columbian Diquís culture.

First Noticed in the 1930s: These spheres came to the attention of the wider world during the 1930s when the United Fruit Company began clearing land in the area for banana plantations.

Size and Weight: The spheres vary in size, with diameters ranging from a few centimeters to over two meters, and some weigh up to 16 tons.

Craftsmanship: They are noted for their high degree of perfection, with some almost perfectly spherical and smooth.

In 2014, the stone spheres were included in the UNESCO list of World Heritage Sites, under the name "Precolumbian Chiefdom Settlements with Stone Spheres of the Diquís."

The spheres have become a national symbol for Costa Rica, featured in local lore, tourism promotions, and cultural displays.

In the heart of Costa Rica's lush landscape, the Stone Spheres have been a source of wonder and speculation. Here are three prevailing theories about these enigmatic creations:

1. Celestial Calculators: Some believe these spheres were the ancient world's astronomical tools. Picture this: centuries before apps and telescopes, these stone globes might have aligned with the stars, the sun, and lunar cycles, serving as a pre-Columbian star chart. Who needs Google Earth when you have giant stone globes to navigate the cosmos?

2. Symbols of Swag: Bigger and smoother spheres might have been the ultimate status symbol among the Diquís elite. Imagine these as the ancient equivalent of a fancy chariot parked outside a noble's dwelling. A massive, perfectly round stone sphere in your courtyard was probably the ancient way of saying, "I've made it big!"

3. Sacred Stones: The spheres might have had deep religious or ceremonial significance, representing deities or used in sacred rituals. Each sphere could have been as central to their rituals as the secret ingredient in a family's heirloom recipe. "Come one, come all, to the grand sphere for our yearly rain dance," they might have proclaimed.

Remember: While the exact purpose and method of construction of the Costa Rican stone spheres remain a mystery, they serve as a remarkable testament to the skill and ingenuity of ancient cultures. **You may never need to know** the detailed history of these enigmatic artifacts, but their existence adds to the rich tapestry of human cultural heritage and the enduring fascination with ancient civilizations.

95. The Legend of the Lost City of Z

The Lost City of Z, a tantalizing tale of exploration and mystery, chronicles the quest for an ancient city hidden in the uncharted jungles of the Amazon. This legend captures the allure of the unknown and the human desire to uncover the world's secrets.

The story centers around British explorer Percy Fawcett, a real-life Indiana Jones, who in the early 20th century became obsessed with finding a fabled lost city he called "Z." His expeditions were driven by reports of a sophisticated civilization deep in the Amazon, with tales of gold and grandeur.

Fawcett embarked on multiple expeditions, gathering clues and piecing together evidence. His determination was fueled by ancient manuscripts and indigenous stories of a flourishing city hidden amidst the dense foliage.

The intrigue of the Lost City of Z deepened when, in 1925, Fawcett, along with his son and a friend, vanished without a trace during an expedition to find the city. Numerous rescue missions and speculative expeditions followed, but no sign of Fawcett or the mythical city was ever found.

Fawcett's disappearance and his quest for the Lost City of Z have inspired books, movies, and countless adventurers. His story speaks to the enduring fascination with the unknown and the allure of ancient civilizations.

The Amazon Basin, where Percy Fawcett sought the Lost City of Z, is a vast and complex geographical area, spanning across several South American countries. It's the world's largest rainforest, known for its incredible biodiversity and the sprawling Amazon River. This dense jungle landscape is a labyrinth of rivers, creeks, and flooded forests, with a canopy so thick that the forest floor is often shrouded in perpetual twilight.

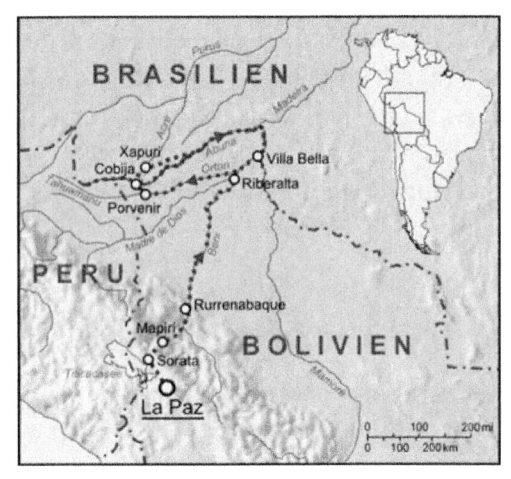

The geography of the Amazon is as challenging as it is diverse. The rainforest is home to an estimated 390 billion individual trees divided into 16,000 species. Its river systems are equally complex, with the Amazon River alone having over 1,100 tributaries. These waterways were both highways and obstacles for explorers like Fawcett. The region's climate adds to the challenge, characterized by high humidity and significant rainfall, which can lead to sudden and severe flooding, transforming the landscape dramatically. This environment, while teeming with life, poses numerous hazards, from dangerous wildlife to diseases like malaria.

- **Fawcett's Inspiration:** Fawcett was inspired by ancient Greek historian Herodotus and conquistador tales of El Dorado.
- **Royal Geographical Society:** Fawcett was a member and received funding from this esteemed British organization for his expeditions.
- **Initial Disbelief:** Initially, Fawcett's tales of the Amazon were met with skepticism by the scientific community.
- **Ancient Manuscript:** Fawcett based his theories on a document he referred to as "Manuscript 512," housed in the National Library of Rio de Janeiro, which described a city rich in gold and silver.
- **Lost Companions:** Accompanying Fawcett on his fatal expedition were his son, Jack, and Jack's friend, Raleigh Rimmell.
- **Last Communication:** Fawcett's last known communication was a letter sent to his wife from Dead Horse Camp, asserting his confidence in finding Z.
- **Numerous Search Parties:** Over the years, more than 100 people perished or disappeared while searching for Fawcett and Z.
- **The Fawcett Mystery:** Some believe Fawcett and his companions were killed by indigenous tribes, while others think they succumbed to the harsh conditions of the jungle.
- **Cinematic Adaptations:** The story of Fawcett's search for Z was adapted into the 2016 film "The Lost City of Z," directed by James Gray.
- **Fawcett's Theory of Z:** Fawcett theorized that Z was the remains of an ancient, advanced civilization with complex agriculture and architecture.
- **The City of Kuhikugu:** Recent archaeological discoveries in the Amazon, like Kuhikugu, suggest the existence of large, sophisticated pre-Columbian societies, lending some credence to Fawcett's theories.
- **Influence on Pop Culture:** Fawcett's story has influenced various works, including Arthur Conan Doyle's "The Lost World."

- **Fawcett's Background:** Before becoming an explorer, Fawcett had a military career and served in Sri Lanka and North Africa.
- **Fawcett's Mapping:** Fawcett contributed significantly to the mapping of South America, particularly Bolivia and Brazil.
- **Spiritual Beliefs:** Fawcett was deeply interested in spiritualism and the occult, which influenced his views on the lost civilization.

While you may never need to know the exact truths behind the legend of the Lost City of Z, this story serves as a testament to human curiosity and the eternal quest for discovery, reminding us that some mysteries of our world continue to elude even the most daring explorers.

96. The Unexplained Disappearance of the Eilean Mor Lighthouse Keepers

The Eilean Mor Lighthouse Keepers' Disappearance remains one of the most puzzling and eerie mysteries in maritime history. Eilean Mor is a small, uninhabited island in the Flannan Isles, located off the west coast of Scotland. The island, known for its rugged terrain and the isolated lighthouse built in 1899, became the scene of a baffling event that has intrigued and baffled people for over a century.

In December 1900, the lighthouse keepers stationed on Eilean Mor —Thomas Marshall, James Ducat, and Donald MacArthur— vanished without a trace. The circumstances surrounding their disappearance were strange and left more questions than answers.

The Last Records: The last entries in the lighthouse logbook, made by Thomas Marshall, described severe storms and high winds, although records from nearby areas didn't report such severe weather. The entries also mentioned that Ducat was quiet and MacArthur was crying, which was unusual given their experienced and tough backgrounds.

The Disappearance: The relief keeper arrived on December 26th to find the lighthouse deserted. The beds were unmade, the clock was stopped, and a meal was left uneaten. The lamp was in working order, and there were no signs of a struggle or accident in the lighthouse.

Various theories have been proposed to explain their disappearance, ranging from a freak wave washing them away to abduction by foreign spies, a sea monster, or even alien activity. Some suggest that one of the keepers went mad and killed the others before throwing himself into the sea.

Despite the supposed severe weather, no distress signals were sent from the lighthouse. This fact, combined with the absence of any bodies or wreckage, deepened the mystery.

Over the years, several investigations have been conducted, but no conclusive evidence has been found to explain what happened to the three men. The lighthouse was eventually automated in 1971, leaving the island uninhabited once again.

The Eilean Mor Lighthouse Keepers' disappearance continues to fascinate and perplex. The lack of concrete evidence and the eerie circumstances of their vanishing ensure that this mystery remains a topic of speculation and storytelling. While **you may never need to know** the truth behind what happened to the lighthouse keepers of Eilean Mor, their story is a haunting reminder of the sea's unpredictable nature and the mysteries that it still holds.

97. The Oslo Hotel Murder Mystery

Jennifer Fergate, is a name associated with a mysterious and unsolved case that has intrigued detectives and the public for years. The case revolves around the death of a woman using the name "Jennifer Fairgate" in one of the most luxurious hotels in Oslo, Norway.

On June 3, 1995, the body of a woman was found in a locked room at the Oslo Plaza Hotel. She had been dead for several days, and the cause of death was a gunshot wound. The room was registered under the name "Jennifer Fairgate."

Investigations revealed that "Jennifer Fairgate" was a false identity. The woman had checked into the hotel without any luggage, and the name and address she provided did not exist.

The circumstances of her death were mysterious. There were no signs of struggle in the room, and the weapon used was found in her hand. However, there were several oddities: her fingerprints were not found on the gun, there was no gunshot residue on her hand, and the room's security lock was engaged from the inside.
No personal belongings, ID, or passport were found in the room, making it difficult to identify her. Even the labels on her clothes were removed.

The investigation faced numerous challenges, including language barriers, the lack of CCTV footage, and the absence of any witnesses. The hotel staff could not provide much information about her, as she had minimal interaction with them.

Over the years, various theories have emerged, including espionage, suicide, murder, and involvement in criminal activities. The possibility of her being a spy or involved in illicit activities was considered due to the nature of her stay and the false identity.
Efforts have been made to identify her using forensic techniques, including facial reconstruction and DNA analysis. However, her true identity remains unknown.

The case has attracted significant media attention and has been featured in various documentaries and crime investigation shows. It remains one of the most enduring mysteries in Norway.

Theories Regarding Jennifer Fairgate's Death

- **Espionage Theory:**

Rationale: The lack of personal belongings, the absence of fingerprints, and the use of a false identity have led some to speculate that Jennifer might have been involved in espionage.

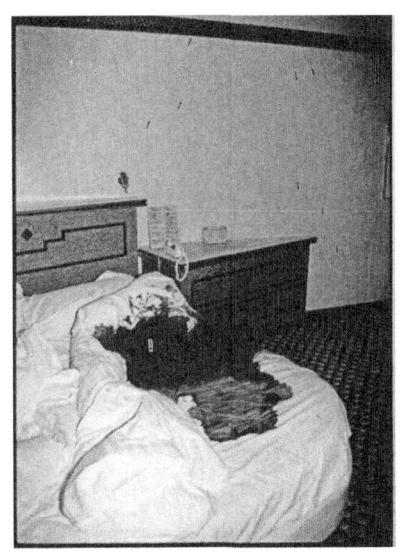

- **Supporting Points:** The meticulous way in which she seemed to cover her tracks, the professional execution of her death, and the fact that she chose a high-profile hotel are often seen as indicative of spy activity.
- **Counterarguments:** There's no concrete evidence linking her to any intelligence agency, and the scenario might be considered too obvious for a trained spy.

Suicide Theory:

- Rationale: The position of the body and the gun in her hand have led some investigators to consider suicide.
- Supporting Points: The locked room from the inside suggests a lack of external involvement. Additionally, her solitude and the absence of luggage might indicate a planned end.
- Counterarguments: The lack of gunshot residue on her hands and the absence of fingerprints on the gun raise questions about this theory.

Murder Disguised as Suicide:

- Rationale: Some believe that her death was a murder made to look like a suicide.
- Supporting Points: The oddities like the absence of fingerprints on the weapon and the lack of gunshot residue are unusual for a suicide case.
- Counterarguments: The locked room from the inside complicates this theory, though it's not impossible for a skilled perpetrator to stage the scene.

Discovery of the Body

- **Location**: Jennifer's body was found in a locked room at the Oslo Plaza Hotel, which she had checked into under a false identity.
- **Condition of the Body:** She had been dead for several days. The cause of death was identified as a gunshot wound.
- **Position and Scene:** The body was found sitting against the bed, with a gun in her hand. There were no signs of struggle in the room, and all personal belongings were conspicuously absent.
- **Investigation Challenges:** The room's security lock was engaged from the inside, making it difficult to understand how someone else could have been involved if it were a case of foul play.

The case of Jennifer Fairgate is a perplexing one, filled with more questions than answers. While you may never need to know the true identity or the story behind Jennifer Fairgate, her case is a fascinating example of how some mysteries continue to evade even the most determined investigative efforts.

98 - Crazy Laws of Europe

Europe's legal landscape isn't a single tapestry, but rather a quilt woven with threads of history, quirky traditions, and a dash of humor.

Europe's patchwork of laws comes from centuries of independent kingdoms and evolving cultures. Think of it like a family recipe passed down for generations, each country adding its own secret ingredient (and occasionally forgetting a pinch of salt). In Italy, the Roman emphasis on order and public decorum still echoes in laws like the anti-skirt rule and the mandatory smile (except when faced with life's lemons). In Switzerland, Sunday's tranquility is fiercely protected, even if it means silencing laundry lines and toilet flushes.

Cultural quirks take center stage: From Denmark's child-under-the-car check to Sweden's paint-license requirement, Europe isn't afraid to prioritize unique cultural values. These laws reflect a focus on safety, aesthetics, and preserving a certain way of life. Remember, Europe is home to countless towns bursting with history and charm, and sometimes, the laws bend to protect that special character.

Humor sometimes gets a seat at the table: Sure, Europe has its serious laws, but there's also a touch of whimsy woven in. France's "marry-a-dead-person" law stemmed from a real-life tragedy, but its wording adds a quirky twist. And who can deny the absurdity of Belgium's oxen-and-dog-powered-army-vehicles law? It's a reminder that even in the world of legalese, a little laugh can't hurt.

It's not just about individual states: Unlike the US with its separate federal and state laws, Europe has the European Union, where some rules apply across the continent. This adds another layer to the legal landscape, creating a blend of national quirks and EU-wide regulations. Think of it like a larger pot boiling over the national stoves, occasionally adding its own broth to the dish.

So, while the US legal system might be a streamlined highway, Europe's is a winding village road, full of unexpected turns and charming detours. It's a system shaped by history, culture, and a touch of eccentricity, which, let's be honest, makes it all the more fascinating. And hey, even if you can't wear a skirt in Milan or play music in a Finnish taxi, there's no denying that exploring Europe's legal quirks is an adventure in itself!

- **Italy**: Men, be careful with your fashion choices in Italy. It's illegal for men to wear skirts. Also, in Milan, it's a legal requirement to always smile, except during funerals or hospital visits.

- **Switzerland**: Late-night bathroom users, take note. In Switzerland, flushing the toilet in an apartment after 10 pm is considered illegal.

- **Sweden**: Planning to give your house a fresh coat of paint? You'll need to get a license first. This law is designed to maintain aesthetic harmony, particularly within city bounds. Also, don't even think about posting a picture of Swedish Krona; it's protected by copyright.

- **Finland**: Long taxi ride? Don't expect any background tunes. In Finland, playing music in a taxi without paying a copyright fee to the Finnish Composers Copyright Society is against the law.

- **Denmark**: Before driving off, it's compulsory in Denmark to check under your car for children. This thorough pre-driving check is a unique legal requirement.

- **Netherlands**: If a burglar breaks into your house, think twice before locking them in the bathroom. Depriving a burglar of their liberty, even when they're stealing your stuff, is against the law in the Netherlands.

- **Belgium**: In a throwback to times of war, dogs and oxen can be requisitioned to propel army vehicles. This law, dating back to 1939, still exists in the Belgian military code.

- **Luxembourg**: Driving a car without windshield wipers? That's illegal in Luxembourg, even if your car doesn't have a windshield!

- **Germany**: Running out of fuel on the Autobahn is not just a travel faux pas; it's actually illegal. This law is in place because stopping on the highway for preventable reasons, like running out of fuel, is considered a hazard.

- **UK**: Handling salmon in suspicious circumstances is actually against the law, as per the Salmon Act of 1986. This peculiar wording relates to illegal fishing activities.

- **France**: In a rule that seems more storybook than legal code, it's legal to marry a dead person in France, provided there's evidence of plans to marry before their death. This law was introduced after a tragic incident in 1959.

- **Denmark**: Before setting off in your car, you must check under it for children. This thorough check is a unique Danish legal requirement to ensure safety.

- **Portugal**: Thinking of relieving yourself in the sea? Better think twice in Portugal, as it's illegal to pee in the ocean.

- **Netherlands**: Surprisingly, it's against the law to lock a burglar in your toilet during a break-in. This law is centered on the principle of not depriving someone of their liberty, even if they are committing a crime.

- **Greece**: High heels are banned at archeological sites in Greece. This is to prevent damage to these historically important locations.

- **Italy**: In the Isle of Capri, wearing noisy sandals is a no-go. This law is aimed at maintaining a certain level of decorum in this picturesque location.

- **Switzerland**: Be cautious when doing laundry on a Sunday. Hanging clothes out to dry is not allowed, reflecting the country's appreciation for tranquility on this day of rest.

- **Germany**: It is legal to break out of prison, an interesting reflection of the country's legal perspective on the freedom of individuals.

- **Sweden**: During the winter darkness period, it's illegal to complain about wishing it were sunny. This law reflects the country's approach to coping with its long, dark winters.

- **Austria**: Don't get caught sleeping naked on a balcony in Austria. Public nudity, even in the comfort of your own home, is considered a disturbance of the peace.

- **Spain**: In parts of Spain, chewing gum is a sticky situation. Some towns banned it due to concerns about litter and sidewalk cleanup. So, keep your chomping discreet!

- **Croatia**: Feeling patriotic? Don't burn the Croatian flag, even unintentionally. This act of disrespect can land you in hot water.

- **Ireland**: Public intoxication is no laughing matter in Ireland. Even walking under the influence can earn you a fine. So, pace yourself at the pub!

- **Iceland**: Need a new hamster? Forget about it. Importing live hamsters to Iceland is strictly prohibited, aimed at protecting the island's fragile ecosystem.

- **Hungary**: Forget singing along to Hungarian national ant in a public place, unless you're at a special ceremony. Belting it out casually can be seen as disrespectful.

- **Norway**: Thinking of naming your child "Bob"? Not so fast in Norway. Naming authorities have the power to reject names they deem unfit, aiming for linguistic and cultural appropriateness.

- **Czech Republic:** Feeling stressed? Don't scream in silence. In some Czech towns, making excessive noise after 10 pm, even indoors, can result in a fine. Respect those bedtime hours.

- **Scotland**: It's against the law to be drunk and disorderly in a chargehouse, which is basically a drunk tank. Seems like a redundant rule, but apparently, things can get wild even in a holding cell.

- **Poland**: Want to take a selfie with a pigeon? Think twice. Feeding or attracting wild pigeons in public spaces is prohibited in some Polish cities due to concerns about hygiene and nuisance.

- **Spain**: In some Spanish towns, throwing bread on the ground is a no-no. Respecting food is a big deal, so treat those crusts with dignity!

- **France**: Planning a picnic in the Palace of Versailles? Hold your horses (not literally, they're banned too!). Eating on the palace grounds is strictly forbidden.

- **Germany**: Need to blow your nose in public? Do it quietly. Loudly honking your snot rocket is considered disruptive and rude.

- **Denmark**: Don't even think about wearing slippers outside your house in Denmark. Shoes are mandatory for public appearances, even if you're just popping out for a quick stroll.

- **Italy**: In Venice, feeding the pigeons is a bad idea. Not only is it messy, but the city has implemented hefty fines to deter feathered freeloaders.

- **Switzerland**: If you're a dog owner in Switzerland, be prepared for some doggy duties. Leaving your pup's poop unbagged on the sidewalk is an offense punishable by a fine.

- **Netherlands**: Want to go skinny dipping in Amsterdam? Think again. Public nudity is prohibited in most waterways and beaches, so keep your birthday suit private.

- **Finland**: Need some new furniture? Building your own wooden chair? In Finland, you'll need a permit before you hammer away. This ensures construction aligns with aesthetic standards.

- **Sweden**: Dying for a quick tan? Sunbathing on balconies in some Swedish cities is illegal. Apparently, soaking up rays in your undergarments can disturb the neighbours' peace.

- **Portugal**: In Portugal, driving with flip-flops is a no-no. Safe footwear is mandatory for hitting the road, so ditch the beachy vibes for your driving adventures.

- **Greece**: In some Greek islands, throwing confetti is strictly forbidden. Apparently, celebrating a bit too enthusiastically can lead to a tidy-up battle.

- **Ireland**: Need to silence a noisy neighbour? Don't crank up the music in retaliation. Playing loud music between 11 pm and 8 am in Ireland can land you in legal trouble.

- **Austria**: In Vienna, don't even think about painting your front door pink. Building regulations dictate specific colour palettes for different districts, so choose your hues wisely.

- **Belgium**: Forget about using a leaf blower on Sundays in Belgium. Disturbing the peace with noisy tools is forbidden on the day of rest.

- **Luxembourg**: Need to take a quick shower after a gym session? Be aware that in some Luxembourg towns, showering between 10 pm and 6 am is illegal. Apparently, late-night water usage is frowned upon.

- **Germany**: In some German cities, walking across a red light after a pedestrian signal turns off is technically legal. However, proceed with caution, as jaywalking is still generally discouraged.

- **France**: Planning a road trip? Make sure your car has two breathalyzers on board. In France, drivers are required to carry these devices in case of police checks.

- **Spain**: Need to take a quick siesta? In some Spanish towns, closing stores for the afternoon siesta is mandatory. So, embrace the laid-back rhythm and join the snooze fest!

- **Norway:** Don't wear camouflage clothing in Norway, especially near military installations. Blending in with the troops can be misconstrued as a security risk.

- **Czech Republic:** Want to name your baby "Lucifer"? Not happening in the Czech Republic. Names deemed offensive or detrimental to the child's well-being are off the table.

Europe, a continent steeped in history and tradition, also has its fair share of laws that range from the quaint to the quirky. As we traverse this tapestry of nations, we encounter rules that reflect the deep-rooted customs and contemporary concerns of its people. From bans on naming pigs after heads of state to rules about wine production, these laws paint a colorful picture of European life. So, while you may never need to know that in parts of Italy, building sandcastles might be frowned upon by the law, these eccentricities offer a charming insight into the European way of life, blending the old with the new in fascinating ways.

99. Georgia Guidestones

The Georgia Guidestones, often referred to as America's Stonehenge, are a modern-day enigma wrapped in a set of ten guidelines inscribed on the structure in eight different languages. Located in Elbert County, Georgia, these massive granite stones were erected in 1980 and have since been a subject of curiosity and conspiracy theories.

Commissioned by a person or group under the pseudonym "R.C. Christian," the true identity and intentions behind these stones remain unknown.

The anonymity of the sponsors adds to the mystique and various interpretations of the monument's purpose and significance.

The Guidestones carry a set of ten guidelines or principles, which are viewed by some as a framework for humanity, and by others as controversial messages.

Some of the more contentious instructions include maintaining the human population under 500 million and guiding reproduction wisely.

The guidelines are inscribed in eight modern languages, with shorter messages in four ancient languages (Babylonian, Classical Greek, Sanskrit, and Egyptian Hieroglyphs). This multilingual aspect emphasizes a universal message, meant for all of humanity.

New World Order

Those who subscribe to this theory believe that the Guidestones are a physical manifesto laid out by an elite, secretive group with intentions of establishing a world government that exerts total control over the population.

The New World Order, in conspiracy lore, is often depicted as an emerging totalitarian world regime.

Proponents of this theory argue that the Guidestones' call for maintaining humanity under 500 million is a clear indication of this group's intent to enforce population control. This guideline, in particular, is seen as a sinister plan for mass depopulation, with critics arguing that such a goal could only be achieved through catastrophic means or authoritarian population management.

Additionally, the notion of "guiding reproduction wisely" is perceived as a call for eugenics or selective breeding, further fueling the belief in a dystopian future where individual freedoms are heavily restricted under a global regime.

Critics of the NWO theory point out that it is steeped in paranoia and a misunderstanding of the Guidestones' broader messages about conservation and sustainability. They argue that the guidelines are more about living in harmony with nature and each other, rather than a literal set of commands for a future authoritarian government.

This theory reflects a broader mistrust in institutions and elite groups, tapping into fears of loss of autonomy and freedom. The Guidestones, through the lens of the NWO theory, become a symbol of these anxieties, representing the potential dangers of unchecked power and the need for vigilance against threats to personal freedoms.

While their true meaning and the identity of those behind them remain unknown, they continue to fascinate and provoke debate. Remember: **you may never need to know** the intricate symbolism of the Georgia Guidestones, but their enigmatic presence offers a unique window into the complexities of human thought and the diverse interpretations of our collective future.

100. Why Do Cats Purr?

Cats purring is one of those charming enigmas that pet owners adore, yet it's a phenomenon that has puzzled scientists and cat lovers alike. Let's delve into this feline mystery with a blend of facts, humor, and the acknowledgment that some cat behaviors might just be beyond human understanding.

A Sign of Contentment:

The most common interpretation of a cat's purr is that it's a sign of contentment. When your furry friend curls up in your lap and starts that motor running, it's often taken as a sign they're happy and relaxed. Picture it as a cat's way of giving a thumbs-up, but with a sound that's much more soothing than a human saying, "I'm chill."

Healing Vibrations:

Cats purr at a frequency between 25 and 150 Hertz, which is a range known to be medically therapeutic for many illnesses. Purring has been linked to lowering stress, reducing the chance of having a heart attack, and even strengthening bones. So, not only is your cat a cuddly companion, but it might also be a tiny, purring, four-legged doctor.

Communication Tool:

Purring is a form of communication, especially in kittens. Kittens can purr when they're only a few days old, and it's a way for them to let their mother know they're okay or they're hungry. It's like a baby's cry but much less likely to keep you awake at night.

Self-Soothing Mechanism:

Cats also purr when they're frightened or hurt, leading some to believe that purring is a self-soothing mechanism that helps them to calm down or even heal.

It's akin to humans humming a tune to themselves to feel better, except cats probably have a better sense of pitch.

Seeking Attention:

Some studies suggest that cats have a special type of purr, known as the "solicitation purr," which is more urgent and less pleasant. This purr is often used to wake you up for breakfast and is slightly more annoying than their usual purr – it's basically a polite but firm way of saying, "Hey human, the food bowl isn't going to fill itself."

It's Just a Cat Thing:

Lastly, and perhaps most importantly, cats might purr just because they can. It's one of those enigmatic behaviors that remind us that as much as we try to understand our feline friends, they'll always have a bit of mystery about them.

So, while **you might never need to know** the exact scientific explanation behind why cats purr, understanding this charming behavior can deepen the bond between you and your feline friend. It's a reminder that sometimes, the simplest joys in life come in the form of a purring cat.

101. Steve Jobs Commencement Speech

Steve Jobs' 2005 commencement speech at Stanford University is one of the most cited and remembered speeches of our time. It was a speech that not only provided guidance and inspiration to the graduating students but also offered insights into Jobs' own philosophy on life, work, and overcoming challenges.

Let's break down this iconic speech:

Connecting the Dots

Jobs recounted his birth to a young, unwed graduate student and subsequent adoption by a working-class couple. This part of his life story laid the foundation for his message about the unpredictability of life and how unforeseen events can shape our destinies.

Jobs shared his experience at Reed College, where he dropped out after six months but continued to audit classes for another 18 months. One of these classes was calligraphy, which he took purely out of interest, with no practical application in sight. Jobs later connected this experience to the elegant typography that became a hallmark of Apple computers.

He emphasized that when he was taking the calligraphy class, he could not possibly have seen how it would affect his future. It was only a decade later, when designing the first Macintosh computer, that he realized the class's significance. This experience became a crucial aspect of Apple's success.

The crux of Jobs' message in this section was about trusting that the dots in one's life will somehow connect in the future.

He urged the graduates to believe in something – their gut, destiny, life, karma, whatever – because believing that the dots will connect down the road will give them the confidence to follow their heart, even when it leads them off the well-worn path.

Jobs' narrative highlighted the importance of having faith in life's journey, even when it doesn't make sense in the moment. His story was a testament to the fact that life's most significant and beneficial experiences may not always seem relevant or important when they occur.

Death

The most poignant part of the speech was when Jobs talked about his diagnosis of pancreatic cancer. He described staring death in the face and how it forced him to confront his own mortality. This experience led him to stress the importance of remembering that we are all going to die, which is the best way to avoid the trap of thinking you have something to lose. Jobs urged the graduates to live each day as if it was their last, as one day it surely would be.

Jobs concluded his speech with the farewell message from the final edition of The Whole Earth Catalog: "Stay Hungry, Stay Foolish." He wished the same for the Stanford graduates, emphasizing the importance of maintaining one's curiosity and adventurous spirit.

- **Ouster from Apple:**
  - In 1985, a power struggle within Apple led to Jobs being forced out of the company he co-founded. This was a significant blow to Jobs, as Apple had been the center of his professional life. His departure was a result of conflicts with John Sculley, the CEO he had personally recruited, and the Apple board. This period was marked by internal disagreements over the direction of the company, particularly regarding the Macintosh's future.
- **New Ventures and Learnings:**
  - After leaving Apple, Jobs didn't cease his pursuit of innovation. He founded NeXT, a company focused on producing high-end computers for the education sector. Although NeXT was not a commercial success, it was significant for its advanced technology. In parallel, Jobs acquired The Graphics Group (later renamed Pixar), which revolutionized animation with hits like "Toy Story". This period was a time of both personal and professional growth for Jobs, as he navigated the challenges of starting anew.
- **Return to Apple:**
  - In 1997, in a twist of fate, Apple acquired NeXT, which led to Jobs returning to the company. This return marked the beginning of a historic turnaround for Apple. Jobs revitalized the company with a series of successful products, including the iMac, iPod, iPhone, and iPad, re-establishing Apple as a leader in innovation.
- **Battle with Illness and Death:**
  - In 2003, Jobs was diagnosed with a rare form of pancreatic cancer. Despite his illness, he continued to lead Apple until August 2011, when he resigned as CEO due to health reasons, naming Tim Cook as his successor. Jobs passed away on October 5, 2011. His death was widely mourned, marking the loss of one of the most visionary leaders of the modern era.

Remember: While you may never need to know the detailed timeline of Steve Jobs' professional ups and downs or his health struggles, his story is a poignant reminder of the human capacity for resilience and innovation, even in the face of daunting challenges.

Thank You for Reading

As we close this eclectic ensemble of esoteric tidbits, we hope you've enjoyed this whimsical whirlwind tour through the corridors of the curious and the halls of the humorous. "Trivia Book: 101 Random Stuff You Never Need to Know" was a labor of love and laughter, designed to sprinkle a little joy and wonder into your day.

Thank you for joining us on this quirky quest for knowledge. Whether you've chuckled at the oddities, marveled at the mysteries, or simply shook your head in disbelief, we're delighted to have shared this journey with you.

Remember, the world is full of incredible stories, strange facts, and unbelievable tales, waiting just around the corner. Keep your curiosity alive, your sense of humor handy, and your mind open to the endless possibilities that life has to offer.

Until next time, keep pondering the peculiar and celebrating the strange. Who knows what delightful discoveries await us next?

BNW
PUBLISH

Join us on your favourite platform, Scan the QR code on your phone or tablet

Thank you

Please review on Amazon

★★★★★

B N William

Printed in Great Britain
by Amazon